CONTEMPORARY JEWISH AMERICAN WRITERS *and the* MULTICULTURAL DILEMMA

Judaic Traditions in Literature, Music, and Art
Ken Frieden *and* Harold Bloom, *Series Editors*

CONTEMPORARY JEWISH AMERICAN WRITERS AND THE MULTICULTURAL DILEMMA

THE RETURN OF THE EXILED

ANDREW FURMAN

SYRACUSE UNIVERSITY PRESS

First Edition 2000
00 01 02 03 04 05 6 5 4 3 2 1

The paper used in this publication meets the minimum requirements of American National Standard for Information Sciences – Permanence of Paper for Printed Library Materials, ANSI Z39.48-1984.∞™

Library of Congress Cataloging-in-Publication Data
Furman, Andrew, 1968–
Contemporary Jewish American writers and the multicultural dilemma : the return of the exiled / Andrew Furman.
p. cm.—(Judaic traditions in literature, music, and art)
Includes bibliographical references and index.
ISBN 0-8156-2843-9 (cloth : alk. paper) ISBN 0-8156-2846-3 (pbk. : alk. paper)
1. American fiction—Jewish authors—History and criticism. 2. Jewish fiction—United States—History and criticism. 3. Jewish fiction—20th century—History and criticism. 4. Jews in literature. I. Title. II. Series.
PS153.J4F86 2000
813'.54098924—dc21 00-022488

Manufactured in the United States of America

To my wife,

Wendy,

and to our son,

Henry Asher

Andrew Furman is an assistant professor of English at Florida Atlantic University and the author of *Israel Through the Jewish-American Imagination* (1997). He has published numerous articles, essays, and reviews on Jewish American writers and on other topics in a variety of periodicals such as *Forward, MELUS, Contemporary Literature, Midstream, Tikkun, Response, Studies in American Jewish Literature, Modern Jewish Studies, Jewish Currents* and the *Miami Herald.* He is a contributing editor of *Tikkun*.

Contents

Acknowledgments

Although I wrote this book alone, it is just as true that I would not have been able to do so without the enthusiastic support of several friends and colleagues. In this regard, I have been especially blessed and would like to acknowledge my warmest appreciation for Daniel Walden, Sanford Pinsker, Alan Berger, Gloria Cronin, Sarah Blacher Cohen, Sandra Doopan, Krishna and Ben Lewis, Oliver Buckton, Laurice Campbell, Bill Covino andd Debbie Covino, Marianne Sanua, Rabbi Daniel Levin and Aimee Levin, Andrea Lewis, Graham Davis, Davis Houck, Clevis Headley, Marina Banchetti, Ben Lowe, Patricia Kollander, Julia Serebrinsky, Henry Abramson, David Keplinger, Dirck Aumiller, Robert Stone, Monica Giacoppe, and Matthew and Evelyn Sobrinski.

Special thanks also to Traci Klass and Stuart Clarry for their computer expertise.

Finally, I would like to thank my students at Florida Atlantic University. Through their energy and intelligence, they continue to inspire me toward ever richer readings.

Earlier versions of or significant excerpts from some of these chapters have appeared in various publications. For permission to reprint the material here I am grateful to *Midstream,* the Johns Hopkins University Press, *English Academy Review, Forward,* and *Shofar.*

CONTEMPORARY JEWISH AMERICAN WRITERS *and the* MULTICULTURAL DILEMMA

1

Introduction

Jewish American Fiction and the Multicultural Curriculum; or, What Is *Contemporary Jewish American Fiction?*

"Books are for the scholar's idle times," Ralph Waldo Emerson declared with temerity in the oration he delivered before the Phi Beta Kappa Society at Cambridge, which he later republished as "The American Scholar" (50). "When he can read God directly," Emerson continued, "the hour is too precious to be wasted in other men's transcripts of their readings" (50). As far as this particular transcendentalist was concerned, books existed for nothing but to inspire.

I invariably feel pangs of anxiety and self-consciousness when I review these classic Emerson lines with undergraduates: anxiety because the last thing most of my students need is the encouragement Emerson lends to their already unbookish inclinations, and self-consciousness because books, after all, have claimed a far greater stake on my recent "scholarly" existence than Emerson evidently had in mind. It was not too long ago that I completed both a doctoral program in English and the search for gainful academic employment. Inspiration, to be sure, is always a nice fringe benefit of reading in graduate school—one should embrace inspiration where one can find it, yes?—but the subject tends not to work its way into the "conversation" at a job interview at the Modern Language Association Convention. Which is simply to say that the subtitular question above has been anything but rhetorical for me. "What *is* Jewish American fiction?" is one of those questions I had to anticipate, along with a host of others such as, "What are the theoretical moorings of your dissertation?" and "Do you see yourself primarily as a researcher or a teacher?" and (my personal favorite) "What scholarly project are you working on *now?*" As the possibility of actually completing my dissertation seemed more and more a surety, I was forced to consider seriously how the literature on which I had decided to cut my academic teeth—the Jewish American novels of Abraham Cahan, Anzia Yezierska, Henry Roth, Saul Bellow, Cynthia Ozick, Philip Roth, and others—could fit harmoniously into our current paradigms of literary study. Put simply, I wanted a job. (This point cannot be overemphasized.)

I can claim little excuse for pursuing such "unfashionable" writers, for I was warned at every step of the way that writing a dissertation about Jewish American fiction on Israel was not exactly the way to garner dossier requests, writing sample requests, first interviews, second interviews, and, ultimately, job offers at prestigious research institutions (the type of position toward which any graduate student worth his or her salt aspires). The Graduate Studies Committee at my university reluctantly accepted my dissertation proposal and only after expressing their reservations, for the record; the director of Graduate Studies in the English department, a prominent Jewish scholar of literary modernism, advised me that few schools would be interested in an Americanist specializing in Jewish American fiction; even mentors who had carved out eminent careers for themselves as scholars of Jewish American literature expressed concern, somewhat cryptically, about the number of arrows in my quiver. Everyone was trying benevolently enough to tell me that although multicultural American literature (defined narrowly as Latino/a American, Asian American, American Indian, and African American literature—just look at the postings in any recent *MLA Job Information List*) is, in a word, hot, Jewish American literature is decidedly not. And although the gainfully employed Mark Shechner could observe with a modicum of detachment that "in the MLA . . . list of job openings, the demand for instructors in minority literature or 'multiculturalism' is clamorous, while nobody is looking for teachers of Jewish American literature" ("Is This Picasso" 39), this fact on the ground was enough to make my blood run cold as I prepared my first job application letters. Despite the prodigious number of articles I had published already, the book contract I managed to secure just in time to announce it prominently on my vita, and the absence, as far as I could tell, of any pronounced character flaws, it was no great surprise to me when my first time around the job search block yielded few interviews and no job offers.

Fair enough. However, what concerns me today is not so much the tepid academic interest in Jewish American writers but that scholars of American literature have ceased to consider them multicultural or minority writers at all. As Joseph Epstein observes, "In more recent years, whenever the words 'minorities' or 'minority groups' were mentioned, it was understood that the Jews were not included among them; however 'multi' culture was supposed to be in America, Jewish culture was generally never really considered a part of it" (12). This recent exclusion of Jewish culture from multicultural contexts, including curricula, is especially disconcerting because few academics consider our contemporary Jewish American writers part of the so-called mainstream either. Cynthia Ozick cogently describes this double bind on contemporary Jewish American writers like herself: "Whatever the reasons, the fact remains that there is clearly no room for Jewish writers at the multicultural table. They are not welcome there. . . . Then what about the mainstream? Do Jewish writers, major or minor, today sit at the mainstream table? No longer" ("Making Our Way" 11).

The exclusion of Jewish voices from the multicultural curriculum stings Evelyn Torton Beck even more so perhaps than it stings Ozick, for Beck does not believe that the Jew was ever truly welcome at the mainstream table. She argues, *"Jewish contributions to culture have never been included in the Eurocentric curriculum that has perpetuated the most blatant Jew-hating stereotypes. So we are about to be excluded when we were never included in the first place"* (166, emphasis in original). The very title of the collection in which Beck's chapter appears, *The Narrow Bridge: Jewish Views on Multiculturalism* (1996), and the title of a more recent collection of essays on the same topic, *Insider/Outsider: American Jews and Multiculturalism* (1998), evoke the recognition (if not the fear) voiced by several of the contributors, who are from a variety of disciplines, that contemporary multiculturalists increasingly ignore the Jewish voice. Beck and Ozick offer a prescient account of the marginalization of the Jewish American voice on course syllabi. Demographics, they both observe, would seem to certify the minority status of Jewish Americans (Jews represent roughly 2 percent of our country's population). Moreover, Jews certainly have a "recognizable cultural matrix," to borrow Ozick's phrase ("Making Our Way" 11), distinct from American mainstream culture. So what gives?

A combination of factors, I believe, has conspired to inflict this double bind on the Jewish American writer. First, the mainstream success of Jewish

American novelists in the 1950s and 1960s currently discourages multiculturalists from including contemporary Jewish American fiction in the curriculum. During this brief period (which we might as well call the golden age of Jewish American fiction), Saul Bellow, Philip Roth, and Bernard Malamud brought widespread academic and public attention to the development of the Jewish American novel, but as Leslie Fiedler observes, "by the late sixties, though many of them continued to write and would for the next couple of decades, Jewish American writers had ceased to seem central" (xii). After this mainstream love affair with the Jewish American novel was over, however, the work of a younger cohort of Jewish American writers was no longer championed by the predominant cohort of multiculturalists interested, above all, in marginalized voices (I elaborate on this brand of multiculturalism below). In 1990, Paul Lauter, a pioneer of literary multiculturalism, remarked that "[i]n prose, the writing of men like Emerson, Thoreau, Hawthorne, Melville, James, Eliot, Hemingway, Faulkner, and Bellow constitute the mainstream" ("Literatures" 9). When a distinctively Jewish American writer such as Bellow, a son of Yiddish-speaking immigrants, finds himself lumped together in the literary "mainstream" with such blue-blooded American writers as Emerson, Melville, and Thoreau, what hope can there be that a younger Jewish American writer penning her first novel in the 1990s will find her book adopted for undergraduate courses in multicultural or minority literature? Which is simply to say that the success of their predecessors has hemmed in contemporary Jewish American writers to a near invisible territory of literary limbo between the mainstream and the multicultural realm of literary discourse.

Moreover, it seems clearer by the day as I keep my ear to the academic ground that a socioeconomic factor—the disproportionate flow of Jewish Americans into the professions and the concomitant material success of Jewish Americans since World War II (although several poor Jews do exist)—plays a significant role in the exclusion of contemporary Jewish American writers from the multicultural canon. Several Jewish American writers and critics have noted this disconcerting trend. "I hear reports from campuses," Norma Rosen reflects, "that there is a new resistance to teaching Jewish writers in the multicultural mix. We are not regarded as a *suffering minority.* We are thought to have made it, both in American society and in literature (13, emphasis added). In the foreword to his recent collection of Jewish American stories, Ted Solotaroff observes that "Jews today, rightly or wrongly, are perceived to be part of the white mainstream. Their formerly marginal position is now occupied by the people of color. . . . The multicultural movement passes them by and anti-Semitism is mostly a demagogic way of attacking the power structure" (xx). Even more pointedly, the editors of *Insider/Outsider: American Jews and Multiculturalism* note that "there are some extreme advocates of multiculturalism, especially in the African American community, who have singled out the Jews among the generalized category of 'whites' for special criticism, criticism that is sometimes hard to distinguish from anti-Semitism" (Biale, Galchinsky, and Heschel 4).

Implicit in this "special criticism" is the assumption that Jews in America—unlike African Americans and other minorities currently considered "people of color"—have simply not suffered enough of late to be considered a minority or multicultural group. As Julius Lester (an African American and Jew By Choice) argues, "No black denies that Jews suffered in Europe, but the Jewish experience in America has not been characterized by such suffering. The black experience has" (173). Indeed, it is difficult not to see the inscription on the dedication page of Toni Morrison's *Beloved* (1987), "Sixty Million and More," as the author's self-conscious trumping of Jewish victimhood. Six million Jews may have perished in the Holocaust, Morrison implicitly suggests, but the Middle Passage claimed more than ten times that number in African lives.

Gregory Jay's distinction between two multicultural approaches proves helpful in explaining further the new resistance to include Jewish American writers in the multicultural context. As Jay observes, the first approach "celebrates the diversity of cultural groups," but it gives way to an "oppositional rather than pluralist" approach, which "is less interested in celebrating difference than in resisting oppression" ("Taking Multiculturalism" 103–4). To oppositional multiculturalists, then, victimhood (and the more current the victimization the better) represents a crucial criterion to qualify a writer as "ethnic," "multicultural," or "minority" (see Biale, Chicago Cultural Studies Group, and Hughes). "In multicultural politics," Michael Walzer cannily observes, "it is an advantage to be injured" (89). Hence, Sander L. Gilman's lamentably unrhetorical questions in a recent *PMLA* Symposium on Ethnicity: "In a culture of victims, does being ethnic mean being oppressed? Can successful ethnics still be ethnic? Do ethnics have to be subalterns? Or can they be good bourgeois . . . ?" (23).

Whatever one may think of the oppositional approach, one can glean that practitioners of this au courant version of multiculturalism would not likely include Jewish American writers on their syllabi because Jewish Americans, as a group, have suffered little economic or political oppression of late. Jewish American writers, the logic goes, may represent a minority population, demographically speaking, but their recent experience in this country can hardly be characterized as a true "minority experience" (read: oppression)—hence, the virtual elimination of the contemporary Jewish American writer from the multicultural curriculum.

Indeed, one need only scan the entries in recent anthologies devoted to minority and multicultural writing to verify these gloomy observations. Paul Lauter's *Heath Anthology of American Literature* (three editions to date: 1990, 1994, and 1998) arguably represents the single most influential book in establishing a multicultural literary curriculum. Lauter and his editorial advisory board explicitly (and laudably, I believe) set out to "represent as fully as possible the varied cultures of the United States" (xxxv). To be sure, they succeed on a great many fronts, especially through their inclusion of numerous entries by American Indian, U.S. Latino/a, and Asian American writers. However, although earlier twentieth-century Jewish American writers appear in the collection (e.g., Yezierska, Cahan, Bellow), a reader would search in vain for contemporary Jewish American writers, even in the third edition, just released in 1998. Thus, for the reader unfamiliar with our powerful young Jewish American voices, the latter sections of the *Heath Anthology* give the dangerously false impression that Jewish American fiction simply fizzled out after the generation informed by the immigrant experience (an experience that reached its statistical peak long ago—in 1907).

Redefining American Literary History, published by the Modern Language Association in 1990 and edited by A. LaVonne Brown Ruoff and Jerry W. Ward, presents a more egregious oversight of Jewish American fiction. The editors of the volume seek to establish a new American literary history, as the title suggests, "based on multiethnic and multiracial, rather than a European, theory of culture" (2). Thus, they include in the collection several fine essays devoted to African American, Asian American, American Indian, Chicano, and Puerto Rican writers. They also include, at the end of the volume, rather comprehensive bibliographies devoted to each of these groups of minority writers. I embrace the essential goals of *Redefining American Literary History* and believe that the book is an invaluable resource for any scholar of multiethnic fiction and that it has gone a long way toward enhancing our pedagogical approach toward that "patchwork quilt we call American literature" (Ruoff and Ward 2).

That said, the spectrum of colors emblazoned on the cover of *Redefining American Literary History* finally provokes only the "two cheers" response, for, speaking as one who possesses a keen interest in those Jewish American squares of the quilt, I cannot help wondering how and (more disconcertingly) if contemporary Jewish American writers fit into the "redefinition" of American literature that the editors have in mind. The exclusion of Jewish American writers from a volume ostensibly devoted to minority and multiethnic voices seems especially bizarre given that Ruoff and Ward redefine American literature explicitly to challenge Robert E. Spiller's earlier Anglo-American conception, which, in their words, "excludes blacks, *Jews,* and immigrant groups coming late to this country" (2, emphasis mine).

Finally, the Jewish American experience is conspicuously excluded from *The Graywolf Annual Five: Multi-Cultural Literacy* (1988), edited by Rick Simonson and Scott Walker. Importantly, the editors of the volume seek to amplify the "contributions of repressed cultures" (x) and thereby affirm Jay's observations concerning the current oppositional rather than pluralist multicultural agenda. I am quite certain that the editors of both the *Heath Anthology* and *The Graywolf Annual Five* value Jewish American writers' contributions to American culture, but these writers evidently occupy a space outside the paradigm of multicultural fiction. All of which affirms Jay's recent contention:

> The exclusion of Jewish American experience and literature from dominant accounts of multiculturalism and antiracism can be confirmed by a glance at the major books and anthologies in the field. None give these topics substantial coverage. Even very recent edited collections such as *Multiculturalism: A Critical Reader* and *Off White: Readings on Race, Power, and Society* say barely a word about Jews. . . . Much evidence points to a consensus that Jews do not belong on the multiculturalism syllabus. ("Jewish Writers" 8)

Given such pervasive exclusions, it should be of little surprise that "[t]he Modern Language Association . . . has consistently denied petitions to create a national Division of Jewish American Literature, or of Jewish Literary and Cultural Studies, despite the creation in the last fifteen years of Divisions of Black American Literature and Culture, American Indian Literatures, Women's Studies in Language and Literature, Ethnic Studies in Language and Literature, and Gay Studies in Language and Literature" (Horowitz 118). Further, it was no great shock (although disappointing all the same) to discover in my first year as an assistant professor that the ethnic studies program at my university included my course on Toni Morrison, Ralph Ellison, and William Faulkner under their list of offerings, but not my course on Jewish American literature.

Ethnic and multicultural studies departments and programs, it seems to me, have yet to face the dilemma built into their titles. That is, are not *all* writers ethnic? As Allegra Goodman recently noted, "Ultimately, I believe, all writing is ethnic writing, and all writers are ethnic writers grappling with great ambitions and a particular language and culture. . . . Faulkner used Shakespeare and southern dialect together" ("Writing Jewish Fiction" 274). Insisting on the inclusion of Jewish material in ethnic studies programs, Beck argues similarly that "everyone has an ethnicity," and she instructively recalls the way in which I. B. Singer tersely put it: "everyone has an address" (170). Indeed, in addition to Jewish American writers, many Polish American, Italian/American (they have eschewed both the hyphenated and open forms), Irish American, and other ethnically specific Euro-American writers exist who currently receive short shrift by departments purporting to study ethnic voices. Such inclusions and exclusions, it is worth noting, directly affect the number of students who can pragmatically enroll in a course, given English department curricula that increasingly include a multicultural or ethnic studies requirement. For example, the first course I offered in Jewish American literature—excluded from the ethnic studies program—barely "made," to use the academic expression.

The rarely articulated but growing assumption that Jewish Americans have somehow forfeited their minority status because they have "made it" in America naturally places Jewish American writers and scholars of Jewish American literature (who are not necessarily Jewish or American for that matter) in an awkward position when the thorny issue of the multicultural curriculum crops up at English department meetings. That scholars of Jewish American fiction were among the first to rally behind an inclusive multicultural curriculum in the 1960s and 1970s adds a significant measure of irony to the situation. (Daniel Walden, for example, the longtime editor of *Studies in American Jewish Literature,* helped found the Society for the Study of the Multi-Ethnic Literature of the United States. I should also note here that *MELUS*, the journal of this society, still actively publishes articles about Jewish American and other Euro-American writers, against the grain of our current multicultural zeitgeist.) To ask anyone with a stake in Jewish American fiction to support the multicultural curriculum in its current manifestation runs akin to asking multiculturalists to support funding for another course on the "Great Books."

That Daniel Green recently lauded Steve Stern as "a worthy successor to these great Jewish writers [Bernard Malamud and Isaac Bashevis Singer]," but qualified his declaration by cautioning that "our interest in his work, as with theirs, should not be restricted to its value as an addition to the multicultural potluck" (967) exemplifies the Jewish American literature scholars' antipathy toward the capriciousness of the multicultural agenda. At a recent American Literature Association symposium, "Revisioning Jewish American and Holocaust Literature," the panel I organized and chaired, "Jewish American Literature and the Multicultural Curriculum," also reflected this multicultural ambivalence on the part of Jewish American literature scholars. Although each of my panelists expressed their longstanding commitment to an inclusive multicultural literary curriculum (one panel member described his persistent efforts during the late 1960s to carve out a niche for "black literature" in the English Department curriculum at his large university), they all came armed to the teeth with journals such as *Multicultural Education* and with scores of university press flyers advertising multicultural studies titles to prove that Jewish American material was being systematically excluded.

Unlike the contributors to my panel, Cynthia Ozick gives an unblinking fish eye to academic multiculturalism: "Multiculturalism is intellectual deceit. Indifferent to the singularity of genius, it prides itself on rescuing groups from the margin (with the exception of Jews), and ends by marginalizing nearly everyone. Trampling on writers' autonomy, it pretends to be about literature, and engages in social work based on population ratios and bloodlines" ("Making Our Way" 12).

I must confess that Ozick's uncompromising intellectual stand smacks of good sense to me, that all the hoopla over "majority" and "minority" writers threatens, as Ozick suggests, to leave out literature altogether, whereas perhaps "cultural and historical particularity can flourish undamaged" (Ozick, "Making Our Way" 12) in an academic environment where literary standards dictate literary inclusion. We will have to wait to see, of course, whether a curriculum fashioned from purely aesthetic criteria can defy its less than enviable track record to foster the cultural and historical particularity of our country's racial and ethnic minorities; the multicultural curriculum, like T. S. Eliot's etherized patient, has spread itself out on our academic table and won't be cleared off anytime soon. That the very term *multiculturalism* mysteriously lost its hyphen in recent years goes a long way toward showing how rapidly the academic community has warmed to the phenomenon. (As Nathan Glazer sardonically puts it in the title of his recent book, we are all multiculturalists now.) To be sure, one can scarcely make it these days as a "mainstream" writer. As Allegra Goodman has noted, "It is difficult to be a literary giant in the global village, to be ambassador without portfolio" ("Writing Jewish Fiction" 270).

Ideally (and this is the point I wish to belabor in the pages to follow), Jewish American writers and scholars of Jewish American writing should have little reason to bemoan this fact. A multiculturalism true to the inextricable promises of its name cannot effectively advocate a "resistant politics of the marginalized" (Jay, "Taking Multiculturalism" 106) while it simultaneously silences other minority voices that contribute to our cultural conversation. That is, Jewish American writers (and, for that matter, other ethnically distinct Euro-American writers) must be included in the multicultural mix because they have their own distinct voice or portfolio peculiar to their sociocultural experience outside the mainstream.

In her plea for Jewish literacy, Nessa Rapoport also implicitly offers a corrective to those who would conflate Jewish American economic success with cultural and artistic assimilation: "In an era in which people are struggling to grant each ethnic tradition its cultural and moral due, we had best not mistake our material and sociological acceptance in this country for an entirely identical literary history" (xxix). Norman Finkelstein, another prominent voice in literary matters Jewish, weighs in with Rapoport: "Sociologically speaking, Jews may well feel as at home as any other American minority (and we are by now a nation of minorities), but sociology, whatever tools it may provide for the literary critic, can never fully account for the vicissitudes of literary creation. . . . Jewish American *culture* is still a culture of exile, and I see little reason to either hope for or expect a change" (139–40, emphasis in original). The work of the contemporary Jewish American fiction writers on whom I have decided to focus in this book reaffirm Finkelstein and

Rapoport's conviction that Jewish American fiction continues to embody the distinct values and preoccupations of a decidedly minority culture.

Allegra Goodman, specifically, affirms the Jewish content of her work in "Writing Jewish Fiction in and out of the Multicultural Context." "I write," she contends, "from the inside . . . an idiom in which ritual and liturgy are a natural part of my fictional world, and not anthropological objects to be translated and constantly explained" (271). Indeed, Goodman's fiction and the work of her peers (which I limn below) suggest that our definition of multicultural literature should not be beholden to the criteria of economic or political history but to more substantive literary and sociocultural stuff.

It is passing strange that the multicultural movement in our universities pays short shrift to contemporary Jewish American fiction at the precise moment that these writers have begun to assert their Jewish identities and values with an unprecedented intensity. Recognizing this trend in Goodman's work and in the fiction of several other Jewish American writers, Alan Berger notes, "Collectively, Jewish novels are increasingly exploring the meaning of being Jewish from within rather than from the perspective of American culture. . . . Orthodoxy seems . . . once again to be a driving force in Jewish American literature" (222–23). A multicultural curriculum sensitive to oppressed voices, yes, but also sensitive to the other ethnically distinct voices that contribute to the ongoing creation of our national character and literature would do well to pay heed to the Jewish American literary voice. Henry Louis Gates Jr. articulates the inclusive ideals of such a curriculum when he suggests that we think of American culture as a conversation among different voices, each conditioned by a different perception of the world (712).  Now, this is a multicultural agenda that I (and most scholars of Jewish American literature, I suspect) can rally behind, for it certainly promises to lean its attentive ear toward the increasingly unique perspective of the Jewish American voice, just as it promises to engage the distinct literatures of African American, U.S. Latino/a, American Indian, Asian and Pacific American writers. I speak as a grateful beneficiary of the multicultural rage. Although Jewish American titles have carved out a formidable niche on my bookshelf, the works of Chitra Banerjee Divakaruni, Charles Johnson, Sandra Cisneros, Ralph Ellison, Gish Jen, Toni Morrison, Sherman Alexie, Julia Alvarez, James Welch, John Edgar Wideman, Cristina Garcia, Jhumpa Lahiri, Chang-Rae Lee, and the works of several other minority writers have laid their claim as well. And although I teach a course on Jewish American literature, I also teach a course on Asian American literature, a more broad-based course on multicultural writers entitled "Fictions of Multiculturalism," and a course in my university's doctoral program on public intellectuals entitled "Writing in the Americas." The writers I read and teach in the latter three courses—many of whom are listed above—have produced fine and often innovative aesthetic works, works that dramatize minority experiences in this country that are strange from my own, though sometimes hauntingly familiar. Listening to these voices, I believe, has broadened my humanity by measures of empathy. I would hate to see students deprived in the millennium ahead of the range of voices afforded to me as a student in the 1980s.

My hunch, however, is that we will continue to wrangle over which of these voices deserve to "count" as minority or multicultural voices. I have broached only one (admittedly self-interested) controversy in focusing on the untenable exclusion of contemporary Jewish American writing from the multicultural category. After all, I am a teacher and critic with a considerable intellectual investment in Jewish American fiction; it would be no small inconvenience to me, to put it mildly, if our paradigm of literary study excluded the body of work toward which I have largely decided to devote my career. So, lest I commit the same oversights that I have decried, permit me to emphasize once again that scholars of other ethnically distinct Euro-American literatures surely have their own ax to grind with our contemporary multicultural curriculum. The mention of Rebecca Goldstein, Melvin Bukiet, and Thane Rosenbaum elicits blank stares from several multiculturalists, but the work of, say, Giose Rimanelli, Nicholas Gage, and Stanislaw L. Baranczak seldom makes its way onto the multicultural American fiction course syllabus either. As Fred L. Gardaphe, a leading scholar of Italian/American literature, recently lamented, "'[W]hat chance could *my* anthology featuring Italian male writers have in this climate? . . . if I'd submitted an anthology on African-American writing, or Native-American writing, or Hispanic writing, or Ethnic Women's writing, or Lesbian or Gay men's writing, I'm confident I'd have found a commercial publisher'" (qtd. in Talese 316).

Still, there are encouraging signs that an increasing, if still outnumbered, contingent of multiculturalists has begun to cast its net a good deal wider of late. Case in point: *New Immigrant Literatures in the United States: A Sourcebook to Our Multicultural Heritage* (1996), edited by Alpana Sharma Knippling. This collection of bibliographic essays might be seen as a corrective to Ruoff and Ward's earlier *Redefining American Literary History,* for in addition to sections devoted to Carribean American, Asian American, and Mexican American literature, Knippling includes several bibliographic essays devoted to the plethora of ethnically distinct Euro-American literatures ignored by Ruoff and Ward: Italian/American, Greek American, Polish American, and others. Knippling even trumps my own expectations by including not only a bibliographic essay on Jewish American literature, but a separate entry on Sephardic Jewish American literature. To be sure, inclusiveness was Knippling's overarching criterion as she sought to represent our multicultural literary heritage as accurately as she could. In her preface, for example, she bemoans the "lack of treatment of Vietnamese-American and German-American literatures (among others)," but explains that she simply could not locate qualified contributors in these areas (xi).

Three recent anthologies of multicultural literature *Imagining America: Stories from the Promised Land* (1991), *Coming of Age in America: A Multicultural Anthology* (1994), and *American Identities: Contemporary Multicultural Voices* (1994)—embody Knippling's (and Henry Louis Gates Jr.'s) more inclusive multicultural precepts. The editors of *Imagining America,* Wesley Brown and Amy Ling, include stories by Jewish and other ethnically distinct Euro-American writers. As Gregory Jay has noted, this editorial approach "invites students to develop a comparative perspective on American history and culture" ("Jewish Writers" 9). Mary Frosch, the editor of *Coming of Age in America,* selects coming-of-age fiction by American Indian, African American, U.S. Latino/a, and Asian American writers, but also includes fiction written by Jewish and Greek American writers. She organizes the material by theme rather than along bloodlines. Thus, in the "Crisis" section of the collection, one reads side by side excerpts from Chaim Potok's *Davita's Harp* and Julia Alvarez's *How the Garcia Girls Lost Their Accents.* Robert Pack and Jay Parini, the editors of *American Identities,* also include selections of prose and poetry from Jewish American and other Euro-American writers. The poignant stories of family life written by Lev Raphael, Ishmael Reed, and Richard Rodriguez (published consecutively in the volume) emerge, as Gates would have it, as a conversation among Jewish, African, and Mexican American voices, each conditioned by discrete perceptions of the world. Brown, Ling, Frosch, Pack, and Parini evidently believe that an anthology devoted to our multicultural literary heritage should reflect the considerable richness of this heritage. The truly polyphonic song that is the contemporary American voice resounds in *Imagining America, American Identities,* and *Coming of Age in America.*

As I hope I have illustrated, however, editorial inclusiveness of this ilk is enough to make the blood of many a multiculturalist run cold. One can almost see advocates of the oppositional multiculturalist approach cringe at Gary Soto's suggestion in the foreword to Frosch's collection that "Whether we are Jews or Catholic Chicanos, grew up on a corn farm or the oil-dark lot of a radiator shop in East Los Angeles, we come to age in the same human ways" (ix). Frosch's own insistence that the anthology will "reflect our commonalities, while never completely subverting our differences" (x) also grates against the sensibilities of this contingent. Oppositional multiculturalists not only believe that our differences far outweigh our similarities, but fear that Frosch's inclusive approach obfuscates the social, political, and economic disenfranchisement of specific minority groups by painting a false portrait of multicultural harmony. Even more distasteful to this contingent is Pack and Parini's assumption "that writers are empowered to acknowledge and explore their individual points of origin—religious, racial, class, sexual—and to freely identify, if they choose, with other identities" (x). Here, Pack and Parini articulate a "postethnic" theory of multiculturalism that challenges the rigid essentialism of the oppositional model (see also Biale, Hollinger, Sollors, and Waters). Oppositional multiculturalists, however—advocating first and foremost an agenda to combat the oppression of specific minority groups—have little use for works that affirm the possibility of "consenting" to an ethnic identity; they are more interested in those works (and there are several, to be sure) that illustrate how inexorable one's fixed descent can be in a country entrenched by racism (in using the terms *consent* and *descent,* I borrow from Werner Sollors's lexicon with regard to the dynamic formation of ethnic identity in America, as expressed in his landmark study *Beyond Ethnicity: Consent and Descent in American Culture* [1986]).

Oppositional multiculturalists, it seems to me, operate under the wrongheaded assumption that we cannot simultaneously adopt an inclusive multicultural curriculum and illuminate the oppression of specific minority groups in America. For them, to mix nonoppressed minority writers with oppressed minority writers on the syllabus is ineluctably to enact an insidious politics through "celebrating" diversity. I refuse to accept this view. Those who claim that inclusive multiculturalists merely celebrate diversity trivialize the intellectual rigor of the multicultural enterprise, for inclusive multiculturalists do not celebrate the diverse voices in multicultural America so much as scrutinize how these voices singularly resound, how they meet and often clash, whether along the gritty streets of New York City or the dusty roads of small town America. To read, for example, Grace Paley's "Zagrowsky Tells" (1985) side by side with such texts as Gloria Naylor's *Bailey's Cafe* (1993), Saul Bellow's *Mr. Sammler's Planet* (1969), Brent Staples's *Parallel Time* (1994), Alan Lelchuk's *Playing the Game* (1995), Nathan McCall's *Makes Me Wanna Holler* (1994), Bernard Malamud's *The Tenants* (1971), Paul Beatty's *The White Boy Shuffle* (1996), and Paul Hond's *The Baker* (1997) is to immerse oneself in a dynamic and often tumultuous cultural conversation between African and Jewish Americans. This particular conversation, I believe, continues to be an important one in our society and one that merits representation in our curriculum.

I fear, however, that this conversation (among many others) will be silenced if the academic zeitgeist casts Jewish American writers out of the paradoxically favored realm of multicultural or minority literature. Indeed, Stephen Sumida—couching in more scholarly prose Allegra Goodman's observations about the cultural "portfolio" that writers seem to need these days—observes how nebulous terms such as *minority, majority,* and *center* have become as minority texts increasingly "become positioned in a space usually occupied by a 'majority.' Centers and margins shift radically, as do ascriptions of 'minority' and 'majority' status" (803). The "repositioning of 'minority' literatures and literary studies at the 'center' of American literary history and criticism . . . [is] actively underway" (804), as Sumida observes, illustrating what is at stake as we seek to define Jewish American fiction. Today, scholars of Jewish American fiction need not search for distinctively "Jewish" American voices. They abound in unprecedented numbers. Instead, we face the more essential task of garnering once again an audience for these writers.

My aim, then, in organizing and writing this study was two-fold. Most broadly, I felt that it was imperative that someone (and, if not I, who?) explore in some depth the work of this largely neglected group of contemporary American writers. Philip Roth is the only widely recognized author in this study. The trajectory of his fruitful career offers an intriguing counterpoint, I believe, because each of the younger Jewish American writers have necessarily written in his long shadow and, as I hope to show, have staked out their own ground. That Jewish American fiction will continue to dazzle audiences long after Roth has written his last sentence might be seen as the overarching point of this study. More specifically, in my effort to carve out a sizeable (rather than delimiting) space for the Jewish American fiction writer in our multicultural curriculum, I intentionally selected a small group of contemporary Jewish American writers whose work bespeaks the diversity and range of the contemporary Jewish American imagination.

Before I limn the emergent preoccupations of these contemporary Jewish American writers, I should pause to note that the blame for the widespread neglect of their work cannot be pinned entirely on oppositional multiculturalists. Indeed, at least two eminent scholars of Jewish American literature were quick to sound its death knell as the first wave of Jewish American writers ran out of steam. Some background might prove helpful. We must recall that it was the nagging sense of alienation and marginality that provided the essential grist for the fictional mills of the dazzling postimmigrant writers who contributed to this golden age: Henry Roth, Grace Paley, Saul Bellow, Bernard Malamud, and Philip Roth, to name but a few. As Jewish Americans gained material success and cultural confidence in the years following World War II, marginality and alienation ceased to define the Jewish American experience and, predictably, could not fuel a second wave of such fiction—hence, Leslie Fiedler's downright cavalier observation in 1986 that "the Jewish American novel is over and done with, a part of history rather than a living literature" (117). Irving Howe argued some ten years earlier and just as implacably that "American Jewish fiction has probably moved past its high point. Insofar as this body of writing draws heavily from the immigrant experience, it must suffer a depletion of resources, a thinning-out of materials and memories. Other than in books and sentiment, there just isn't enough left of that experience" ("Introduction" 16).

Although I am certainly not the first scholar of Jewish American literature to challenge Fiedler's and Howe's pronouncements concerning the demise of Jewish American literature (see Finkelstein; Kremer, "Post-Alienation"; Pinsker, "Dares"; and Stern, "After the Law"), it bears emphasizing that the current outcropping of talented Jewish American fictionists belies their dour predictions. As Sanford Pinsker recently observed, "What Howe hadn't counted on . . . was the staking out of fictional claims on essentially new territories, ones that an older generation of Jewish writers largely ignored or only addressed from oblique angles" ("Dares" 282). Indeed, the writers I have chosen to explore demonstrate, above all, that as the Jewish American experience has evolved, so has Jewish American fiction.

This very evolution of the Jewish American *experience*, I believe, is primarily what Fiedler and Howe did not anticipate. To be sure, the proliferation of Jewish families into increasingly mainstream (read, WASP) neighborhoods, dizzying intermarriage rates, and waning synagogue affiliation in the 1970s and 1980s offered observers like Howe and Fiedler ample evidence that Jewish Americans were well on their way toward complete and utter assimilation. Even secular Zionism no longer seemed to galvanize the Jewish American community around a single purpose, as the Arab threat to Israel's existence seemed less and less palpable. Today, there is no dearth of wary souls who, like Howe and Fiedler, lament the imminent demise of Jewish continuity. Elaine M. Kauvar's recent sobering remarks—"[a]t present, both assimilation and fragmentation threaten the Jews with extinction as a people and leave the future of American Jewish culture in doubt" (340)—exemplify the widespread concern that Jewish Americans have all but abandoned the Jewish side of their hyphenated identities.

Although assimilation will continue, I suspect, to "Americanize" its fair share of Jews in this country, I believe we are in the midst of a powerful countervailing trend toward rediscovery. An unprecedented number of young Jewish Americans, raised largely ignorant of Judaism, have become part of the *baal t'shuvah* (returnee) phenomenon. The subtitles of an ever-increasing number of memoirs—including David Klinghoffer's *The Lord Will Gather Me In: My Journey to Jewish Orthodoxy* (1998), Carol Orsborn's *Return from Exile: One Woman's Journey Back to Judaism* (1998), and even Wendy Shalit's paean to prudery, *A Return to Modesty: Discovering the Lost Virtue* (1999)—betray the growing currency of traditional Jewish values in contemporary America. Further, the Reform rabbis at the 1999 Central Conference of American Rabbis ratified principles encouraging the observance of traditional Jewish rituals, such as keeping kosher.

Nominal Jews, however, are not only "returning" to Jewish Orthodoxy. As this final decade of the twentieth century winds to a close, it seems beyond dispute that a significant number of Jewish Americans continue to "feel Jewish," if I might borrow the subtitle of Sara Bershtel and Allen Graubard's recent study, in an almost limitless variety of ways. In *Saving Rem-*

nants: Feeling Jewish in America (1992), Bershtel and Graubard put their finger on the pulse of contemporary Jewish American culture as they assiduously document this heady Jewish revival:

> Those who seek evidence of such a revival do not have far to look. There are the proselytizing Hasidim of the Chabad movement who invite passersby to pray in their Mitzvah Mobiles; the flourishing Orthodox congregations attended by young, prosperous, well-educated, and worldly people, many of whom have had no previous religious training; the groups of former New Leftists who gather for their own form of weekly Sabbath service combining ancient prayers and Hebrew songs with excerpts from socialist, humanist, and feminist writings. (3–4)

Bershtel and Graubard proceed to note that the reenergized concern with the Holocaust, the Yiddish language and culture, and the thriving gay congregations, among other indicators, "all suggest that more and more Jewish Americans are discovering, rediscovering, or intensifying some impulse to Jewish identity" (4). This renaissance in Jewish American culture does not represent a resurgence of traditional Judaism per se so much as it represents its "transformation," Bershtel and Graubard contend, as contemporary, postalienated Jews in America—thoroughly integrated now into the mainstream realm of society—choose to construct a meaningful Jewish ethos (286). Writing as one who received a fairly lackadaisical Jewish education in a Conservative temple but who currently studies Talmud with a *chevrusa,* I consider myself very much a part (and proof) of this resurgence.

What I, as a literary scholar, find particularly fascinating about this revitalization is how it has manifested itself in a concomitant renaissance in Jewish American fiction. Indeed, practically each locus of Jewish identity that Bershtel and Graubard explore through exhaustive interviews with Jewish Americans has found expression in the contemporary Jewish American fiction I consider in the pages to follow. Robert Cohen, for example, explores in *The Here and Now* (1996) the viability of Hasidic Judaism amid a secular American milieu. Melvin Bukiet's *After* (1996) and Thane Rosenbaum's *Elijah Visible* (1996) and *Second Hand Smoke* (1999) illustrate how the "second generation," to borrow Alan L. Berger's terminology, continues to grapple with the Holocaust in its own distinct and creative ways. Bukiet's first collection, *Stories of an Imaginary Childhood* (1992), and Rebecca Goldstein's *Mazel* (1995) betray a revitalized interest in the vibrant Yiddish world in Europe in the years just prior to its decimation by the Nazis. The trajectory of Rebecca Goldstein's career also offers us a glimpse of one Jewish American woman's ongoing creative endeavor to reconcile her feminist precepts with traditional modes of Jewish practice. A good deal of Allegra Goodman's work pivots about the tensions between traditional Judaism and various contemporary competing influences—including feminism, most notably in the case of her debut novel, *Kaaterskill Falls* (1998)—but I chose to examine how a preoccupation with Israel and Middle East matters generally pervades her recent collection of stories, *The Family Markowitz* (1996). (I explore the emergence of this theme in the work of other contemporary Jewish American fiction writers such as Philip Roth, Tova Reich, and Anne Roiphe in my earlier study, *Israel Through the Jewish American Imagination: A Survey of Jewish American Literature on Israel, 1928–1995* [1997]). In his magical stories, Steve Stern focuses primarily on a motley assortment of Jewish characters living in a Memphis ghetto called the Pinch prior to the Holocaust and World War II. He thereby bypasses the experiences of the alienated, postwar Jewish American generation in his effort to reinscribe the world of the Pinch into our collective memory. Finally, Gerald Shapiro revisits the schlemiel tradition to explore the unique burdens of contemporary Jewish American existence and to test out the possibilities for spiritual return, or *t'shuvah*. If alienation was the Jewish American writer's single "inescapable subject," as Howe put it ("Introduction" 3), in the good old days when the immigrant experience still loomed large, the sheer range of contemporary Jewish American fiction illustrates that many inescapable subjects currently preoccupy the Jewish American imagination.

A cogent definition of Jewish American fiction thus remains elusive. This is not to say that scholars have not ventured definitions. Indeed, a variety of conflictive definitions might be found in the recent collection of essays edited by Hana Wirth-Nesher, *What Is Jewish Literature?* (1994). (See also Alter, "Jewish Voice"; Finkelstein; Wirth-Nesher, "Language"; and the *Tikkun* symposium "The Jewish Literary Revival" in its Nov.–Dec. 1997 issue.) Here, I must own up to my cantankerous side, which bristles against the defensiveness of Jewish American literature scholars who incessantly grope for definitions and redefinitions of the genre. Scholars of other minority American literatures, as far as I can tell, seldom feel that they must prove the legitimacy of their field via definitions. This cantankerous side often wishes to offer the following simple definition and be done with it: a novel written by a Jewish American writer is, perforce, a Jewish American novel.

That said, I realize that such a definition ultimately will not do, for there are a number of Jewish American fictionists who I honestly do *not* consider practitioners of Jewish American fiction. As Wirth-Nesher asks rhetorically in her introduction to *What Is Jewish Literature?* "Do Sholem Aleichem and Nathanael West really inhabit a shared universe in any respect?" (3). Perhaps I should admit here that I am not altogether convinced that a case could not be made for the Jewishness of Nathanael West. His appropriation of that blue-blooded name, Nathanael, betrays a distinctive Jewish self-consciousness that possibly emerges in subtle and intriguing ways in such dystopic "modernist" classics as *Miss Lonelyhearts* (1933) and *The Day of the Locust* (1939). Perhaps it is about time that a scholar explore the Jewish content of West's work (Arthur Cohen's "Nathanael West's Holy Fool," interestingly, skirts the issue of West's Jewishness). I embrace, however, Wirth-Nesher's essential argument. A great many Jewish American writers (some, no doubt, observant Jews) create works that manifest not the slightest concern with Judaism, Jewish culture, or other issues relevant to Jewish identity. To consider such work Jewish American fiction would be to descend into a shabby multiculturalism of bloodlines that I resist, both viscerally and intellectually. As long as Judaism and the Jewish experience continue to evolve, we must constantly revisit and revise our definition of Jewish American literature. As Alyssa P. Quint suggests, "Answers to such questions as 'What is Jewish literature?' must be accepted as provisional and dynamic, as constructions that can be pondered and toyed with, but not set in stone" (26).

Indeed, what makes the essays in this book cohere, I believe, is my pervasive concern with the Jewish content of the work in question. It occurred to me only as I was in the middle of this project that these essays represent, at least in part, a sort of conversation I have been having with myself regarding my own provisional and dynamic definition of Jewish American literature. Each is a journey to one significant outpost of what I currently consider the distinctively Jewish American imagination. Many of the works I discuss will strike most readers as shoo-ins as Jewish American novels. Few, for example, would dispute the Jewishness of Goldstein's *Mazel,* set in three representative Jewish milieux of the twentieth century: the pre-Holocaust Polish shtetl of Shluftchev, the cosmopolitan Warsaw, and the contemporary Orthodox

Jewish suburb of Lipton, New Jersey. However, I test the boundaries of the genre explicitly in my chapter on Robert Cohen. Should Robert Cohen's *The Organ Builder* (1988)—which revolves around a nominally Jewish lawyer who gives little thought to Judaism or Jewish identity—"count" as a Jewish American novel? I argue that it should for a variety of reasons, but do not expect (or even hope, really) that everyone agree, for when critics and scholars debate the arguable "Jewishness" of Jewish American fiction, they necessarily engage the wider theoretical debate over multiculturalism, productively testing and contesting its definition. "Precisely because we believe that the Jews constitute a liminal border case, neither inside nor outside—or, better, both inside and outside," the editors of *Insider/Outsider* argue, "they have the capacity to open up multicultural theory in new and interesting ways that may help it overcome some of the deficiencies that theorists of multiculturalism have begun themselves to see" (Biale, Galchinsky, and Heschel 8). Indeed, examining when and how Jewish Americans write as "insiders" or "outsiders" or both (and interrogating our very definition of these and other dynamic terms and concepts in the multicultural lexicon) is, in part, to envision or revision what an intellectually tenable multicultural curriculum should look like. I have endeavored in this book to articulate my own vision regarding these issues, but I have grown tired of this conversation with myself. Come, won't you join me?

2

What Drives Philip Roth?

"You must change your life."

—Rainer Maria Rilke, in Philip Roth's, *The Breast* and *The Ghost Writer*

"[Y]ou've got to be somebody, don't you? There's no way around that."

—Amy Bellette, in Philip Roth's, *The Ghost Writer*

To pursue fiction writing as a career must surely be considered an act bordering on self-torture. The scarce chance of achieving commercial success and material comfort aside, those aspiring to the literary life can look up to only a precious few role models who managed to refine their skills novel after novel, decade after decade. I am certainly not the first to observe that many of our most cherished literary icons in this century reached their artistic peak early in their careers, then painfully endured the waning of their powers.

One need only scan the names on any twentieth-century American literature course syllabus to glean as much. Ralph Ellison, who spent a lifetime trying (unsuccessfully) to summon up the magic of *Invisible Man* (1952), stands out perhaps as the most tragic case, not least of all because a fire consumed hundreds of manuscript pages written through Ellison's blood and sweat over many years. Writer's block plagued Henry Roth throughout his long life, as well, from the moment that he completed that last dazzling paragraph of *Call It Sleep* (1934). After decades of silence, his final flurry of creativity in the *Mercy of a Rude Stream* series has mostly gone to show that Roth, alas, spent himself in his tour de force of 1934. We celebrate even our more prolific and renown twentieth-century American novelists—William Faulkner, Ernest Hemingway, Edith Wharton, F. Scott Fitzgerald, Richard Wright, and others—primarily for their early efforts. *The Sound and the Fury* (1929), *The Sun Also Rises* (1926), *The House of Mirth* (1905), *The Great Gatsby* (1925), and *Native Son* (1940) will still be read and admired long after, say, *The Mansion* (1959), *Across the River and into the Trees* (1950), *Hudson River Bracketed* (1929), *Tender Is the Night* (1934), and *Lawd Today* (1963) have faded from memory.

To his credit, Philip Roth has managed to elude this seemingly ineluctable quandary of the novelist writing in America. Now well into his sixties, he continues to top himself—to extend his artistic reach and, more importantly, his grasp. In his three most recent novels, *Operation Shylock: A Confession* (1993), *Sabbath's Theater* (1995), and *American Pastoral* (1997), his voice bursts from the pages more urgently and audaciously than ever, as several critics have observed. (Roth's *I Married a Communist* [1998] and Human Stain [2000] were published too late for consideration in this chapter.) *Operation Shylock* garnered for Roth the prestigious PEN/Faulkner Award. Cynthia Ozick lauded the work as "A stupendous thing, before which much current American fiction will seem diminished, shrunken. Roth has a *subject,* an obsession; put it that he's possessed. He's now the boldest American writer alive" ("Interview" 370, emphasis in original). *Sabbath's Theater* inspired its share of kudos, as well, and earned Roth yet another National Book Award for fiction. The reviewer for the *New York Times Book Review* called it his "richest, most rewarding novel" (Pritchard 6), and *Tikkun*'s fiction editor, Melvin Jules Bukiet, concurred: "If Roth's previous works once seemed brilliant and substantial, *Sabbath's Theater* makes them look like (finger) exercises prior to this quantum leap into the highest realms of art" (86). It is not without a trace of envy that Bukiet observes, "for all his continually expanding accomplishment, it's not enough for Roth" (85). As if to prove Bukiet right, Roth topped himself once again by winning the Pulitzer Prize for his next novel, *American Pastoral.* Indeed, just as we might have begun instinctively to brace ourselves for Roth's creative well to run dry (given the track records of those writers I previously mentioned), his latest efforts leave us wondering what depths he might still plumb. More to the point, these novels raise the question: What drives Philip Roth?

One might begin to search for answers by looking at some of Roth's most notable failures. In the decade between his critically acclaimed debut collection of stories, *Goodbye, Columbus* (1959), for which he won his first National

Book Award, and the immensely popular *Portnoy's Complaint* (1969), Roth's career seemed to be headed along roughly the same general trajectory as that other Roth of American letters, Henry. This is not to say that Philip Roth experienced an extended period of writer's block. Hardly. The consummate professional, he has produced the goods consistently from the start. However, the two novels that followed *Goodbye, Columbus*—*Letting Go* (1962) and *When She Was Good* (1967)—were something of a disappointment. In these works, Roth left the Jewish suburbs of New Jersey behind to explore the distinctively American Protestant terrain of the Midwest (the home turf of his first wife, Margaret Martinson Williams). Although clearly the work of a competent craftsman, these novels lacked the energy, the bite, the sheer brio of his early stories. As Hillel Halkin has recently noted, they are "ploddingly social-realistic" (43).

Roth's most pronounced artistic failures, *Our Gang* (1971) and *The Great American Novel* (1973), came hard upon the success of *Portnoy's Complaint* (1969). And, like his earlier lackluster novels, they represent a departure from his direct engagement with the issue of Jewish American identity. Roth, setting the crosshairs directly on Richard Nixon, takes a shot at political satire in *Our Gang* and, tellingly, has not returned to the genre since. Through a fantastical baseball league in *The Great American Novel,* Roth attempts glibly to explore "American" (read, WASP) myths. It seems that as much as Roth wanted to be the "Jew who got away," to borrow a phrase from his familiar protagonist Nathan Zuckerman, his fictional meanderings through America's heartland and inside the beltway have invariably been recipes for disaster.

The non-Jewish elements of Roth's weaker efforts would not emerge as so salient a feature if it were not for the distinctively Jewish characters, themes, and locales that earmark his more accomplished works, for it was not until Roth once again engaged the Jewish American milieu in *My Life as a Man* (1974), *The Professor of Desire* (1977), and *The Ghost Writer* (1979) that he reemerged as a force on the American literary scene. Moreover, he has sustained his momentum in his latest works through fictional voyages to Israel in *The Counterlife* (1986) and *Operation Shylock* and through that quintessential Jewish theme—the beleaguered family—in *Sabbath's Theater* and *American Pastoral.* The first twenty or so years of Roth's career, then, summon up for me the image of a precocious acting talent who could not shake the yen to direct, but found himself drawn back time after time to his true vocation.

But to say merely that "the Jewish question" drives Roth won't get one very far. One must dig deeper to answer the question implicit in Ozick's provocative comment: Just what is Roth's "subject," his "obsession," and how does it account for the enduring power of his artistic vision? If Roth's recent works embody a heightened, even obsessive, Jewish self-consciousness amid often hostile environments (e.g., the Middle East, England, the blue-blooded exurbs beyond Newark), they betray in equal measure Roth's commitment toward aesthetic innovation. In short, they are works that the odd detractor tends to scorn as "experimental"—after all, an experiment is a tenuous, unpolished thing—while advocates extol them as "postmodern."

In *The Counterlife* (1986), Roth stretches the boundaries of what we understand to be the novel. Put simply, his characters refuse to remain dead. In one section, Nathan Zuckerman's brother Henry dies of a heart attack. In the next section, he is holed away on a militant Zionist settlement on the West Bank and (healthwise, at least) seems to be doing just fine. Later, it appears that it has been Nathan all along who died of the heart attack (but wasn't it just Nathan who was telling us this story?). If such contradictions do not prove troubling enough, Roth's characters dare to break through what might be called fiction's fifth wall. That is, they have the gall to know that they are fictional characters. At one point, Nathan Zuckerman's English lover, Maria, calls it quits not just with Zuckerman but with her role in the novel as well. "Dear Nathan," she writes, "I'm leaving, I've left. I'm leaving you and I'm leaving the book. . . . I know characters rebelling against their author has been done before, but . . . I have no desire to be original and never did" (*TC* 357). Now, to immerse ourselves in those lives on the written page, we as readers (though an ever-increasing cohort of academic sophisticates would deny it) generally agree to overlook the purely fictional nature of the whole enterprise. Essential to the art of fiction is that "interior collaboration of writer and reader," as the young novelist Jonathan Franzen recently put it, "in building and peopling an imagined world" (41). Roth flouts this implicit contract between writer and reader in *The Counterlife.*

The experimental and postmodern touches in *Operation Shylock* are tamer insofar as the dead obediently remain dead. Still, Roth again pulls the rug out from under us by obfuscating the realms of fact and fiction. To wit: "Philip Roth" is the novel's protagonist. He travels to Israel to interview his friend and colleague, Aharon Appelfeld, and gets more than he bargains for when he encounters his double, who usurps his identity to tout "Diasporism," an anti-Zionist ideology. He also runs into a Palestinian friend,

George Ziad, from his graduate school days; mistaking Roth for his anti-Zionist double, Ziad feels an instant affinity once again for his Jewish American friend. Roth, the protagonist, usurps his impostor's identity, at first just to make good sport with Ziad, but toward the end of the novel to expose, for the Mossad, Jewish financial supporters of the PLO in Athens.

Ample enough reasons exist to treat Roth's novel as fiction and be done with it. For starters, Aharon Appelfeld has disavowed the content of the conversations between himself and Roth that appear in the novel, and (I've done my homework on this) there never was an advertisement in the *Jerusalem Post* for a Philip Roth lecture at the King David Hotel entitled "Diasporism: The Only Solution to the Jewish Problem." As for the Mossad business, well, Roth might just as believably claim that the New York Yankees called on him to pitch relief (to save both Israel and the Yankees is, after all, an enduring fantasy of the American Jew). Interestingly, Roth has stood by the veracity of much of his "confession." In a curious *New York Times Book Review* article that appeared shortly after the novel's publication, he insisted that he was, in fact, stalked by a Diasporist-proselytizing double in Israel and that he could now identify with those Jewish readers who had taken him to task for his own acts of Jewish mischief via fiction. His harrowing experience served to forge, according to Roth, "an astonishing affinity between myself and the audience that has long considered me exactly what I considered him: deformed, deranged, craven, possessed, an alien wreck in a state of foaming madness" ("A Bit of Jewish Mischief" 20).

Roth fashioned for himself a most amusing scenario when he sat down to write a novel about Philip Roth and penned the following lines in the preface: "The book is as accurate an account as I am able to give of actual occurrences that I lived through during my middle fifties and that culminated, early in 1988, in my agreeing to undertake an intelligence-gathering operation for Israel's foreign intelligence service, the Mossad" (*OS* 13). Throughout his entire career, Roth has insisted that he was writing fiction, only to be accused of writing autobiography (Roth *was* Alexander Portnoy for most readers—like Jacqueline Susann, for example, who told Johnny Carson on the *Tonight Show* that she would like to meet Roth but wouldn't want to shake his hand). If his readers wanted autobiography, Roth surely mused, he would give it to them. In *Operation Shylock,* he "'fesses up" as the novel's subtitle suggests. A tough admission, to be sure. "Oh, all right," one can almost hear Roth snicker while pecking away at his keyboard, "I worked for the Mossad.

I saved Israel! There, now I'm writing autobiography. Are you happy?" What thanks does Roth get for letting his guard down? No one believes him.

One would think that Roth's postmodernism would encourage caustic attacks from Jewish critics. Jewish scholars and laypeople alike, especially in the wake of the Holocaust, have been sensitive to the trickiness of language and to the nefarious uses toward which such trickiness can be and have been put. Jewish American writers such as Saul Bellow, Bernard Malamud, and Cynthia Ozick (along with our latest outcropping of social novelists such as Barbara Kingsolver, Toni Morrison, James Welch, Leslie Marmon Silko, and John Edgar Wideman), acutely aware of the power they wield with the written word, can be counted among the few writers since World War II who unabashedly use language toward moral and, yes, didactic ends. Both Jewish writers and critics have excoriated those blathering on about the indeterminacy of language, a postmodernist precept that illusorily extricates fictionists from any moral concern and allows them to construct a language that revels merely in itself, utterly detached from the felt lives of readers. To Ozick, what passes for such postmodern "experimental" fiction smacks of idolatry: "the writers who insist that literature is 'about' the language it is made of are offering an idol: literature for its own sake, for its own maw: not for the sake of humanity" ("Innovation" 247).

Yet Ozick, as I have noted, reserves her highest praise for Roth's most experimental novels. She regarded *The Counterlife* as his most Jewish novel (i.e., his best novel) before having to deem it his second most Jewish novel after the release of *Operation Shylock*. Moreover, Ozick's praise embodies the spirit with which Roth's Jewish audience at large has embraced his recent efforts. The postmodernism of *The Counterlife* did not preclude it from winning the National Jewish Book Award for fiction, along with the National Book Critics Circle Award. Granted, there were those who took Roth to task for his pronounced experimentalism. One reviewer of *The Counterlife* wondered why Roth's revival of Henry passed for "experimentalism" in the first place, considering that the producers of the television show *Dallas* brought back Bobby Ewing using the same "trick" (Pinsker, "Lives" 54). However, the fact remains that, in the eyes of most readers, Roth has treaded of late through the quagmire of Jewish identity with a moral rigor unparalleled by *Portnoy's Complaint,* that knee-slapping lampoon of the Jewish American family. (Irving Howe's uncompromising attack of this novel in "Philip Roth Reconsidered," published in *Commentary,* reflected only the more localized but no less voluble grumblings that were emanating from synagogue pulpits and from B'nai B'rith and Hadassah meetings alike.)

A connection, then, surely exists between Roth's absorption in the issue of Jewish identity and the aesthetics of postmodernism. Determined to get to the bottom of it, I decided that there was only one thing to do. I chaired a panel on Philip Roth at a 1996 regional conference of the MLA. Hoping to prompt inquiry into the relationship between Roth's postmodernism and his Jewishness, I added a subtitle to the panel, "Jewish Mischief Maker or Postmodern Master?" In a brief synopsis of the panel's goals that I sent dutifully to English departments throughout the northeast, I rather more straightforwardly encouraged prospective contributors to explore this relationship.

Although I had hoped to stimulate inquiry concerning the interplay between Roth's Jewish consciousness and his postmodernism, the prospective contributors shed a great deal more light on the "ism" side of the equation. Most did make an effort to square one side of the equation with the other; few, thankfully, took my either/or subtitle literally. Still, most of the abstracts I labored over offered me more knowledge on the theories of various postmodernists and, in the end, precious little about what has driven Philip Roth (steeped more than ever in matters of Jewish identity) to draw on these theories. I realize now that by encouraging writers to focus on Roth's *recent* work, I had pretty much precluded the type of submissions for which I had hoped, for we cannot begin to speculate on the relationship between Roth's Jewish consciousness and his intensified postmodernism of late without taking a closer look at some early manifestations of what we might call postmodernism in his fiction.

Now, let me state clearly that I do not wish to give the impression that I have gotten to the bottom of what drives Roth—that I was blind, but now I see. I hope only to place Roth's recent postmodern aesthetics in the larger context of his career to suggest the consistency of his artistic vision. It is my contention that from the very start of his career, Roth has displayed a fascination with the slipperiness of Jewish identity, which he has only lately illustrated through an overtly postmodern aesthetic especially conducive to such slipperiness. I explore some of Roth's early work in a moment, but first I would like to account for his career-long obsession with the tenuous nature of Jewish identity. The musings of Shuki Elchanan, Nathan Zuckerman's Israeli friend in *The Counterlife,* prove instructive:

> Whenever I meet you American-Jewish intellectuals with your non-Jewish wives and your good Jewish brains, well-bred, smooth, soft-spoken men, educated men who know how to order in a good restaurant, and to appreciate good wine, and to listen courteously to another point of view, I think . . . we are the excitable, ghettoized, jittery little Jews of the Diaspora, and you are the Jews with all the confidence and cultivation that comes of feeling at home where you are. (82)

Elchanan describes a self-assured, even complacent Jewish American ethos for which Zuckerman (and Roth, I would argue) would die. Such an identity represented, in large part, the promise that Zuckerman's Galician grandparents envisioned in a democratic, pluralistic America. Faithful to his grandparents' dreams, Zuckerman tries mightily to exude such "confidence." While in Israel to rescue his brother Henry from making aliyah and, worse, from joining Mordecai Lippman's right-wing Settler movement, Zuckerman boasts of his family's full-fledged Americanness. Henry, he believes, has no business taking on the Zionist struggle because "in our family the collective memory doesn't go back to the golden calf and the burning bush, but to 'Duffy's Tavern' and 'Can You Top This?' Maybe the Jews begin with Judea, but Henry doesn't and he never will. He begins with WJZ and WOR, with double features at the Roosevelt on Saturday afternoons and Sunday doubleheaders at Ruppert Stadium watching the Newark Bears" (149). Would that Zuckerman's consciousness remain wedded solely to such happy, prosaic stuff of Americana. If it would, however, we would have no novel. The hundreds of subsequent pages consist largely of Zuckerman's energetic, even exhausting reflections on and renunciations of Lippman's messianic Zionism (eerily evocative of Baruch Goldstein and Yigal Amir); Elchanan's dovish Middle Eastern precepts; the lunacy of a would-be Jewish hijacker, Jimmy Lustig, who wishes to save the Jewish state by blowing up Yad Vashem—"ZIONISM WITHOUT AUSCHWITZ!/JUDAISM WITHOUT VICTIMS!!" (189); and the insidious anti-Semitism of his lover's home country, England. Thoughtful American Jews, it seems, cannot cultivate their own gardens, à la Candide, given the nagging precariousness of Jewish existence elsewhere in the world. This, above all, seems to be the point of *The Counterlife.* Contra Elchanan's perceptions, Zuckerman is hardly "at home" in America. His tortured meditations on the polemical topics listed above embody the psychic dislocation and consequent torment that define the Jewish American ethos.

To be a Jewish American in the twentieth century is to ask a series of "what if" questions. What if I had been born in 1933 in Germany or Czechoslovakia or Poland? What if my parents or grandparents fled to Israel rather than to the United States? It has been Roth's charge, I would argue, to speculate on such possibilities in his fiction. Reflecting on the counternarratives in *The Counterlife,* Roth once remarked, "Life, like the novelist, has a powerful transforming urge" ("An Interview" 253). Small wonder that Zuckerman cannot ignore any one of the disparate Jewish perspectives embodied in a Lippman, Elchanan, or Lustig; they each represent tangible counterlives that might easily have been his own. This in mind, it seems less and less important as we read *Operation Shylock* to distinguish fact from fiction, to ask the real "Philip Roth" to stand up. If not in the flesh, if only through his artistic consciousness, Roth *is* the "Philip Roth" of the novel, who engages the greatest moral quandary of contemporary Jewish existence, the Middle East.

As I have suggested, one could see Roth dramatize the slipperiness of Jewish American identity early on in his work. One of his first stories, "Eli the Fanatic," serves as an apt example. The eponymous protagonist, Eli Peck, lives in Woodenton, where he and his fellow Jews, having rejected the "extreme practices" of their religion, live "in amity" with their gentile neighbors ("Eli" 189). Naturally, they fear what the goyim might think—that ubiquitous Jewish American concern—when an Orthodox yeshiva moves into the neighborhood. They fret little over the fact that the eighteen yeshiva students and their teacher recently survived the Holocaust; what concerns them is the Hasidic instructor who strolls down the street in his black caftan and hat. Surely such a flagrant display of Jewishness will provoke the scorn of their gentile neighbors. (Interestingly, we never find out what the gentiles think of the yeshiva, if they think of it at all.) A convenient zoning ordinance restricts boarding schools in residential areas, so the assimilated Jews of Woodenton leave it up to Eli, a lawyer, to encourage the yeshiva to pull up stakes and leave town peacefully.

Eli, however, cannot shrug off a nagging sense of responsibility for the welfare of his fellow Jews and manages to placate his assimilated Jewish neighbors by convincing the Hasidic instructor to don secular clothing, one of Eli's own suits. More to the point of this essay, Eli *identifies* with the plight of the Hasidic survivor of Hitler's camps. Roth dramatizes his protagonist's affinity for the Hasid as Eli defiantly adopts the religious clothing—underwear and all—that the Hasid surrenders on his doorstep. He strolls through the town offering hearty "sholoms" to every mortified Jewish passerby. But then he and the Hasid come face to face, each in the other's clothing, whereupon "Eli had the strange notion that *he was two people. Or that he was one person wearing two suits.* The greenie looked to be suffering from a similar confusion" (209, emphasis mine).

Roth, then, began exploring "counterlives" from the start. Eli Peck, like Roth himself, knows that only the cunning of history accounts for the disparate fates of those Woodenton Jews enjoying their lush lawns and those newcomers struggling to carve out their own niche amid hostile brethren. Haunted by such knowledge, Roth's protagonists would go on to envision alternative fates, counterlives, long before it would occur to Roth to adopt the term as a title for his most postmodern novel. Those "what if" questions persisted and continued to drive Roth's artistic imagination. What if a Czech Jewish writer, Sisovsky (modeled roughly upon the Polish Jewish writer, Bruno Schulz), managed to complete his masterpiece before the Gestapo murdered him? This possibility burdens Zuckerman in the epilogue to *Zuckerman Bound* (1985), and he travels to Prague to rescue the lost manuscript. What if Kafka had not died of tuberculosis and had managed to survive the Holocaust and emigrate to America, asks the narrator of "'I Always Wanted You to Admire My Fasting'; or, Looking at Kafka" (1973). In Roth's meditation on such a counterlife, Kafka, the refugee, becomes a lowly Hebrew schoolteacher, endures the spitballs of disrespectful nine-year-old boys, squanders his only chance of marriage to the narrator's aunt by venturing a sexual advance, and dies alone as a stone at seventy, leaving no survivors, "no *Trial,* no *Castle,* no diaries" (326).

In *The Ghost Writer* (1979), Roth gives his imagination an even freer rein to contemplate alternative Jewish fates. Specifically, Zuckerman imagines that Amy Bellette, the assistant to his literary idol, E. I. Lonoff, is Anne Frank, who survived the concentration camps only to see that, thanks to her diary, she has been immortalized as a martyr. Critics have made much hay over Zuckerman's envisioning of Bellette/Frank as a bride who will assuredly garner for him the approbation of his Jewish family. "'I met a marvelous young woman while I was up in New England,'" Zuckerman imagines himself saying to his parents, and the delicious dialogue continues: "'We are going to be married.' 'Married? But so fast? Nathan, is she Jewish?' 'Yes, she is?' 'But who is she?' 'Anne Frank' . . . *Oh, how I have misunderstood my son. How mistaken we have been*" (*TGW* 195–96, emphasis in original). Talk about bringing home the Jewish girl! One, indeed, would be hard-pressed to argue with those who read the whole Anne Frank business in *The Ghost Writer* as Zuckerman's (and Roth's) fantasy of one-upping those Jewish readers who dared to scorn him for his tell-all fiction, certain to be "bad for the Jews."

That said, if Zuckerman sees Bellette/Frank as a potential wife, she also emerges as his double. When he reads Anne Frank's diary, he is taken in not so much by the horror that looms over Frank's innocence, but by her elegant use of the relative clause. "Suddenly she's discovering reflection," Zuckerman marvels, "suddenly there's portraiture, character sketches, suddenly there's long intricate eventful happening so beautifully recounted it seems to have gone through a dozen drafts" (209). He sees the diary primarily as a portrait of the artist as a young woman, the relic of a snuffed out talent. Frank's tragic fate, he realizes, might have been his own had he been the Jewish artist cutting his teeth on the rattle and hum of Amsterdam's streets rather than Newark's.

It should come as little surprise that Zuckerman projects himself into the drama he imagines for Bellette. Bellette/Frank's preoccupations as a burgeoning artist startlingly parallel Zuckerman's: "*I have now reached the stage that I can live entirely on my own, without Mummy's support or anyone else's for that matter. . . . I don't feel in the least bit responsible to any of you. . . . I don't have to give an account of my deeds to anyone but myself*" (174). Zuckerman's declaration of independence to his mother—"'I am on my own!'" (136)—resonates, of course, in this declaration he imagines for Bellette/Frank. He realizes, ultimately, that he entertains his own counterlife when he fashions one for Bellette/Frank. "No," he reflects, "the loving father who must be relinquished for the sake of his child's art was not hers; he was mine" (207). Before intuiting as much, Zuckerman plays the fantasy out to the end. Barely surviving the Holocaust, Zuckerman's Bellette/Frank wishes to "forget her life," so takes on a new identity, Amy Bellette, and chooses not to reveal herself once she sees the impact that her diary has had on the world. Alive, she reflects, her diary would be little more than an adventure story, "But dead she had something more to offer than amusement for ages 10–15; dead she had written, without meaning to or trying to, a book with the force of a masterpiece to make people finally see" (181). Would Zuckerman have sacrificed his identity for art? Would he have been selfless enough to choose the illumination of humankind over his own life? These, of course, are the questions he poses as he imagines a counterlife for Anne Frank and for himself.

Roth, of course, participates vicariously in Zuckerman's retrieval of Anne Frank's legacy. The very word *retrieval,* as I hope I have shown, is an eminently useful word to keep in mind when considering Roth's work as a whole. In fact, the epilogue to Roth's *Zuckerman Bound,* according to Hana Wirth-Nesher, marks a transition in Jewish American literature "from a literature of immigration and assimilation into a literature of retrieval" ("From Newark" 228). She views Zuckerman's search for Sisovsky's lost manuscript in Prague partly as a metaphor for Roth's own search for his Eastern European literary roots. To Wirth-Nesher's canny observation I would add only that Roth has set out to "retrieve" not only a European Jewish *literary* legacy, but the legacy of European Jewry itself. He commemorates the significant Jewish dead in Europe when he imagines counterlives for Anne Frank and Franz Kafka, and he engages the living legacy of Europe's Jews when he contemplates Israeli counterlives to Jewish life in America.

Roth's latest novels, *Sabbath's Theater* and *American Pastoral,* illustrate that although Europe and Israel weigh heavily on Jewish American consciousness, Jewish American novelists have plenty of retrieving to do within America's borders. The novels might be seen, in part, as a stay against the postmodern confusions of Roth's Israel novels, *The Counterlife* and *Operation Shylock.* Confining his protagonists to more familiar turf—the shores of the Atlantic rather than the Mediterranean—Roth, it appears, need not flirt with alternative realms of reality. *Sabbath's Theater* achieves its most powerful climax (a loaded phrase, I realize, while discussing Roth's work) as its alienated and suicidal protagonist, Mickey Sabbath, travels to the New Jersey shore of his childhood to revisit his Jewish roots. First, he visits the dilapidated cemetery where his parents and brother lie buried. Indicative of how hopelessly adrift Sabbath has been throughout a life of debauchery, he discovers that his Aunt Ida has usurped his burial plot next to his family. Nonetheless, amid the headstones of those "original seashore Jews" (*ST* 363)—beloved mothers, fathers, grandfathers, grandmothers, wives and husbands, as he reads on headstone after headstone—Sabbath feels almost whole again: "He felt himself at last inside his life, like someone who, after a long illness, steps back into his shoes for the first time" (357). "'You've got to find a place for me,'" he pleads with the cemetery superintendent (355).

Sabbath's retrieval of his past just begins at the cemetery. For Sabbath, the past merges with the present, in all its Faulknerian eeriness, when he discovers his one-hundred-year-old cousin alive in his home. Yet it is not enough for him to find the past alive in his cousin, Fish. He must establish his own place along the continuum of Jewish history by jarring Fish's memory of both their generations:

> "Do you remember your mother and father, Fish?"
>
> "If I remember them? Sure. Oh, yes. Of course. In Russia. I was born in Russia myself. A hundred years ago."
>
> "You were born in 1894."
>
> "Yeah. Yeah. You're right. How did you know?"
>
> ". . . *And you don't remember Morty and Mickey? The two boys. Yetta and Sam's boys."*
>
> *"You're Morty?"*
>
> *"I'm his kid brother."* (390, emphasis added)

Though Sabbath cannot jar Fish's memory, he reconnects himself to his past when he discovers his brother's possessions in a box marked "Morty's Things." The death of Morty, who was shot down in the Pacific by the Japanese during World War II, devastated the Sabbath family, even drove Sabbath's mother insane. In retrieving his brother's "things"—his track letter, an abridged prayer book for Jews in the armed forces, a red, white, and blue yarmulke, the American flag that was draped over his coffin, among other paraphernalia—Sabbath rescues both his brother's memory and himself. As he muses, "How could he kill himself now that he had Morty's things?" (415). He returns to his home in New England with the most tangible artifacts commemorating his brother's existence and validating his own.

These are the fragments that Sabbath shores against his ruins. Before leaving the New Jersey coast, he wraps himself in his brother's flag and dons his patriotic yarmulke. These artifacts, of course, are the deeply personal fragments of his Jewish past. Sabbath, however, also shares a common history with scores of Jewish American families. In the cemetery, he stumbles across a number of gravestones like this one: "Beloved son and dear brother killed in action at Normandy July 1, 1944 age 27 years you will always be remembered Sergeant Harold Berg" (375). World War II represents nearly a Wordsworthian "spot of time" for Roth. Revisiting his old Newark stomping grounds recently, Roth gazed at a spot on the sidewalk and remembered "standing right here the day, the hour that World War II began. . . . We were playing a game against the stoop on that Sunday afternoon. There was a football game on the radio. The Brooklyn Dodgers were playing the New York Giants. I was 8 years old, and they announced Pearl Harbor had been bombed" (qtd. in Rothstein 278). Roth's reflections suggest simultaneously the good fortune of being an American rather than European Jew during the 1940s and the sacrifice that his generation of Americans, Jews and Gentiles, would nonetheless make. That Roth's eight-year-old counterpart in Poland surely was not fortunate enough to have been listening to a ball game on the radio on this Sunday afternoon has haunted Roth throughout his career and has driven him to imagine Jewish counterlives and fates from the start. But, as Roth well knows, Jewish Americans have far from escaped the maw of humankind's most brutal century. Pearl Harbor, to which he alludes, wrenched America from its stupor, and the subsequent war in Europe exacted a mighty toll from an entire generation. It is this psychic toll that Roth explores through Mickey Sabbath's journey of retrieval in *Sabbath's Theater.*

Roth continues to reconstruct Jewish American counterlives in his most recent novel, *American Pastoral.* Whereas the manifold and warring Jewish identities in Israel (from messianic ultranationalist to secular dove) preoccupied Nathan Zuckerman in *The Counterlife,* some ten years later he is absorbed in the life of his childhood hero from Newark, Seymour "the Swede" Levov. Levov's athletic prowess, combined with his Nordic good looks and effortless charm, propelled him to near mythic stature among his fellow Newark Jews, children and adults alike:

> The Jewishness that he wore so lightly as one of the tall, blond, athletic winners must have spoken to us too—in our idolizing the Swede and his unconscious oneness with America, I suppose there was a tinge of shame and self-rejection. Conflicting Jewish desires awakened by the sight of him were simultaneously becalmed by him; the contradiction in Jews who want to fit in and want to stand out, who insist they are different and insist they are no dif-

> ferent, resolved itself in the triumphant spectacle of this Swede who was actually only another of our neighborhood Seymours whose forebears had been Solomons and Sauls and who would themselves beget Stephens who would in turn beget Shawns. (*AP* 20)

In short, the assimilationist immigrant dreams of Newark's Jews culminate in the heroic figure of the Swede. His distinctively American brand of *spretzaturra* goes a long way toward convincing Zuckerman and his cohorts that they just might transcend the status of "jittery little Jews of the Diaspora," as Shuki Elchanan predicts in *The Counterlife* (82). That Levov goes on after college to marry Miss New Jersey, to take over his father's thriving glove-manufacturing business, and to move to the decidedly blue-blooded exurb of Old Rimrock convinces Zuckerman further that the idyllic, American pastoral life is no longer off limits to the Jew in America.

Upon seeing Levov's brother at their forty-fifth high school reunion, however, Zuckerman discovers that the Swede has recently died of cancer and that there was more to his hero's life than he had dared to imagine—that eschewing the immigrant Jewish ethos for a blue-blooded pastoral existence might have contributed to the tragedies that darkened the Swede's existence. Specifically, he learns from Jerry Levov that the Swede's daughter, Merry, was the "Rimrock bomber" who blew up the town's post office to protest the Vietnam War and unwittingly killed an innocent civilian. She subsequently went into hiding to escape arrest and essentially shattered the Swede's pastoral existence. As Jerry Levov puts it, "My brother thought he could take his family out of human confusion and into Old Rimrock, and she put them right back in. . . . Good-bye, Americana; hello, real time" (*AP* 68–69).

From the sparest of details that Jerry Levov furnishes, Zuckerman sets out to reconstruct the Swede's life. He would "think about the Swede for six, eight, sometimes ten hours at a stretch, exchange my solitude, for his, inhabit this person least like myself, disappear into him, day and night try to take the measure of a person of apparent blankness and innocence and simplicity, chart his collapse, make of him, as time wore on, the most important figure of my life" (74). Indeed, through the prism of the Swede's consciousness (as Zuckerman constructs it), Roth meditates on the utter turmoil of the late 1960s and early 1970s: the violent demonstrations against the Vietnam War, the inner-city race riots, the Black Panther movement, the libidinous excesses, the Watergate scandal. Roth creates Zuckerman, who in turn creates the Swede, and herein Roth offers us a glimpse of a society torn almost completely asunder.

Put simply, Roth seems very much up to his old tricks in *American Pastoral,* for, as I hope I have made clear, it has been his charge as a writer to address the most pressing issues bearing down on Jewish American identity by imagining a host of counterlives. Through an older, more contemplative Zuckerman in *American Pastoral,* Roth articulates eloquently what has consumed his artistic imagination throughout his long career:

> And yet what are we to do about this terribly significant business of *other people,* which gets bled of the significance we think it has and takes on instead a significance that is ludicrous, so ill-equipped are we all to envision one another's interior workings and invisible aims? . . . The fact remains that getting people right is not what living is all about anyway. It's getting them wrong that is living, getting them wrong and wrong and wrong and then, on careful reconsideration, getting them wrong again. That's how we know we're alive: we're wrong. Maybe the best thing would be to forget being right or wrong about people and just go along for the ride. But if you can do that—well, lucky you. (35)

How short a distance, really, from Eli Peck's moment of disorientation in "Eli, the Fanatic" to Roth's blurring of identity altogether in his Israel novels, *The Counterlife* and *Operation Shylock,* and finally to his return to the American terrain in *Sabbath's Theater* and *American Pastoral.* Which is simply to say that the postmodern aesthetic has allowed Roth only greater freedom to express artistically what he has known and dramatized all along—that consciousness, especially Jewish consciousness in our century, is unstable, fractured, fragmented. "The treacherous imagination," Zuckerman contends in *The Counterlife,* "is everybody's maker—we are all the invention of each other, everybody a conjuration conjuring up everyone else. We are all each other's authors" (164). If Roth's "treacherous imagination" might be said to run constantly in overdrive, he has the starkly contrasting but often interweaving fates of the twentieth-century Jew to thank for it. In a career-long effort to keep his finger on the pulse of the Jewish American ethos, Roth must "invent" and "conjure" more than his share of Jewish (counter)lives: Israeli, European, and American. His incessant drive belies Shuki Elchanan's view of a complacent, self-assured Jewish American identity in *The Counterlife* and the

Mossad agent's more irascible spin on the matter in *Operation Shylock*: "Go wherever you feel most blissfully unblamable. That is the delightful luxury of the utterly transformed American Jew. Enjoy it. You are that marvelous, unlikely, most magnificent phenomenon, the truly liberated Jew. The Jew who is not accountable" (352). It is to Roth's credit that he has never fit such a description. Through his imagination, he has journeyed to those places few other Jewish American writers have dared to travel: the morally corrupt Jewish suburbs in America, the West Bank in the Middle East, post-Holocaust Europe. He has decidedly *not* gone to those "blissfully unblamable" places, but to those polemical realms of Jewish consciousness certain to elicit jeers from certain quarters.

To be sure, the din of disapproval from the Jewish ranks continues to dog Roth, if at a lower pitch. That *Operation Shylock* won the PEN/Faulkner Award didn't keep Daphne Merkin from panning it: "If I were living in Israel—if I were my sister, say, who lives in Jerusalem with her American husband and four American-born children despite ongoing doubts and criticism—I would despise this book" (44). *The Ghost Writer* generally enjoyed favorable reviews, but there were those (as there surely would be) who opined that Roth exploited the Holocaust through the Anne Frank subplot. "Is Roth not utilizing the Holocaust to give himself legitimacy in the Jewish community?" asked Alan Berger rhetorically (160). Finally, no sooner does Roth win the National Book Award for *Sabbath's Theater* than the reviewer for the prominent Jewish magazine *Midstream* trotted out this old anti-Roth chestnut: "Roth's characters have little Jewish identity. They rarely—if ever—go to synagogue. They do not contribute to UJA. They do not worry about intermarriage" (Teicher 46) and on and on and on. Although these statements still represent legitimate concerns, sociologically speaking, one would think that criticism on Roth had moved beyond unreflective and downright unliterary censure of this ilk.

True, Roth's protagonists stand little chance of earning lifetime service plaques from their local UJA chapter; they don't wrap tefillin each morning, nor do they even attend synagogue, as the *Midstream* reviewer bemoans. Fair enough. To close this meditation on what drives Philip Roth, I would qualify such dour criticism only by arguing that no other Jewish American writer feels a greater burden concomitant to the "freedom" defining his or her existence as an American. Those readers who still chastise Roth as self-absorbed have simply not been paying attention, for what most absorbs Roth's artistic consciousness is not his own identity but the plethora of alternate, often tragic, Jewish identities and fates throughout the Diaspora and in Israel. One sees what drives Roth not so much in the lascivious adventures of Portnoy, but in Zuckerman's travels to Prague, Jerusalem, and the Newark of his youth, in "Roth's" trip to the West Bank, and in Sabbath's journey to the Jersey shore.

3

The (Mischievous) Theological Imagination of Melvin Jules Bukiet

The work of Melvin Jules Bukiet goes a long way toward proving that Jewish American fiction continues to embody the distinct values and preoccupations of a minority culture. In three powerful works—*Stories of an Imaginary Childhood* (1992), *While the Messiah Tarries* (1995), and *After* (1996)—Bukiet has transported us to a pre-Holocaust shtetl in Poland, to contemporary Orthodox and secular Jewish milieus in America, and back to the European Jewish terrain just "after" the Holocaust. (Bukiet's *Signs and Wonders* [1999] was published too late for consideration in this chapter.) Bukiet is a child of a Holocaust survivor, and the European catastrophe has thus far served to a definite degree as a ubiquitous referent around which his precocious artistic imagination whirls. Indeed, through his artistic journey to various outposts of Jewish existence in the twentieth century, Bukiet explores the viability of a meaningful Jewish identity in a post-Holocaust world.

Bukiet's depiction of the shtetl—replete with Jews, Gypsies, and dybbuks—and the surreal nature of his work, generally, have compelled several critics to note the resonances of I. B. Singer's work in his fiction (see especially Berger 72 and Cheyette 21). Although I would be hard-pressed to dispute Singer's presence in Bukiet's work, I would argue that the predecessor discussed in the previous chapter, Philip Roth, informs Bukiet's artistic vision in more subtle and illuminating ways. One can see the anxiety of influence emerge in Bukiet's essay "Looking at Roth; or 'I Always Wanted You to Admire My Hookshot.'" In the essay, the title of which refers to Roth's dazzling essay/story "'I Always Wanted You to Admire my Fasting'; or, Looking at Kafka," Bukiet waxes elegiac over Roth's artistic command:

> Roth is hilarious and smart and just about the world's most beautiful writer, delighting in the path any single sentence follows, making palpable the perfect turn of thought that finds echo in the perfect turn of phrase. It's not a hookshot now, but a bank off the backboard, the angle of incidence equalling the angle of reflection, finding the basket almost every time. Roth's is a fiction of exquisitely counterbalanced incident and reflection. Newark is the ball.
>
> Swish. ("Looking" 125)

A faint but discernible trace of envy, I believe, permeates Bukiet's reflections on Roth, both in the passage above and in his more recent laudatory review of Roth's *Sabbath's Theater* (1995; see Bukiet, "Master"). Indeed, making that perfect swish with each sentence is as important to Bukiet as it is to Roth. I would argue, moreover, that the same countervailing forces that have dogged Roth throughout his career have also preoccupied Bukiet. I am thinking, specifically, of the recurrent tension in Roth's work between his (or his protagonists') artistic consciousness and his filial and tribal obligations. In *The Ghost Writer* (1979), for example, one might recall that Roth's familiar protagonist and alter ego Nathan Zuckerman inspires his father's vehement disapproval after writing a story based on a money feud between relatives. Dr. Zuckerman tells his son, "Nathan, your story, as far as Gentiles are concerned, is about one thing and one thing only. . . . It is about kikes. Kikes and their love of money" (94). Rather than renounce his story for the sake of public relations, rather than succumb to the pressures of his tribe, Zuckerman sticks to his artistic guns. "I am on my own!" (109) he tells his mother adamantly in an especially poignant scene.

One sees a similar tension at the center of Bukiet's fiction. The essential and equally instructive contrast is that Bukiet's uncompromising artistic vision engages the theological quandaries that beset the Jew in both a pre- and post-Holocaust world, whereas Roth has explored largely the predicament of secular (albeit not wholly assimilated) Jews in America. The stakes, consequently, seem much higher in Bukiet's work. In *Stories of an Imaginary Childhood,* the adolescent narrator's artistic consciousness threatens to rip him away from the redemptive Jewish world of his ancestors; the characters in *While the Messiah Tarries* brazenly challenge the validity of Jewish Law amid a post-Holocaust world; finally, in *After,* Bukiet outstrips Roth's Jewish brand of mischief by fashioning a thoroughly unconventional Holocaust novel in his effort to challenge a silent God.

In "American Jewish Writing, Act II," a perspicacious article that appeared in *Commentary* in 1976, Ruth R. Wisse observed that more and more Jewish American writers (who took the Jewish side of their hyphenated identities seriously) had begun to transport their protagonists to European or Israeli soil. The increasingly assimilated American terrain, it appeared, had grown too delimiting for the Jewish imagination. Hence, "Writers like [Cynthia] Ozick and [Hugh] Nissenson, who feel the historic, moral, and religious weight of Judaism, and want to represent it in literature, have had to ship their characters out of town by Greyhound or magic carpet, to an unlikely *shtetl,* to Israel . . . to other times and other climes, in search of pan-Jewish fictional atmospheres" (45).

Wisse recognized no less than a paradigm shift in Jewish American writing, given that an earlier wave of writers such as Abraham Cahan, Anzia Yezierska, Henry Roth, Saul Bellow, and Bernard Malamud put Jewish American fiction on the map by situating their protagonists amid numerous gritty urban environments in America. As Murray Baumgarten aptly notes in his influential study *City Scriptures: Modern Jewish Writing* (1982), "American Jewish writers . . . marked Brownsville, Brooklyn, 'uptown,' and later the Bronx, New Rochelle, Scarsdale, Newark, Chicago, and Montreal as their ground" (10–11). Wisse recognized, then, that the work of Ozick and Nissenson heralded in a new generation of writers who would stake out new ground beyond America's shores. Although America continues to be a fruitful site for the Jewish American imagination, it is worth noting that in the twenty-odd years since her essay appeared, a plethora of Jewish American writers have followed Ozick's and Nissenson's lead to explore the European and Israeli Jewish setting in their work. The writers who immediately flash on one's mental screen in this category include Philip Roth, Rebecca Goldstein, Curt Leviant, Tova Reich, Anne Roiphe, E. M. Broner, Nessa Rapoport, and, more to the point of this essay, Melvin Jules Bukiet.

Indeed, Bukiet's *Stories of an Imaginary Childhood* (winner of the 1992 Edward Lewis Wallant Award) exemplifies Wisse's thesis. Through the perspective of an unnamed twelve-year-old narrator (on the precipice of manhood according to Judaic belief), Bukiet brings to life the Polish shtetl, Proszowice, the setting for each of the twelve interrelated stories. The year is 1928, and the imminent Holocaust thus looms hauntingly throughout the collection right up until the final lines of the last story, "Torquemada," as the narrator's father comforts his son, psychologically disoriented by a recent anti-Semitic assault. "We have each other," the father assures our narrator, "and it's the twentieth century of civilized man. There, there. What harm could possibly come to us in 1928?" (*SIC* 197). To be sure, Bukiet carefully constructs the stories in the collection to evoke the Holocaust allusively and to elicit responses such as the following by Lawrence L. Langer: "As a member of the post-Holocaust generation, I was unable to banish from consciousness the sense that I was reading about a doomed people. . . . In a very subtle way, Bukiet builds this complicated response into his fiction" (75). In the very title of his collection, Bukiet evokes the Holocaust; these are stories, he suggests, of an imaginary childhood in Europe, which might have been his own childhood if not for the cunning of history.

Small wonder that *Stories of an Imaginary Childhood* has been seen as Bukiet's artistic attempt to retrieve a world torn asunder by the Nazis: "Bukiet attempts to inscribe his life as it might have been in a Jewish world now vanished. In so doing, he retrieves a portion of that world, with all its hopes, illusions, and prayers" (Berger, *Children* 72). As Alan Berger suggests, Bukiet (re-)creates the Jewish pre-Holocaust Proszowice with scrupulous care. He peoples the shtetl with thoroughly unique Jewish characters, including Zalman the gravedigger; Rebecca the whore; Shivka Bellet, a shrew who bestows all her pent up loving-kindness on a stray dog; Jacob Lester, a brainy rebel who yearns for America; and a fraudulent but thoroughly winning "millionaire," Isaac. It is to Bukiet's credit that, by the time one finishes reading the collection, one intimately knows the Jews of Proszowice, their idiosyncratic religious rituals and superstitions. What is more, one cannot help but bemoan the imminent decimation of that shtetl and the countless other Jewish villages in Europe whose unique characters and stories have yet to be "imagined."

Having said this much, I would like now to focus on the specific stories in which the artistic consciousness of the adolescent narrator emerges most forcefully, for if it is true that Bukiet sets out to reconstruct and retrieve an entire shtetl in *Stories of an Imaginary Childhood,* it is just as true that he renders an incisive portrait of a Jewish artist as a young man. As I have suggested, Bukiet dramatizes the conflict between the young narrator's artistic consciousness and the communal, religious mores of Proszowice in several stories. A brief passage in "A Woman with a Dog" illustrates what the independent, artistic consciousness is up against in the shtetl: "Proszowice was a town of talkers. . . . Silence was automatically suspect. It was considered arrogant, enigmatic; worst of all, it was private. We felt as if we had a right to each other's pains and pleasures. The notion of the individual was anathema to that of community" (*SIC* 89).

This emphasis on community, consistent with Judaic principles, bears down heavily on the narrator's fiercely independent artistic consciousness. In "The Virtuoso," Bukiet engages this tension as the narrator tries to find a way to extricate himself from violin lessons. The rub is that the violin is not a mere instrument, but a tangible artifact linking the narrator to his Jewish ancestors: "The instrument had been my father's and his father's before him. Legend had it that it originally came from fifteenth-century Spain, where it had played to the accompaniment of the Exile. It had led the column of Jews to the border, out, and across Europe, adopting the rhythms of the countries through which it passed" (3–4). The narrator's parents' obdurate insistence that he continue his lessons, despite his marginal talent, represents their way of forcing their son to accept his place in the continuum of their familial, Jewish history. The narrator, however, does not accept his legacy. Although he does not yet know where his talent lies, the pig squeals he elicits from the violin are enough to convince him that he will never be the next Heifetz. Importantly, he recognizes that the choice that faces him is "the same old battle between obligation and independence" (11). In depositing the violin in a tree's hollow for a prodigy of the future, the narrator boldly chooses independence over obligation.

In the second story of the collection, "Levitation," the narrator eschews more specifically religious obligations in his effort to assert his independence. Early on in the story, he acknowledges his petulance: "I cannot abide limits. I don't know when to stop. I have always, imagine that I always will, want to see or do whatever is prohibited—for precisely that reason" (18–19). It comes as little surprise, after such a confession, that the narrator defies Jewish ritual on Rosh Hashanah by gazing into the eyes of the Kohanim—the descendants of the priestly caste—during their reading of the Shema Yisroael. Later, during the Tashlikh ritual (in which Jews traditionally throw bread into a body of water to cast off their sins symbolically), the narrator more brazenly defies the traditional religious rituals of the community. Rather than wash away his sins contritely, Proszowice's special version of the Tashlikh tradition, he attempts to fly from the river, to levitate. He wishes to transcend the ignoble condition of his community, "to shed the yoke that bore us down, to harness that magnificent lack, to meet the perfect contradictions of the Almighty on his own ground—that was my goal" (21). Bukiet emphasizes that the narrator's singular (and futile) efforts to levitate form a rift between himself and his more traditionally adherent parents. At story's end, the parents gaze at their son "with the inexpressible ignorance born of love and the rending knowledge that there is nothing we can do to help each other" (29).

Bukiet imbues both "The Virtuoso" and "Levitation" with tremendous emotional intensity by emphasizing the very real pull of familial and religious obligation that the narrator painfully resists. Upon surreptitiously hearing his violin instructor play, for example, the narrator recognizes the redemptive power of the instrument. "She played the song of Jews," he acknowledges, "of the remembered past and the redeemable future" (13). He does not gaze blithely upon the Kohanim in "Levitation," but forces his eyes open, half expecting the Devil to "reach through the floor of the shul and drag me under" (19). Moreover, his desire to levitate represents not a rejection of Judaism per se, but a rejection of the traditional modes of religious expression. As he reflects, "My family would take my aspirations amiss, but, like them, I was in search of the presence of the holy. Only our maps differed" (20). In these first two stories, then, Bukiet depicts the emergence of the narrator's creative, independent consciousness against a backdrop of powerful familial love and religious ardor. The narrator resembles Philip Roth's young Nathan Zuckerman insofar as he, too, wishes to be "the Jew who got away" (*The Ghost Writer* 50). However, familial and religious obligations, I would argue, exert more sheer force in Bukiet's pre-Holocaust shtetl than in Roth's post-Holocaust Newark.

Nonetheless, the artistic imagination of Bukiet's narrator cannot be held in check by tribal pressures any more than Nathan Zuckerman's imagination can be held in check by Judge Leopold Wapter's ten admonitory questions (e.g., "Can you honestly say that there is anything in your short story that would not warm the heart of a Julius Streicher or a Joseph Goebbels?" [Roth, *The Ghost Writer* 103–4]). The distinctively literary nature of Bukiet's adolescent narrator emerges in "Sincerely, Yours." In the story, Bukiet charts the boy's rapid development as a writer, from his highly imaginative advertisements for his father's wares—whose herring, he touts, will "'tickle the most fickle of taste buds'"—to the belletristic love letters that he ghostwrites for Isaac the Millionaire (*SIC* 65). The latter endeavor, the narrator reflects, transforms him "from Proszowice's second greatest liar into a writer" (66).

His father encourages his literary imagination by giving him a book of poetry as a Hanukkah gift, but he clearly hopes to channel his son's talent toward religious pursuits. Perhaps, the father muses, his son will write prayers.

While this remains a remote possibility in "Sincerely, Yours," it seems practically impossible in "New Words for Old," in which Bukiet depicts the narrator's literary imagination as more clearly antithetical to the pious sensibilities of the shtetl. The story revolves around a famous Jewish poet's stay in Proszowice while his carriage is being repaired. The narrator, a burgeoning poet himself, admires the renowned poet, Kimminov, tremendously. Bukiet takes pains, however, to emphasize Proszowice's ambivalence toward Kimminov and, importantly, the narrator's recognition of this ambivalence: "To most, poetry was an aberration, inspired by lazy, no-good gadabouts with self-proclaimed emancipated tendencies. Strangely, they did appreciate Kimminov. He was a half-breed partaking of both idol and pariah, a religious man, a literary man. Jewish successes in the non-Jewish world were few, and therefore to be treasured. Not emulated, but treasured" (133).

The narrator realizes, then, that many in his shtetl consider poetry an idol and poets, perforce, idol worshipers. Still, Kimminov's visit only fuels his literary aspirations. As the narrator orates for his village the poetry that a feeble Kimminov whispers into his ear, he marvels at its transformative power. "Kimminov," he reflects, "had created a world that swept over the moment like the shadow of a cloud. It was a miracle. Or a trick" (139). His wish to emulate Kimminov manifests itself as he begins to revise the elder poet's words during the reading. He gradually begins to ignore Kimminov completely and instead recites his own poetry: "My voice rang out my own poems with my own words in my own rhythms, my own vision taking the souls of the people of Proszowice for a flight out of the tiny shul into space, and then returning them safely to tremble in their pews" (143). This is the indomitable voice of a Jewish artist as a young man. The young narrator realizes that his artistic consciousness threatens to isolate him from the loving, religious world of the shtetl. He knows that imaginative writing of Kimminov's ilk might be a devil's "trick," but he must take this chance. He cannot suppress the literary imagination that so eloquently renders the Proszowice of Bukiet's *Stories of an Imaginary Childhood.*

I would no sooner argue that Bukiet *is* the adolescent narrator of *Stories of an Imaginary Childhood* than I would argue that Philip Roth is Nathan Zuckerman. That said, the narrative voice of Bukiet's second collection of stories, *While the Messiah Tarries,* does evoke the independent artistic consciousness of the narrator in Bukiet's earlier collection—a voice defiant of religious pieties but deadly serious about theological issues. Put another way, if the adolescent narrator of Bukiet's first collection of stories were to survive the imminent Holocaust, he would no doubt go on to write a book like *While the Messiah Tarries.* The stories in this collection are not as closely interrelated as the stories in Bukiet's first collection; they are not limited to a single narrator or locale. This approach allows Bukiet to touch on a broader range of concerns. For example, he dramatizes the alienation of Orthodox Jewish characters who must find their footing on increasingly secular American terrain; he enacts midrashim, revelatory commentaries or rereadings of biblical stories; he envisions his contemporary Jewish American characters' various, often morally ambiguous responses to the Holocaust (see Berger, *Children* 73–75); and he takes on an emergent theme in Jewish American fiction when he explores the subject of Jewish identity against a post-perestroika Russian backdrop. Although these areas of inquiry are fruitful, it is Bukiet's insistent and often surreal exploration of the role of Jewish Law in the lives of his post-Holocaust, American characters that permeates *While the Messiah Tarries* and betrays his mischievous theological imagination.

The burden of abiding by the Jewish Law, of leading a covenanted existence, has long been a preoccupation of established Jewish American fictionists such as Hugh Nissenson, Cynthia Ozick, Saul Bellow, and, I would add to the list, Bernard Malamud (though his protagonists embrace a highly secularized covenant). In a recent essay, "The Jewish Voice," Robert Alter adumbrates how this preoccupation with the Law manifests itself in the work of that quintessential Jewish writer of the twentieth century, Franz Kafka: "In his writing, he would ponder again and again the imperative authority of the law, its possible arbitrariness, the necessity of constant interpretation it imposed, the impossibility of living without it. These are compellingly Jewish concerns" (42). Kafka's tortured meditations on the Law interestingly and even eerily resonate in Bukiet's second collection of stories. Granted, Bukiet's contemporary urban American milieu hardly affords him a measure of alienation and psychic terror that rivals Kafka's as a Germanophone Jew in prewar Czechoslovakia. Nonetheless, the burden of the Law bears down on Bukiet's artistic consciousness so inexorably that one might justifiably use that overused descriptor "Kafkaesque" to characterize his most recent stories. Bukiet, less obliquely than Kafka, holds the Law up to constant interpretation in his work as he explores its viability in a gritty post-Holocaust world that would seem to preclude any redemptive possibilities. Like his college student protagonist in "Postscript to a Dead Language," he refuses to partake in the "blind observance of ritual" (*WMT* 153). Indeed, the title of Bukiet's collection, if couched as a question, might stand the revision, "How Should a Jew Live While the Messiah Tarries?" (As it stands, Bukiet's title echoes the words of the Ani Ma'amim, the Jewish testament of faith recited by some Holocaust victims on the way to the gas chambers.) Bukiet pits his characters against fantastic circumstances to entertain answers to this question. In "Himmler's Chickens," a disaffected Jewish lawyer must decide what to do with home movies of Heinrich Himmler madly shooting his chickens with a pistol; a prominent Columbia University archaeologist unearths the birthplace of God in "Old Words for New"; a rabbi in upstate New York squares off against Satan himself in "The Devil and the Dutchman."

Philip Roth, himself influenced by Kafka, commented during his first public interview, "My fiction is about people in trouble" ("The NBA Winner" 2). The same might be said of Bukiet's "people" in *While the Messiah Tarries,* though, as the sketches above suggest, they grapple with crises of a more theological, less corporeal ilk than the crises of Roth's memorable protagonists. One reviewer of the collection identified the stories as "theofictions, ruminations—simultaneously playful and deadly serious—on the nature of divinity in our post-Holocaust condition" (Pinsker, "Earthly Brushes" 44). "The Golden Calf and the Red Heifer" epitomizes Bukiet's theological imagination (his Kafkaesque meditations on Law and covenant) and, to my mind, stands out as the most forceful story in the collection. "If there is the tiniest discernible nick in the blade, the slaughter is considered unkosher" (*WMT* 72). One need only read this first sentence of the story to locate Bukiet's overarching concern and that of his protagonist, Kleinberg. Through Kleinberg's perspective, Bukiet explores the moral viability of kashruth, Judaism's fastidious dietary laws. It falls on Kleinberg, as the only kosher butcher of Spritzendyville, an insulated Orthodox Jewish suburb of New York, to uphold these sacred, inviolable laws. The contemplative butcher, however, suffers from a crisis of faith; he doubts the ethical propriety of kashruth. The perceptive reader can infer as much before finishing the first paragraph as the narrator draws our attention to the hypocrisy of the aforementioned kosher law:

> This stricture derives from a humanitarian impulse, for the being so nobly sacrificing its life and aspirations in order to satisfy the human appetite for flesh must be dispatched as painlessly as possible, so saith the law, which envisions pain commenced and concluded with the quality of the blade, eliding the fact that twenty-five hundred pounds of steer is shackled, hung upside down, and terrorized before the perfectly whetted edge is drawn in a single wild swipe across its throat. The law states what it requires and the rest is optional. (72)

The passage evokes Philip Roth's own brand of scathing irony, an irony that has virtually become the stylistic trademark of postwar Jewish American writers (see Alter, "Jewish Voice" 43). Roth, in fact, has taken his jabs at the kosher laws in *Portnoy's Complaint* (1969). However, whereas Roth engages the subject primarily for comic effect, Bukiet holds these laws up to serious scrutiny in "The Golden Calf and the Red Heifer." He dramatizes the net result of kashruth's "humanitarian" laws as Kleinberg slaughters a lamb. The disquieting scene merits a lengthy quotation:

> The rows of animals stared mournfully at him, as if waiting for him to choose the scapegoat who would pay the price for his discomfiture. He stroked the chin of the shy lamb he had taken to calling Molly, and led her across to the rear where the shackles and trough lay. . . . Molly was an idiot, prancing vainly before the others, delighted by her temporary release from her restraints, oblivious to the end of the path of such freedom. . . . He hung Molly up, ignoring the pathetic eye contact the upside-down lamb attempted to make with the man who had housed her, named her, fed her, and been her benefactor, and now slit her throat and jumped back lest his canvas soles be soiled by her blood. (79)

The kosher laws, Judaism's compromise with the ideal of vegetarianism, obfuscate the very real cruelty of animal slaughter. For this reason, perhaps, Bukiet's kosher butcher swears off the eating of meat. The kosher laws, he recognizes, contain serious logical flaws as well. The Levitical injunction "Thou shalt not seethe a kid in its mother's milk"—which "tacitly grants the doomed creatures a maternal sensibility" (75)—might make just enough sense to validate the separation of cow's milk from beef. Kleinberg, however, is hard-pressed to extend the logic to the separation of chicken meat and dairy, and muses, "Do not ask what bird ever gave birth to a calf and why therefore chicken paprikash is taboo" (75).

One wonders why Kleinberg, perturbed by what he perceives as the ethical and logical flaws of kashruth, stops at vegetarianism and does not choose a different occupation to boot. The answer, I believe, lies not primarily in his unquestionable greed, but in his talmudic sensibility, that text-centered sensibility that dictates that one "turn it [the Torah] over and over, for everything is in it" (Alter, "Jewish Voice" 43). Kleinberg—whose reflections and re-reflections on the rabbis' talmudic debates on the law "carried him near to sundown" (*WMT* 77)—remains a butcher to immerse himself in the depths of the moral conundrums of kashruth.

Having exhausted the textual approach, Kleinberg loses faith utterly and flouts the kosher laws (he cheats his customers and, worst of all, refuses to replace his nicked slaughtering blade). His gradual slide into corruption provokes a visit from a golem in the form of a nubile woman. She tempts the butcher to complete the arc of his sins and guides him from one sin to the next with admirable efficiency. In short order, she coaxes him to gaze directly upon her lovely face, slaughter a pig, provide her with bacon, and join her in the sexual act. Kleinberg, to his credit, carries out the golem's wishes not merely for the earthly pleasures that they afford (money and sex), but because he realizes that his descent into sinfulness might bring about illumination, even at the price of God's wrath. He sees the red-headed woman as a contemporary equivalent of a biblical red heifer that the nomadic Jews sacrificed to atone for their sins in the desert: "Kleinberg the mundane butcher felt himself to be in the presence of the sublime. He had no choice but to follow the heifer wherever it led" (80). God does, ultimately, unleash wrath upon Spritzendyville's "kosher" butcher shop as it burns to the ground while Kleinberg couples with his red heifer, who urges the butcher, "Forget me. . . . Think of the other animals," and perishes in the conflagration (85).

Although the residents of Spritzendyville cast the blame for their lost kosher butcher shop squarely on their butcher's shoulders (they discover Kleinberg's nicked, unkosher slaughtering blade amid the charred ruins), the story offers ample evidence that their own spiritual complacency provokes God's fury in at least equal measure, for only Kleinberg's actions, whether sinful or not, seem motivated by a conscious moral intent. Indeed, only Kleinberg is religious in the strictest sense. His neighbors in Spritzendyville might follow the letter of the Law more assiduously than he does, but (like so many of the peripheral Jewish characters in Bukiet's collection) they fret little over the spirit of the Law: "Spritzendyville's residents were continually on guard for impurity within the confines of their miserable shanties, where hordes of ill-clad children shared a room while double sinks and double stoves and double refrigerators and double garbage cans graced the kitchen, lest even the refuse of meat and dairy mix" (75). Kleinberg's neighbors seem unperturbed by the apparent incongruity of the Jewish Law, which affords more square footage to household appliances than to human beings. What is more, such complacent adherence to ritual flies in the face of Jewish values. As two prominent Judaic scholars suggest, "The Bible consistently warns that the person-to-God laws can have but minimal moral effect when observed without the intention of becoming moral. The Prophets vehemently attacked those Jews whose mechanical observance of these laws betrayed a lack of concern for the ethical principles underlying them" (Prager and Telushkin 68–69). Jeremiah, one of these most conspicuous prophets, warned his fellow Jews against mechanical observance, and, interestingly, Bukiet alludes to him and to the "'sins of the people' that had lead to the Babylonian exile" (*WMT* 79). Lamentably, the citizens of Spritzendyville duplicate the sins of Jeremiah's fellow Jews.

"The Red Heifer and the Golden Calf" might best be understood, then, as a midrash on the book of Jeremiah, an indictment against unreflective, mechanical obedience toward Jewish Law. Only Kleinberg realizes that the red heifer sacrifices herself for the town's sin of complacency in ritual as well as for his active defiance of ritual. Neither Spritzendyville's rabbi nor the rest of the townspeople perceive the holiness of her ashes, "spread as loam to repent the sins of the past and to mitigate the sins of the future" (87). Kleinberg alone understands the "inherent morality of the flesh, its weakness and its strength. Only Kleinberg, who had sinned in the midst of sanctity, was now capable of finding sanctity in the midst of sin" (87). To stir his cohorts from their stupor, to redeem them, he sacrifices himself with one deadly stroke of the blade, "which, when it fell to the ashes, was as straight as the line from Adam to Moses" (88).

Although *Stories of an Imaginary Childhood* and *While the Messiah Tarries* announce themselves as the work of a mischievous theological imagination,

Bukiet significantly ups the mischief ante in his most recent work, *After.* Before I explore this novel, however, it is worth pausing to note that a rich mischief-making tradition in Jewish culture informs Bukiet's penchant for mischief and that this penchant represents yet another affinity between Bukiet and Roth. Mischief, embodied from time to time in the impish alter ego of Moishe Pipik (Moses Bellybutton), has seemed to play a continuous and prominent role in Jewish culture, which, perhaps, should come as no surprise given the countervailing Jewish emphasis on the Law. As Philip Roth recently noted,

> Perhaps because of the abundance of prescriptions both internally and externally generated by Jewish history, perhaps because of the singular sort of care that living as a Jew has generally required, perhaps because of the exaggerated seriousness with which a thoughtful Jew is often burdened, Jewish mischief—as couched, say, in the inexhaustible jokes about their peculiarities that Jews themselves so much enjoy—flourishes, surprisingly enough, in even the most superdignified Jewish circles. ("Bit" 1)

Now, there is mischief and there is *mischief.* That is, certain Jewish mischief—like the countless jokes to which Roth refers—brings immeasurable joy to Jewish audiences (while often eliciting only nervous laughter from non-Jews). Jokes about the *nebbisheh* Jew, the cunning Jew, or the parsimonious Jew, told *by* Jews, subvert the dominant culture's use of these stereotypes. They do not so much challenge the veracity of the stereotypes as they strip them of their venom through appropriation.

But as long as Jewish mischief of this ilk continues to inspire kudos from even the most superdignified Jews, there will be that other type of Jewish mischief that inspires condemnation rather than praise from within Jewish circles. Early on, Philip Roth emerged as the preeminent maker of this scurrilous variety of mischief, at least in the eyes of several critics and laypeople. In the wake of his first collection of stories, *Goodbye, Columbus* (1959), Roth was attacked for creating adulterous Jews ("Epstein"), goldbricking Jewish soldiers ("Defender of the Faith"), crass, materialistic Jews ("Goodbye, Columbus"), and thoroughly assimilated Jews who wish to give the boot to Holocaust survivors settling in their lush suburban neighborhood ("Eli, the Fanatic"). When Roth dared, ten years later, to create a lascivious Jew in *Portnoy's Complaint* (who sought to put the *id* back into *Yid*), even Irving Howe, who initially praised *Goodbye, Columbus,* had had enough. In a landmark essay, "Philip Roth Reconsidered," Howe attacked Roth's novel and "reconsidered" his earlier views of Roth's first collection. Roth's characters were, in the final analysis, merely caricatures—the product of Roth's "thin personal culture" (73). Aesthetic considerations aside, what clearly rankled most of Roth's Jewish detractors was the highly unsavory image of the Jew that Roth presented to the mainstream public, who were only too willing (so the fearful logic goes) to believe that Jews were money grubbers, adulterers, sexual predators—the list goes on and on. In short, Roth's brand of Jewish mischief was considered by many to be bad for the Jews. Roth's tumultuous relationship with his Jewish audience, of course, has been both his burden and his muse (for further elaboration on this subject, see Cooper). One will recall, for example, that in *The Ghost Writer,* Nathan Zuckerman must assert his artistic independence from his disapproving father and from a prominent local judge after he pens a story about "Kikes and their love of money," as Zuckerman's father puts it (94).

At this point, allow me to shift my attention to Bukiet's *After.* One wonders how Nathan Zuckerman's father would have responded to this work of fiction had young Nathan presented him with a prepublication copy of the manuscript. The novel opens just "after" Isaac Kaufman's liberation from Aspenfeld, a subcamp of Buchenwald. In one sense, then, *After* is precisely what the elder Zuckerman (and a great many of Roth's early readers) wishes that Zuckerman/Roth would write. Insofar as the Holocaust—that watershed catastrophe of twentieth-century Jewish life—fuels Bukiet's creative enterprise in *After,* the novel is a decidedly Jewish work. That said, though, when one of the American "liberators" pops out of his tank in the middle of Aspenfeld asking, "'Hey youse. Is this the way to the Grand Concourse?'" (*After* 4), we know that we are in store for a Holocaust novel markedly different from what we have come to expect given the solemnity of, for example, Saul Bellow's *Mr. Sammler's Planet,* Edward Lewis Wallant's *The Pawnbroker,* and Arthur A. Cohen's *In the Days of Simon Stern.* As Pinsker notes, "Bukiet upends the apple cart of piety that has until now attached itself to hushed discussions of the Holocaust" ("Dares" 285). In so doing, Bukiet outstrips Roth's version of Jewish mischief. He out-Roths Roth.

Indeed, Bukiet's distinct brand of mordant humor pervades the work in ways that would assuredly make the elder Zuckerman as well as several contemporary Jewish and even non-Jewish readers squirm in their reading chairs. During one scene, for example, an emcee on board a party ship—in one of the novel's more surreal sections—warms up the crowd with the following joke: "'So what did Hitler say to Mussolini when the Italian premier paid him a surprise visit? . . . 'If I'd known you were coming, I would have baked a kike'" (*After* 262). My hunch is that several readers of Bukiet's novel will simply find nothing amusing about such moments. That Bukiet does not intend such moments to be "funny" per se might seem beside the point to this contingent.

What is more, Bukiet's survivor protagonist, Isaac Kaufman, is not the type of protagonist that Nathan Zuckerman's father would likely embrace. Having just been liberated, Isaac does not search tirelessly for lost relatives, nor does he take up the Zionist struggle ("'Eighty million Arabs and a desert: who needs it?'" [237]). Rather, Isaac and his cohorts—most notably Marcus Morgenstern, a dentist "before" surviving Dachau, an expert forger "after," and Fishl, a saintly schlemiel, who "retained every line of liturgy, history, and commentary he had ever heard" (52)—set off to score big on the black market. They turn over sizable profits by manufacturing and distributing straw-filled cigarettes; they somewhat incredulously scare up a market for Dead Person Identification Cards (DPIDs); and they even manage to sell broken watches by entombing live buzzing bees in the mechanism, which simulate the sound of a functioning timepiece for just long enough before suffocating.

It is, of course, just this type of resourcefulness that enables Isaac and his partners in crime to survive the *lager,* and one hesitates to judge them for acting on their survival instincts after the Holocaust. Still, their resourcefulness often comes across as just plain greed. Marcus will supply forged travel documents to fellow Jewish survivors only for just the right price; Isaac wishes to use Jewish skin, flayed by the Nazis, to forge more persuasive worker IDs; and, most disturbingly, he plans to confiscate eighteen tons of golden ingots created from fillings ripped out of Jewish mouths by the Nazis. Upon discovering the tightly guarded ingots, Marcus reacts as one might expect—"Think of all the pain" (101). Isaac, however, has little patience for such sentimentality and replies, "Screw the pain. Think of the money" (102).

"Gevalt!" one can almost hear Zuckerman's pop shout. "Congratulations boychik!" he might continue sarcastically. "You've just written a novel about kikes and their insatiable lust for money. The goyim will love it!" After all,

isn't this novel just more grist for the propaganda mills of anti-Semites? The answer, as one might have guessed by now, is no. Bukiet, to be sure, is up to some mischief in *After*, but if he shares Philip Roth's proclivity for mischief, his mischief is, ultimately, more deadly serious than Roth's. If, as Irving Howe suggested, "the cruelest thing anyone can do with *Portnoy's Complaint* is to read it twice" ("Philip Roth Reconsidered" 74)—whereupon, according to Howe, one would glean the thinness of the novel beneath its witty one-liners—the very opposite holds true for Bukiet's *After* (Howe 74). Only upon a second reading, perhaps, can one—now inoculated against the sting of Bukiet's caustic humor—begin to approach the depth of Bukiet's concerns. Whereas Roth unleashes his mischief to satirize Jewish American and plain-old American culture (*Goodbye, Columbus, Portnoy's Complaint, The Ghost Writer, Sabbath's Theater*) or to question the viability of Zionism (*The Counterlife* and *Operation Shylock: A Confession*), Bukiet creates his motley crew of Holocaust survivors and tracks their decidedly impious exploits to engage the theological crisis "after" the Holocaust. The rootless, dizzying, surreal, and profoundly amoral postwar zeitgeist, he suggests, is what a world suddenly devoid of redemptive possibilities looks like.

This is not to say that Bukiet pays short shrift to human culpability for the Holocaust. His sardonic take on human motives permeates the novel. The American "liberators" of Aspenfeld, including one Jewish American soldier, treat the survivors "like pets. . . . It was obvious that the Jews were no more people in their eyes than they were to the Germans. The substantial difference was that they were objects of sympathy rather than malice" (*After* 13, 16). The American public at large exhibit a voyeuristic rather than humane fascination with the European atrocity. Even worse, American newspapers are only too happy to slake the morbid thirst of the public by printing graphic photographs of the dead and near dead, while leading American intellectual quarterlies scurry to discover and publish the "authentic voice of despair" (181). Evidently, wrenching Holocaust memoirs make for good copy (read: sales). Bukiet even casts an acerbic eye on the Jewish volunteer relief workers, hopelessly naïve and, above all, late. Indeed, there are decidedly few good people in *After*.

Still, God is the real villain of the novel. The reader should be advised not to hunt for Nazi villains, for none exist (interestingly, a Ukrainian Kapo, not a German Nazi, sadistically offers Isaac a cup of scalding coffee that shatters his frozen teeth into enamel bits). The most memorable, if not the only, Nazi we meet is Sturmmann Hans Lichter, who does not manage to flee Aspenfeld before the Americans arrive. An American soldier discovers Lichter hiding in terror amid the stench of his own defecation. Subsequently, the Jewish survivors parade him around on an upraised chair in an eery revision of a Jewish celebration ritual (commonly practiced at weddings and bar mitzvot) and then hang him.

Rather than vilify the Nazi, Bukiet focuses on the spiritual descent of Judaism after the Holocaust. Isaac reflects, importantly, that "[Lichter] was a quiet fellow who hardly ever killed any of the prisoners. He had even been known to give leftover bread from his sandwich to a hungry child" (25). Bukiet simply refuses to offer up the easily digestible, even cathartic scene of good triumphing over evil, for the Big Question "after," he implies, is not so much whether the Nazis were evil (they certainly were), but whether the atrocity marks the irreparable rupture of Jewish continuity. There certainly seems to be little hope of Jewish renewal, or *t'shuvah*. A synagogue in Ostrowiec "had been transformed into a variety store that sold sundries arranged in piles set upon the cardboard cartons in which they had been shipped: spinning tops, mirrors, thimbles, sponges" (63). More hauntingly, on his mission to locate a paper source for their forging schemes, Fishl visits a museum turned paper factory where the workers are busy melting down the archives of the Jewish community of Lodz:

> the acid hit the covers and turned them to a mash the consistency of oatmeal, and [Fishl] felt his heart clutch. He could almost feel the release of the words within. "Shma Yisroel" rising from the pulp to the heavens as the same words had risen from the owners of those books as they were placed into a different processing center. . . . Large wooden paddles sloshed the brew around, and the letters floated off the surface of the pages to the surface like the noodles in alphabet soup. (210)

Despite Fishl's immediate shock, the destruction of these quintessential Jewish texts seems scarcely to rattle him: "the fact that the stuff was to be made into more paper to be covered with more words was a comfort" (210). The reconstitution of, say, Tanakh into travel visas disturbs the reader a good bit more than it disturbs Fishl, so deeply religious "before." Small wonder that Isaac himself ponders whether any Jews actually survived the Holocaust: "Did Jews survive? I don't know what a Jew is anymore. I don't think that I bear any resemblance to my father or my grandfather or some ancestor with camels. Things are different now" (157).

One, finally, need not subscribe to Isaac's gloomy observations. Bleak as the novel may be, Bukiet intimates during several magical moments that the flame of the Jewish soul will never be extinguished. Jewish continuity survives in the birth of Fishl and Rivkeh's baby, initially reluctant to enter the world; in the surreal manifestations of Isaac's indomitable brother, Alter; in the tale of the Last Jew on Earth who becomes the First Jew; in the unfolding of the plot concerning the golden ingots (calf?); and in Isaac's mercy (or *rachmones*) toward the son of a Nazi from Aspenfeld. So that he may achieve a "perfect emptiness . . . create himself anew" (83), Isaac resists his urge to murder the boy. The scene illustrates, however, that he cannot "empty" himself of his Jewish soul, which (though he refuses to acknowledge it) is what really precludes his act of ruthlessness. This moment and the other moments described above burst upon the eye like flashes of light from this canvas of seemingly inexorable darkness.

The mischievous theological imagination of Bukiet, I strongly suspect, will continue to raise the hackles of many a reader. After Philip Roth, Jewish American readers may not be so willing to tolerate another Moishe Pipik pushing the boundaries of acceptable mischief. The Holocaust itself has been the one subject relatively off limits to the Jewish American mischief maker (Art Spiegelman's and Philip Roth's work aside), but perhaps it is about time that Moishe Pipik take center stage to challenge the ways in which we currently write and think about the atrocity. More broadly, Moishe Pipik could serve as a provocative vehicle through which the contemporary Jewish American writer might engage the manifold outposts of Jewish identity as we near the twenty-first century. Which is simply to say that the work of Melvin Jules Bukiet shows us how far we have come since the immigrant novels of Cahan and Yezierska, and it ushers in a wealth of innovative Jewish American fiction now barely visible on the horizon.

4

Thane Rosenbaum's *Elijah Visible*

Jewish American Fiction, the Holocaust, and the Double Bind of the Second-Generation Witness

> [M]y parents, no longer alive but continually reinvented, revised, hostage to my own private therapy. The Holocaust survivor as myth, as fairy tale, as bedtime story. I had created my own ghosts from memories that were not mine. I wasn't there, in Poland, among the true martyrs. Everything about my rage was borrowed. My imagination had done all the work—invented suffering, without the physical scars, the incontestable proof.
>
> —Adam Posner, in Thane Rosenbaum's *Elijah Visible*

Whether or not the artistic imagination can ever be brought to bear on the Holocaust—in a way that does not betray the feebleness of the former while simultaneously diminishing the true horror of the latter—has been a source of contention ever since news of the atrocity belatedly reached the widespread public. Lionel Trilling put his finger on an often repeated moral quandary when he noted that "there is no possible way of responding to Belsen and Buchenwald. The activity of mind fails before the incommunicability of man's suffering" (256). Given the incommunicable nature of the suffering experienced by the Nazis' victims, if we agree to accept Trilling's assertion for a moment, perhaps silence represents the only morally tenable response to the genocide. Elie Wiesel ponders this question most directly in *The Oath* (1973), but one might read Wiesel's entire oeuvre as a tortured meditation on the "power of silence" argument and ultimately as a repudiation of it. Although the narrators of Wiesel's work are painfully aware of the ineffable nature of the Holocaust, they find that they must bear witness through recounting their experiences. Language, as limited as it may be, is all that they have.

That the questionable morality of depicting the Holocaust in literature has dogged Wiesel, a survivor of the Nazi death camps, suggests how much thornier the issue becomes when the Holocaust bestirs the imagination of *Jewish American* fiction writers. Artists who attempt to represent the Holocaust when their knowledge of the event is second- or thirdhand or transmitted by other cultural artifacts can expect their work to elicit a special kind of scrutiny from academic and nonacademic readers alike. Cognizant, perhaps, of this slippery moral terrain, Jewish American writers have proved especially reluctant in the wake of the Holocaust to dramatize the atrocity in their fiction. The role of the Holocaust in the work of Saul Bellow and Bernard Malamud exemplifies this reluctance. Bellow dared to dramatize the Holocaust only allusively in his 1947 novel *The Victim* before mustering up the artistic confidence to depict it more directly in *Mr. Sammler's Planet* (1969) in the horrifying recollections of his survivor protagonist, Artur Sammler. Bellow's Jewish American protagonist in *The Victim,* Asa Leventhal, must endure only the seemingly innocuous anti-Semitic barbs of a physically weak antagonist, Allbee. But, as Lillian Kremer has observed, images associated with the Nazi persecution of European Jews—from asphyxiation by gas to resettlement trains—pervade the novel to suggest the relationship between Allbee's blithe anti-Semitism and its culmination in the Holocaust (see Kremer, *Witness* 36–45).

Like Bellow, Bernard Malamud chose to approach the Holocaust from a safe distance in his novel *The Fixer* (1966). Although the blood libel trial of Mendel Beilis fueled Malamud's plot most directly, critics were quick to recognize that through exploring the plight of Yakov Bok, a Jew rotting away in a czarist jail for a murder he did not commit, Malamud meant to dramatize the virulent and pervasive European anti-Semitism that would culminate in the Holocaust. Indeed, Malamud suggested as much himself: "To his [Beilis's] trials in prison I added something of Dreyfus's and Vanzetti's, shaping the whole to suggest the quality of the affliction of the Jews under Hitler. These I dumped on the head of poor Yakov Bok" (qtd. in Hicks 37). Given the reluctance of two such prominent Jewish American novelists to dramatize the Holocaust directly, it should come as little surprise that as late as 1966, Robert Alter could bemoan the dearth of Jewish American imaginings of this watershed event defining the twentieth-century Jewish experience:

"With all the restless probing into the implications of the Holocaust that continues to go on in Jewish intellectual forums . . . it gives one pause to note how rarely American Jewish fiction has attempted to come to terms . . . with the European catastrophe" ("Confronting" 67).

Since the 1960s, however, we have enjoyed a rather steady outcropping of Jewish American fiction on the Holocaust—enough novels and short stories to merit book-length studies on them, most notably Alan Berger's *Crisis and Covenant: The Holocaust in American Jewish Fiction* (1985), S. Lillian Kremer's *Witness Through the Imagination: Jewish American Holocaust Literature* (1989), and the recently released *Women's Holocaust Writing: Memory and Imagination* (1999). This is not to say that the controversy surrounding the Holocaust as subject for Jewish American fiction has abated as the event recedes further and further into the past. Scholars and critics continue to cast a wary eye on how Jewish American writers "imagine" the Holocaust. For example, upon reading Philip Roth's *The Ghost Writer* (1979)—wherein Nathan Zuckerman imagines that Amy Bellette, the assistant to his literary idol, is Anne Frank and that he is bringing her home as his fiancée—Alan Berger had to say enough is enough. "Is Roth not utilizing the Holocaust to give himself legitimacy in the Jewish community?" he asked rhetorically (*Crisis* 160). More recently, he excoriated *The Ghost Writer* as a "literary exploitation" of the Holocaust ("American" 226). Although Berger did not use the term *Americanization,* what clearly raised his hackles was the way in which Roth (according to Berger's reading of the novel) appropriated the archetypal human story of the European catastrophe for the self-absorbed purpose of bolstering his personal reputation in the American Jewish community (see chapter 2 for my contrastive reading of Roth's Bellette/Frank subplot).

Additional controversies abound regarding the Jewish American writer's treatment of the Holocaust. For example, most scholars and critics lauded Art Spiegelman for his innovative and courageous artistic approach to the Holocaust in his Pulitzer Prize–winning *Maus.* Michael E. Staub's recent assertion that *Maus* presents a story of the Holocaust "that is much more accessible to a general audience than many other accounts, because it is particularly effective at inviting emotional involvement" exemplifies this critical approval (33). Cynthia Ozick, however, cast a more critical eye on *Maus* when she limned the metaphorical difficulty of Spiegelman's comic-book evocation of the Holocaust (he depicts Nazis as cats and Jews as mice). She recognized that Spiegelman meant to invite the reader's visceral involvement through depicting the Jews as the Germans' prey, "[b]ut prey," she perspicaciously argued, "is legitimate in nature; you can't argue with cats when they catch mice and kill them. It's killing, not murder. . . . The Germans were not cats and the Jews were not mice; both were human. And *that* is the *real* point in contemplating the Holocaust" ("Interview" 381, emphasis in original). Small wonder, given the scrutiny to which Ozick holds Jewish American dramatizations of the Holocaust, that she shelved her own Holocaust story, "The Shawl," for several years before finally submitting it in 1980 for publication in the *New Yorker.*

In fact, Ozick has lamented the appropriation of the Holocaust by imaginative rather than strictly historical writers in America: "I believe with all my soul that [the Holocaust] ought to remain exclusively attached to document and history . . . If the Holocaust becomes commensurate with the literary imagination, then what of those recrudescent Nazis, the so-called revisionists, who claim the events themselves are nothing but imaginings?" ("Interview" 390). Those familiar with Ozick's work might be justifiably perplexed at this point by her resolve. After all, the Holocaust has loomed large in several of her works. When Elaine Kauvar confronted Ozick with the apparent contradiction between her intellectual conviction and her artistic output, Ozick offered an intriguing response that cuts to the heart of the current relationship between the Jewish American fictionist and the Holocaust: "Well, I did it in five pages in 'The Shawl,' and I don't admire that I did it. I did it because I couldn't help it. It wanted to be done. I didn't want to do it, and afterward I've in a way punished myself, I've accused myself for having done it. I wasn't there, and I pretended through imagination that I was" ("Interview" 391). Ozick's response illustrates, above all, how ineluctable the Holocaust has proven to be for the contemporary Jewish American fiction writer. As an American Jew, a nonwitness, Ozick does not believe that she has the right to depict the Holocaust in her work, but the Holocaust pervades her consciousness and bursts upon her written pages—"[i]t wanted to be done." As she explained in an earlier interview, "I want the documents to be enough; I don't want to tamper or invent or imagine. And yet I have done it. I can't not do it. It comes, it invades" ("Art" 184–85). In deciding to publish the Holocaust fiction that "invades" her consciousness, Ozick affirms her belief in the revelatory power of art. Though ever wary of the imagination and its potential as a false idol, she implicitly suggests that the facts alone (those "documents") are finally *not* enough.

Ozick's artistic stance concerning the Holocaust obtains for an ever-increasing cohort of Jewish American writers. Despite its seemingly insurmountable challenge to the American imagination and its concomitant moral land mines, contemporary Jewish American Holocaust fiction has carved out its own niche as a subgenre of Jewish American fiction. The Holocaust is a frequent theme in Ted Solotaroff and Nessa Rapoport's recent collection of contemporary Jewish American stories, *Writing Our Way Home: Contemporary Stories by American Jewish Writers* (1992). Isaac Bashevis Singer's "A Party in Miami Beach," Lore Segal's "The Reverse Bug," and Deirdre Levinson's "April 19th, 1985" represent particularly powerful Holocaust stories that Solotaroff and Rapoport chose from among "many, many others" (Solotaroff, "Open" xxiii). That Solotaroff was compelled to refer to the Holocaust as "the subject that doesn't go away" (xxiii) in his introduction to the collection illustrates the surge in Jewish American Holocaust fiction since Robert Alter's gloomy 1966 observations.

Indeed, some of our most promising young Jewish American writers have imagined the Holocaust in significant ways in their work. The most recent works include, of course, Melvin Jules Bukiet's *After* (1996) and two stories in his earlier collection *While the Messiah Tarries* (1995), "Himmler's Chickens" and "The Library of Moloch," as well as Rebecca Goldstein's "The Legacy of Raizel Kaidish: A Story," collected in *Strange Attractors* (1993), and her novels, *The Late-Summer Passion of a Woman of Mind* (1989) and the dazzling *Mazel* (1995), which won the National Jewish Book Award and the Edward Lewis Wallant Award for fiction. As Lillian Kremer suggests, "Contemporary Jews increasingly feel that, geography aside, they were present at Auschwitz. American Jews carry the psychological burden of Auschwitz and Chelmno and Dachau and Bergen-Belsen and Treblinka and all the other Nazi death factories where their relatives died brutal deaths" (*Witness* 15). Kremer's observation complicates one of the principal arguments voiced by many who disapprove of Jewish American fictional representations of the Holocaust: the atrocity didn't happen in America. Although true in the literal sense, the assertion obfuscates the impact that the Holocaust had and continues to have within the Jewish American community. The Holocaust left an indelible thumbprint on the Jewish American ethos, forging the Jewish population in America as a "people of memory" (Solotaroff, "Open" xxiii). It forced Jews in America to reexamine their own Jewish identities and question the viability of a Jewish existence in *galut* (exile). Perhaps embracing an assimilated American identity was no guarantee against imminent persecution in America. After all, the Jews in pre-Holocaust Germany were, ironically, "the most privileged Jews on the continent—prosperous, fully emancipated, and largely assimilated into German society" (Strandberg 38). Perhaps assimilation was no longer desirable in the first place (why offer Hitler a posthumous victory?). Perhaps a Jew could be safe and spiritually whole only in a Jewish state. These issues are just some of the ones that Jewish Americans faced after the Holocaust.

Although the European atrocity had a deep impact on all Jews in America, the Holocaust affected and continues to affect the children of survivors in special and profound ways. The psychological burden to which Kremer refers weighs most heavily on this "second generation" (here, I am borrowing Alan Berger's terminology) and has manifested itself in the current surge of novels and short stories that they have contributed to the burgeoning canon of Jewish American Holocaust fiction. These second-generation children of survivors engage the Holocaust with an unprecedented intensity as they grapple, through their fiction, with both the seemingly ineffable horrors committed against their parents and the legacy of those horrors visited on themselves.

Importantly, these second-generation works force us to reconsider our criteria for defining Holocaust fiction. One might notice that when Cynthia Ozick admonished herself for "imagining" the Holocaust in her fiction, she referred only to that brief moment in *The Shawl* (1989) when she describes the actual experience of Jews in a concentration camp. She implicitly defines Holocaust fiction rather literally and in a way that excludes much second-generation fiction from the category. As one might expect, most second-generation writers explore not the European Jews' Holocaust experiences, but largely the experiences of the second-generation child who grows up in the wake of the tragedy on more hospitable American terrain. It is my contention not only that such second-generation fiction must be considered Holocaust fiction, but that it represents the most significant and poignant example of the continual development of the genre as the children of survivors illustrate how the Holocaust continues to inform—or haunt, rather—their cultural identities as Jewish Americans. Alan Berger is one of the few scholars to explore this second-generation work in any depth (see his "Ashes," "Bearing," *Children of Job*, and "Memory"). For the balance of this essay, I focus on the fiction of an emergent second-generation writer, Thane Rosenbaum.

In his powerful first collection of stories, *Elijah Visible* (1996), Rosenbaum explores the special burdens of the second-generation in America. To engage these burdens as thoroughly as he can, he creates a single protagonist, Adam Posner, but varies the details surrounding Posner's identity from one story to another. To wit, in one story Posner is a lawyer in an elite New York firm; in other stories, he is an abstract expressionist painter or a teacher. He grows up in Atlantic City in one story, in Miami in another, and New York in still another. In Adam Posner Rosenbaum creates a mosaic figure to capture the complex, nuanced, and, above all, fractured existence of the Holocaust survivor's child in America. The name Adam suggests rebirth or regeneration, and throughout the collection, Rosenbaum scrutinizes the possibility of such continuity. Through the many Posners, he dramatizes the second-generation's vicarious psychological immersion in the Holocaust, their responsibility to reconstruct and remember the experiences of the survivor parents, and their struggle to maintain religious faith in a post-Holocaust America seemingly devoid of redemptive possibilities. Owing largely to the simultaneous breadth and depth of Rosenbaum's vision, his collection represents an invaluable contribution to the canon of Jewish American Holocaust fiction.

In the first story of the collection, "Cattle Car Complex," Rosenbaum tersely dramatizes the vicarious suffering of Adam Posner. The overarching point of this opening story is that the past, specifically the Holocaust experiences of Posner's parents, bears down heavily on this American Adam. The Holocaust has scarred Posner, precluding any meaningful relationships in his life. Not even a pet greets him at his barren apartment. More subtly, the Holocaust guides his career choice. He reluctantly decides to become a lawyer to ensure his own safety: "He played the game reluctantly, knowing what it was doing to his spirit, but also painfully aware of his own legacy, and its contribution to the choices he was destined to make. Above all else he wanted to feel safe, and whatever club offered him the privilege of membership, he was duty-bound to join" (*EV* 4). To be sure, the comfortable trappings of Posner's life and his relative physical safety in America contrasts mightily with his parents' predicament during the Holocaust; they survived cattle cars and concentration camps.

When Posner's elevator breaks down, however, trapping him indefinitely in the "hollow lung of the skyscraper" (3), he suffers a psychological trauma that exemplifies the *presence* of the Holocaust in his life. The claustrophobia of the elevator transports him, psychologically at least, to a Nazi cattle car in Holocaust Europe. When a security guard, understandably confused, urges him to calm down and not make such a fuss over the mere inconvenience, Posner's psychic terror consumes him, and he cries: "This is not life—being trapped in a box made for animals! Is there no dignity for man? . . . You are barbarians! Get me out! . . . We can't breathe in here! And the children, what will they eat? How can we dispose of our waste? We are not animals! We are not cattle! There are no windows in here, and the air is too thin for all of us to share" (8). Rosenbaum takes pains to emphasize (in this story and in others) that Posner had inherited the legacy of suffering from his parents, "inherited their perceptions of space, and the knowledge of how much one needs to live, to hide, how to breathe where there is no air. . . . He carried on their ancient sufferings without protest—feeding on the milk of terror; forever acknowledging—with himself as proof—the umbilical connection between the unmurdered and the long buried" (5–6). To say, then, that Posner suffers "vicariously" for his parents might be to qualify matters overmuch. In his mind, he does not suffer *for* his parents, but assimilates their suffering into his own experience. As Posner finally emerges from the repaired elevator in his soiled clothes, awaiting the pronouncement "right or left" (an allusion to the Nazis' two lines at the Auschwitz train tracks designating either hard labor or immediate execution), we know that we have come a long way in Jewish American Holocaust fiction from Philip Roth's "Eli, the Fanatic" (arguably the most incisive story of Roth's first collection, *Goodbye, Columbus* [1959]). The thoroughly "Americanized" Eli Peck must aggressively seek out a fleeting identification with a Holocaust survivor by donning his Hasidic clothing. We know, moreover, that the merging of Peck's and the survivor's identities is more illusory than real. The clothes, finally, do not make the man. In Rosenbaum's story, Adam Posner does not need to seek out an identification with a Holocaust survivor. He cannot eschew the Holocaust from his psyche no matter how hard he tries. As the child of survivors, he grows up hearing his parents' screams at night and adopts their haunted past. The contrast between these two stories suggests, above all, that second-generation writers have begun to call on their special experiences as children of survivors to forge their own special artistic contributions to Jewish American Holocaust fiction.

Rosenbaum's "Cattle Car Complex" goes a long way toward convincing us that the cultural identity of second-generation Jewish Americans remains inextricably bound to a legacy of Holocaust suffering. Now, few dispute that the Jewish American identity *earlier* in this century was tangled up in this web of suffering. Consider, for example, Leslie Fiedler's recollection of how his grandfather would respond when asked what was happening in the world: "Nothing new, *M'hargert yidd'n.* They're killing Jews. What else?" (160). Although Jewish Americans in the late nineteenth and early twentieth century, like Fiedler and his grandfather, were fortunate enough to elude the Holocaust, the dogs of the Eastern European pogroms still nipped at their heels through memory, through vicarious suffering for those left behind to perish in Europe, or through manifestations of anti-Semitism in America. But given the postwar socioeconomic strides made by Jewish Americans (illustrated by Alfred Kazin's quip, "What's the difference between the International Ladies' Garment Workers' Union and the American Psychiatric Association? One generation"), many non-Jews cannot fathom today the persistent Jewish American ethos of suffering. As Julius Lester observes, "From a black perspective . . . there is something jarring in hearing white-skinned Jews talk about suffering. No black denies that Jews suffered in Europe, but the Jewish experience in America has not been characterized by such suffering" (173).

The stories in Rosenbaum's *Elijah Visible* ("Cattle Car Complex," in particular) challenge Lester's observations, for although it is true that Jewish Americans no longer need endure the palpable suffering wrought by institutionalized anti-Semitism, Adam Posner in *Elijah Visible* nevertheless suffers from the horrors committed against his parents. How could it be otherwise when, for example in one story, he arrives home to find them hiding from the Nazis in the dark corner of their bedroom? The second-generation child who observes his survivor parents trembling in their bedroom becomes the second-generation man with a "cattle car complex." The words of Fiedler's grandfather—*M'hargert yidd'n*—resonate, then, just as strongly for the Jewish child of survivors in contemporary America.

Still, if the Posner of Rosenbaum's collection inherits his parents' Holocaust legacy "through his veins," it is just as true that the experience itself cannot be inherited. A double bind, Rosenbaum suggests, plagues the second generation. Posner cannot get the Holocaust out of his skull, but at the same time he remains painfully aware that the treacherous imagination, rather than memory, burdens him. Thus, in several stories, he must satisfy his inexorable desire to learn all he can about the Holocaust generally and about his parents' experiences specifically. He must uncover the details that will sharpen the frustratingly nebulous images of terror that haunt him. The rub is that his parents and other survivor relatives prove especially reluctant to share their stories with him. The memories are too painful, the truth too horrific for words. Besides, why burden the next generation with such stories?

One sees this relational dynamic emerge most poignantly in two stories, "The Pants in the Family" and "An Act of Defiance." The first story might well be described as a meditation on the incommunicable nature of the Holocaust. A short narrative of a dramatic moment in Posner's childhood frames a central narrative of the circumstances surrounding his mother's death during his adolescence. Through the acuity of a third-person narrator, Rosenbaum describes an episode on the Atlantic City pier when Posner's father abandons his son for a brief but scary moment. Baited by a barker at the shoot-out gallery—"Your kid will remember this day, when his pop chickened out of a fight" (39)—he releases Adam's hand and, replacing it with a rifle, shoots down every one of the animal targets with ease. The tale evokes the estrangement between the Holocaust survivor parent and the second-generation child. At the carnival, the father's past rushes on him in a flash of memory and separates him psychologically and physically from his confused son.

In the story's central narrative, Rosenbaum dramatizes the extent of the elder Posner's psychological disorientation as Adam, now the narrator, must make the final medical decisions for his dying mother. When the doctor tells Adam that he really should speak to his father, Adam cries, "'Leave him alone, he won't be able to handle it. . . . the man's been through enough. He's old and weak, and has been disappointed before by bad news. Just look at him. . . . what else do you need to know?" (41). At sixteen, Adam must wear the pants in the family. His father, emotionally embattled and suffering from heart troubles, simply does not have the strength.

Rosenbaum focuses, however, not so much on the father's physical and psychological trauma as on Adam's continual struggle to penetrate the mystery of his father's agony. This struggle proves especially difficult as his parents both suffer in silence, thus provoking Adam's frustrated curiosity. They do not discuss their Holocaust experiences with their son; understandably, they attempt to shield him from their pain and send him off to an elite preparatory school. Adam, then, must glean all he can through the silence: "I wanted to know more about what had happened to him during the war. It was always such an impenetrable secret—my parents, speaking in code, changing the passwords repeatedly, keeping me off the scent. And he was always so ill. There was never the occasion to catch them off guard, ask the big questions, holding out for something other than that familiar silence" (48). As Adam's father nears his own death, he becomes more communicative with his son and regrets having imposed a silent childhood on him. Still, he does not understand why his son wishes to know about the past: "'You think you need to know. . . . Do you want to know whether I ever killed someone? How will that change anything? What mystery will that answer?'" (50–51). Although we readers sense that certain experiences will remain forever inscrutable, Adam's father realizes an emotional connection with his son by piercing the silence that had defined their relationship. Before he dies, he exposes his heart to his son, who embraces it symbolically as he clutches his father's nitroglycerin pills. These pills, Rosenbaum suggests, represent the "final prize of the carnival" (53) as Adam's father bridges the chasm between himself and the son he initially abandoned on the Atlantic City boardwalk.

Rosenbaum further contemplates the bridges that can and cannot be crossed in "An Act of Defiance." Here, he presents us with an adult Adam Posner, who teaches a course on the Holocaust to an increasingly apathetic and dwindling group of students. The lack of student interest in the subject belies Posner's total immersion in it. That he teaches a Holocaust course bespeaks his need (like the younger Posner's need in "The Pants in the Family") to absorb as fully as possible his parents' experiences in the camps. This older Posner, a Ph.D., possesses a keener, more sophisticated understanding of the double bind that plagues him. As much as he strives to learn about the Holocaust experience, he knows that it will always remain a product of his imagination, which continually reinvents and revises his parents' European lives. "My imagination," he reflects, "had done all the work—invented suffering, without the physical scars, the incontestable proof" (59).

At the point that we meet Posner in "An Act of Defiance," his relentless imagination has left him emotionally fatigued, and he has begun to plot his escape from his Holocaust scholarship. He wishes to retreat to the "imperfect but amiable world" (59). Small wonder that he does not welcome the news that his Uncle Haskell, a Holocaust survivor like his parents, plans to visit him for the first time to "fix," as he puts it, his nephew's life (57). Posner fears that Haskell's arrival will only exacerbate his psychic torment, "feed my guilt, replenish my craving for the soul of survivors" (59). Interestingly, Haskell proves to be quite a different fish than Adam's father. Through him, Rosenbaum, to his credit, complicates our perception of the Holocaust survivor as silent sufferer. Haskell does not care to brood on the past with his nephew ("I should come here, all the way from Belgium, to talk about the camps? This you need?" [65]). Rather, he dates women he knows in New York, strolls through Central Park, coaxes his nephew into riding a tandem bicycle with him, and drags him along while he breaks a casino's bank in Atlantic City.

Haskell's yen for life, we must recognize, does not betray a lack of emotional depth on his part or a scant memory (the colostomy bag he wears serves as a perpetual reminder, certainly, of the physical ravages he suffered). Instead, Haskell embraces the joy of living to retaliate imperiously against the Nazis. He refuses to allow Hitler a posthumous victory by living a joyless life. As he explains to Adam, "I still know survivors who carry on this way, like your father did. Silent suffering. A private death that traveled with him, wherever he went, a ghost always on his shoulder, whispering into his ear, not letting him eat, work, rest. . . . You see, Adam, my life, with all the riches and pleasures that I allow myself, is an act of defiance. I am an assassin to their mission" (66). It becomes clear that Haskell means to "fix" his nephew's life by compelling him to adopt his defiant outlook. He tells Adam that he must find a way to let go of the sadness that defines his existence. "There is *tsouris* [troubles] everywhere my boy," he writes Adam in a cautionary note, "but there is always more if this is all you see" (68).

To be sure, one of Rosenbaum's most persistent points in *Elijah Visible* is that the second-generation survivor in America has great difficulty seeing—or imagining, rather—anything else but the *tsouris* of the real survivors. Like the lawyer Posner of "Cattle Car Complex," the Posner of "An Act of Defiance" vicariously experiences the plight of the survivor when, en route to the airport to greet Haskell, he imagines his interrogation at U.S. Customs: "He fumbles excitedly. Nervous beyond sedation. A Jew with ethnically incriminating papers and a convenient scarlet letter—the shape of a Star of David—patched onto his lapel. Hands move in and out of his pockets. A mad search. Sweat builds on his forehead, then plunges into his eyes. . . . 'Sir, I must see your papers! Now . . . Jew!'" (61). Adam conjures the interrogation so vividly that he alarms his taxi driver by screaming "Stop!" at the imaginary Nazi interrogating his uncle (61). Given the absence of tangible memories, Adam cannot contain his rampant imagination; he continually reconstructs and reinvents their experiences. This reconstruction, Rosenbaum suggests, is the special burden of the second generation Jew in America.

Haskell evidently comes to appreciate his nephew's predicament, for he agrees to visit Adam's class to discuss his family's plight during the Holocaust. While ostensibly rendering the story to the class, Haskell reveals to Adam the horrible truths surrounding his family's Holocaust experiences. Through Haskell's terse, even matter-of-fact narrative, Adam learns that his father's parents were murdered in front of all their children. They were shot after refusing to tell a Nazi where one of their sons, Adam's father, had stowed away weapons in the apartment. Thankfully, Adam's father managed to kill the Nazi with one of his concealed guns before the Nazi could proceed to kill the rest of the family. "There was more to the mystery of my silent father than I had dared realize," Adam reflects upon hearing the story (85). Finally, he learns one truth of his father's experience. A period can replace one of the many ellipses of Adam's imagination, offering him, one hopes, a modicum of peace.

If the unbridgeable chasm dividing memory from imagination in *Elijah Visible* represents Adam Posner's greatest burden as a second-generation survivor in America, the waning of religious faith and adherence following the Holocaust also bears down heavily on him. Alienated from Jewish ritual and belief, Adam Posner cannot turn to religion for solace. True, this theological crisis, in the broad sense, is not peculiar to Americans or to the second-generation survivor for that matter. The God that died on the gallows in Elie Wiesel's first memoir, *Night* (1960), died not only in the eyes of a young Wiesel, but in the eyes of several Jews and non-Jews worldwide. That said, Rosenbaum dramatizes in several stories the especially keen spiritual crisis of the second-generation American through Adam Posner, who must reckon not only with his own post-Holocaust religious doubts, but with an American zeitgeist of secularism and crass materialism that exacerbates his spiritual crisis.

In "Romancing the *Yohrzeit* Light," Rosenbaum evokes the crisis poignantly as Posner's religious alienation wars against a curious exigence to commemorate his mother in a religiously meaningful way on the first anniversary of her death. The Posner of this story, an abstract expressionist painter, arguably represents the most disaffected Posner of the collection. Though his mother, Esther, observes the Sabbath rituals and keeps a kosher home, Adam "ate all manner of spineless fish, and the commingled flesh of unhoofed animals. His hot dogs didn't answer to a higher authority other than his own whim of which sidewalk peddler to patronize" (17). He lives close to several synagogues in New York, but avoids them at all costs "as though they were virtual leper colonies" (17). Not only does he ignore the high holidays, but he does not even know what time of year to expect them.

Posner's mother laments her son's renunciation of Judaism. She realizes that his refusal to observe Jewish rituals proffers Hitler a posthumous victory, and she castigates him when he dons the obligatory black leather of the artist: "'I didn't survive the camps so that you could walk around looking and acting like a camp guard. Look at you. Nothing Jewish that I can see" (20). She also does not hesitate to denounce the paganism of her son's art. She pleads with him to paint something Jewish, to abandon the gloomy nihilism that pervades his work. Pointing to one canvas in particular, she opines, "Thank God your father has been dead all these years—because *this* . . . would have killed him'" (20). Importantly, Posner's mother does not encourage her son's identification with the Holocaust. A Jewish identity, Rosenbaum suggests, should not be rooted solely in one's remembrance of the European atrocity, but in the rich legacy of Judaism that was almost completely snuffed out by it.

Precisely what role the Holocaust should play in forging the contemporary Jewish American identity has been the topic of heated debate within the Jewish American community. Several American Jews have lately criticized the disproportionate attention that the Holocaust (and Israel) receives in the synagogue. In a recent *Commentary* symposium entitled "What Do Jews Believe?" David Klinghoffer, the young literary editor of the *National Review,* goes so far as to describe the Holocaust—"the veneration of whose victims allows Jews to share in the trendy cult of victimhood" (56)—as one of the idols leading contemporary Jews astray from Torah Judaism. According to Klinghoffer, several Jews now in their twenties or thirties were raised ignorant of Judaism in Reform or Conservative temples because Holocaust remembrance dominated the agenda. Thus, he and an unprecedented number of other young American Jews have become part of the *baal t'shuvah* (returnee) phenomenon. That is, they have taken it upon themselves as adults to learn

Torah Judaism. Although I believe that Holocaust remembrance and Israel should play a role in forging the Jewish American identity, I agree with Klinghoffer that the precepts of Torah Judaism must move from the periphery to the center of Jewish education. If the rampant assimilation of Jewish Americans tells us anything, it tells us that a viable Jewish American identity cannot be rooted solely or even largely in Holocaust remembrance and Zionism.

This controversy surrounding the role that Holocaust remembrance should play in contemporary Jewish American life has recently made its way into Jewish American fiction. I will explore in a moment how Rosenbaum addresses it, but it is worth pausing here to discuss how the issue has emerged in the work of other recent Jewish American fictionists as well. For example, in Robert Cohen's recent novel *The Here and Now* (1996), a Hasidic character, Magda Brenner, admonishes the nominally Jewish protagonist for his ignorance of Judaism but easy identification with the Holocaust:

> Here you don't know the first thing about Judaism, not even the basic prayers. But put a number on a man's arm and suddenly you know all about them. . . . Thousands of years of history mean nothing to you, but five years of gas chambers, that means everything. It's perverse, no? The side that suffers and chokes and is defeated, that's the side that feels like a Jew. The healthy part is out playing with the *goyim.* (257)

Here, Cohen lends artistic expression to Klinghoffer's convictions. Magda Brenner argues convincingly that a healthy Jewish identity must be rooted in the thousands of years of Judaic history, not in a perverse identification with Hitler's victims. Philip Roth challenged this cult of victimhood in *The Counterlife* (1986) through Jimmy Lustig's "FORGET REMEMBERING" plan (188). Lustig wishes to dismantle Yad Vashem, Israel's Museum and Remembrance Hall of the Holocaust because he believes that "We are torturing ourselves with memories! With masochism!" (*TC* 189). Although Roth portrays Lustig as more than a little bit nuts, the essential principles Lustig articulates—"JEWS NEED NO NAZIS TO BE THE REMARKABLE JEWISH PEOPLE! . . . JUDAISM WITHOUT VICTIMS!" (188–89)—enjoy an unmistakable currency in the Jewish American community.

To return to "Romancing the *Yohrzeit* Light," Rosenbaum himself emphasizes the importance of Jewish ritual rather than Holocaust remembrance alone. Posner's memory of his mother's implacable religious faith following her Holocaust experiences impels him to honor her on the first anniversary of her death by seeking out a Yohrzeit candle (the plain but long-burning candle that, in accordance with Jewish ritual, mourners light on each anniversary of a loved one's death). The lighting of the Yohrzeit represents, for Posner, his first attempt as an adult to reconnect with his Jewish heritage. Spiritually lost in New York, he abides self-consciously by one meaningful Jewish ritual to alleviate some of his pain following his mother's death. He wonders hopefully whether lighting the Yohrzeit might help him "find his own way back, too?" (22).

Rosenbaum's narrative leads the reader to anticipate a hopeful conclusion. After purchasing the Yohrzeit, Posner's art suddenly loses its characteristic dreariness. He paints discernable figures—including several portraits of his mother—in bright, warm colors. Rosenbaum, however, suddenly deflates one's anticipation of Posner's Jewish renewal (or *t'shuvah*) as carnal impulses compete with his theological stirrings. In short, his passion for a non-Jewish woman, Tasha (a Swedish fashion model no less), interferes with his religious commemoration of his mother. Just after Posner lights the Yohrzeit for his mother, Tasha bursts through his apartment door and, sprawling kittenishly across the kitchen table, informs him that she wishes to consummate their relationship. As she attempts to blow out the Yohrzeit, unaware of its religious significance, Posner contemplates the choice that faces him: "He was unequivocally caught between two worlds—sandwiched between two competing desires. A small blond table had served up two irreconcilable courses on this most emotional of evenings: a Swedish smorgasbord of temptation, juxtaposed with a paltry three ounces of scrupulous wax" (30). As one might guess, Jewish observance stands little chance against such temptation. Posner allows Tasha to suffocate the Yohrzeit—that "paltry three ounces of scrupulous wax"—with a coffee saucer. His "need for Tasha's body had abbreviated the anniversary of his mother's death" (31). More disconcertingly, Judaism seems irretrievably lost afterward. First, Posner's art reverts back to its former gloominess. Then the lure of the pagan realm, embodied by Tasha, proves too strong once again for him to resist. The story concludes as they celebrate a Swedish Christmas in his apartment, replete with smoked ham, *julgrot,* and Swedish Christmas carols. The only candle lit is the one atop Posner's first Christmas tree. Importantly, these decidedly un-Judaic trappings move Posner farther and farther away from spiritual well-being.

Tasha may have transformed his apartment into her own, but Posner is left to wonder, "where was *his* home?" (32). The second-generation survivor, Rosenbaum suggests, cannot embrace Judaism given the competing influences in post-Holocaust America and tragically remains hopelessly lost without Judaism.

Rosenbaum somewhat tempers the cynicism of "Romancing the *Yohrzeit* Light" in the titular story of the collection, "Elijah Visible." The story opens as Adam Posner, celebrating Passover with his cousins, bemoans the thinning of religion in their lives. Exasperated by the Elvis Costello music blaring in the background and the prosaic American fashion magazines littering the Passover table, he cries, "You call *this* a Seder?" (89). Later, he elaborates on the spiritual hollowness of their perfunctory Passover observance:

> To all those in the room, it was a seance of incomprehensible words, the mother tongue of orphans in the Diaspora, pig Latin for nonkosher Jews. . . . For the past ten years, ever since all the parents of these cousins had died, the Seder, which had once been a solemn and sanctified event, was reduced to a carnival. The informality was seductive, rampant—and everywhere. White yarmulkes lay folded on the table like crescent half-moons—untouched, unworn. The occasional mistake—the lighting of the menorah—inspired no alarm, no tremor of religious infraction. . . . The four questions went unasked, as though the Posner family didn't want to know the answers, and were sapped of all curiosity. (89)

The desultory Seder illustrates, above all, the result of the silence between the generation of Posner Holocaust survivors and their children. The survivor parents do not discuss their Holocaust experiences, nor do they educate their children in Torah Judaism. Raised to "ignore the lineage that was unalterably theirs" (95), Adam and his cousins cling to near vacuous Jewish identities. Their lives exemplify the assimilatory trend in postwar America that Arthur Hertzberg so assiduously documents in *The Jews in America: Four Centuries of an Uneasy Encounter, A History* (1989). Especially disturbing, in fact, is the complacent manner with which Jewish parents, according to Hertzberg, directed their children's Jewish education: "What the mass of parents wanted, apart from a decent performance at bar mitzvah, was that the school impart to their children enough of the sense of Jewish loyalty so that they would be inoculated against intermarriage. . . . Once that inoculation had supposedly taken hold, the Jewish child could then be launched on his next task, to succeed in being admitted into a prestigious college" (332).

Adam and his cousins certainly appear to be the product of such an upbringing. However, a letter that Adam and his cousins receive from their cousin Artur, the last surviving relative of their parents' generation, jolts Adam from his spiritual complacency. Illustrative of the presence of the European past within the second generation, cousin Artur (who fled to Palestine after surviving Auschwitz) still lives and wishes to meet his cousins in America. He wishes to tell them about their family's history in Europe. Says Artur in the letter, "Your children should know what happened. They must continue to remind the world. . . . We must learn the lessons from the fire" (97). Although the letter moves Adam, his American cousins believe cynically that Artur intends only to exploit their sympathy so that they will foot the bill for his trip to the United States. Their convictions are rooted in their obscure knowledge of a long-standing feud over money between Artur and their parents.

The story harkens back to Saul Bellow's "The Old System," perhaps the most significant postimmigrant story about Jews and money in America. In Bellow's story, Dr. Braun remembers the bitter money feud between his two older cousins, Isaac and Tina. Their life-long enmity offers him a glimpse into the maw of America as he observes how rampant materialism and sexual wantonness commingle dangerously with an "old system" of Jewish values that extol family cohesiveness above all. In "Elijah Visible," the second-generation Posners must also revisit the money feud between their relatives.

However, the stakes in Rosenbaum's "Elijah Visible" are much higher than in "The Old System." Bellow's Dr. Braun, scarcely younger than his cousins, more or less shared their postimmigrant experience in America and struggles only to make sense of it. By contrast, the second generation of Rosenbaum's story did not participate in their relatives' European experiences and, moreover, possess only a limited knowledge of those experiences. Artur holds the key to a secret past that they can either claim by embracing him or eschew by rejecting his overtures.

Adam's cousins, thinking of Artur's collect calls to their parents and other trivialities, initially choose to continue the grudge against him. They, like their petty and materialistic father, have embraced the "fat gods" of America (to borrow a phrase from Bellow) and perforce have little use for Artur. Their suspicions of Artur's motives aside, these affluent cousins believe that they are doing just fine and cannot readily see how Artur might "save" them. It thus falls to Adam to describe to his cousins what they have indeed lost: "Listen to the music we play around here; we've lost our soul. We don't know who we are, where we come from, why we should care about tomorrow. Your kids are running around here like a couple of zombies; it could be Easter for all they know" (101). As Adam recounts the spare details he knows concerning their parents' Holocaust experiences, he forces his cousins to confront their family's painful history and to accept the burden of remembrance and their concomitant obligation to keep Torah Judaism alive. They cannot afford, they realize, to perpetuate the silence of their parents. "We can't afford," Adam argues, "to do that again. We owe it to the children, to ourselves—there's too much at stake" (102). Their cousin Artur (like Haskell in "An Act of Defiance") represents the final link to a past that they must claim. Even though Elijah does not make an appearance at the Posner cousins' Seder, Artur is on the way by the story's end. The second generation, Rosenbaum suggests, might yet achieve *t'shuvah.*

In *Elijah Visible,* Rosenbaum dramatizes the near rupture of Jewish existence, but he also envisions the restoration of Jewish continuity through the piercing of the silence between Holocaust survivors and second-generation children; through the defiant humor of Haskell, who uses the numbers of his Holocaust tattoo to triumph at an Atlantic City roulette wheel; through the similar defiance embodied in the Holocaust survivors' mantra at Cohen's summer cottages—"Leisure *Macht Frei*"; and through the sizzle of a match that poignantly triggers Posner's memories of his mother over the Shabbat candles.

As a second-generation writer, Rosenbaum realizes painfully the unimaginable nature of the Holocaust. That he can never truly comprehend the horrors experienced by his parents is both his burden and his muse. Most importantly, perhaps, his protagonist's psychological immersion in the Holocaust raises essential questions for both the children of survivors and the broader Jewish American community today: How and to what extent should Holocaust remembrance inform the contemporary Jewish American ethos? Can Holocaust education and Torah Judaism peacefully coexist? Might they even bolster one another to forge a stronger Jewish American identity?

The stories in *Elijah Visible,* as I hope I have made clear, suggest that a meaningful Jewish American identity can flourish only once we Jewish Americans confront our recent painful history, for how can our observance of Jewish rituals—especially the Passover Seder, during which we celebrate freedom, justice, and law—transcend the perfunctory if we do not struggle to extract meaning from the decimation in this century of one-third of the world's Jewish population? Where, then, was freedom, justice, and law? Rosenbaum does not offer an answer to this perhaps unanswerable question. The stories in *Elijah Visible* suggest finally that it is in the fervent search for answers, rather than in the answers themselves, that the key to a meaningful Jewish American identity lies.

A Postscript on *Second Hand Smoke*

"The world had been reborn with Auschwitz," Thane Rosenbaum writes in the opening pages of his recently released debut novel, *Second Hand Smoke* (1999, 18). Judging from this novel and from *Elijah Visible,* Rosenbaum has taken it as his charge to describe what this nascent, post-Holocaust world looks like through the eyes of the Holocaust survivors' child.

A reader familiar with *Elijah Visible* need not dip too far into *Second Hand Smoke* before discovering that Rosenbaum means to revisit—with a renewed and redirected intensity—several of the themes of his first collection of stories. Most broadly, and as his fiercely accurate title suggests, Rosenbaum once again explores the toxic legacy that Holocaust survivors unwittingly but ineluctably pass on to their children. The novel revolves around Duncan Katz, a Nazi hunter for the Operation of Special Investigations and the son of two Holocaust survivors. The silent and inscrutable Yankee (née Herschel) Katz feverishly and mysteriously pecks away at his typewriter but refuses to answer Duncan's query, "Father, what happened to you during the war?" (31). His indomitable wife, Mila, guilt ridden over her abuse and abandonment of an infant son she conceived just after the war, cannot bring herself to raise her second son, Duncan, with loving-kindness, and instead ruthlessly trains him to avenge their shattered lives: "Capeless and without a cowl, or even a phone booth, Duncan knew that what his mother really wanted was not a son, but a comic-book superhero" (32).

The impassive Yankee remains pretty much at the periphery of the novel as Rosenbaum focuses instead on the tortured relationship between Mila and Duncan Katz. Mila sees to it that Duncan forswears traditional Jewish bookishness for a black belt in karate by age nine. To the horror of even her tough cronies in Miami Beach's Jewish Mafia, she constantly tests her son's strength by subjecting him to everything from street brawls in the urban ghettoes of New Jersey to wilderness survival training in the Rockies. Traditional modes of Jewish existence, Mila believes, were discredited and made obsolete with God's silence at Auschwitz. Thus, "Senseis influenced [Duncan] in ways that rabbis could not. A sutra lingered in his mind far longer than anything out of the Talmud and Torah. The samurai son of survivors from Miami Beach" (30).

Here, Rosenbaum engages what has now become a central theme in his work, the rupture and discontinuity that lamentably defines Jewish existence after the Holocaust. The center of Judaism, Torah, evidently cannot hold after the atrocity in Europe. Additional scenes that exemplify this rupture pervade the novel. *Second Hand Smoke* evocatively opens, for example, with Duncan's decidedly "unkosher" *bris* (the Jewish circumcision ceremony): "While embracing God's covenant with Abraham, Mila and Yankee were at the same time also breaking promises, smashing tablets, stepping outside the faith, scavenging around, and bringing back pagan souvenirs. . . . There was a rabbi in the apartment, a modern, athletic-looking clergyman who wore a fabulous tan but forgot to bring his yarmulke" (8). The Holocaust, Rosenbaum suggests here and elsewhere, tragically shatters the most time-honored traditions of Judaism as exceedingly few grandparents, uncles, aunts, or cousins survived to occupy their traditional roles at Jewish holidays and life-cycle events. In addition to Duncan's unkosher *bris,* Rosenbaum depicts Mila's unkosher funeral in Miami Beach, which culminates as Duncan—long estranged from his mother and unfairly reviled by her friends—is deprived of the opportunity to shovel the first bit of dirt on her casket, a duty traditionally reserved for the immediate family of the deceased. The reader winces as this highly ritualized Jewish event descends into chaos and farce: "In frustration over the bottleneck with the shovel, a good number of the mourners stepped out of the line, approaching the grave, and began to topple the earth on their own. Canes were used like putters; walkers became bulldozers; wheelchairs backed right up to the precipice, and tires began to spin, sending crescent streams of soil backward in the grave" (70). To be sure, echoes of *Elijah Visible* resound in such scenes of discontinuity and rupture. Rosenbaum, moreover, depicts a corrupt Passover scene analogous to the Passover scene in the titular story of his first book and resuscitates the faithless, philandering Rabbi Vered, who first appeared in

"The Rabbi Double-Faults" and who still "never missed an opportunity to take a cheap shot at the Almighty" ("Second Hand Smoke" 49).

Importantly, however, there are several crucial distinctions between *Elijah Visible* and *Second Hand Smoke,* differences beyond the novel's more intricate and suspenseful plotting. First, the greater elasticity of the novel form allows Rosenbaum to expand the scope of his artistic vision as he generously depicts three central milieus of the Jewish diaspora: Miami Beach, New York, and contemporary Warsaw (where Duncan travels to locate his brother, Isaac). As Rosenbaum broadens his geographic vision, he also expands his social vision. The narrative eye of *Elijah Visible* is intensely, even obsessively, trained on the tortured psyche of its mosaic protagonist, Adam Posner; in *Second Hand Smoke,* Rosenbaum also focuses on his protagonist's interior, psychological burdens, but the novel also betrays Rosenbaum's increased sensitivity to the broader social implications of his protagonist's deeply personal dilemmas. For example, Duncan's clash with an adolescent neo-Nazi on the *Molly Rubin Show* expands into a impassioned critique against America's pathological hunger for ever more outrageous entertainment and the long line of Jerry Springer types only too willing to sate this hunger: "The real culprit here from Duncan's point of view was Molly Rubin and people like her, who, in the name of ratings points and advertising dollars, provided forums for maniacs to ventilate stupidity on the open airwaves" (121). The dissolution of Duncan's marriage serves as a springboard for Rosenbaum to address, through the voice of one of the novel's minor characters, the shabby values of America's thirty-something generation: "The real problem is that your generation values freedom above anything else. You think everything is supposed to go your way all the time. Autonomy and perfection—no matter what! . . . your generation can't tolerate even the slightest down moment" (130). And the apathy of those aboard a New York bus regarding an unpunished concentration camp guard in their midst embodies America's moral decay, a multicultural and multiage phenomenon, Rosenbaum suggests: "So a Nazi is on the M15? Big deal. He'll blend in well with the transvestite, the crack addict, the welfare mother, the proverbial midnight cowboy, the alcoholic banker, the Hasidic embezzler, the Mafia bagman, the grandmother addicted to Percodan, and the bus driver himself, who no doubt has his own secrets" (104).

If Rosenbaum treads on a much broader geographic and social terrain in

Second Hand Smoke, he also and perhaps most significantly redirects his artistic energies toward a new emotional vista. Whereas the overarching tone of *Elijah Visible* might best be described as elegiac and mournful, as I hope I have shown, Rosenbaum's novel is decidedly more red in tooth and claw. Put another way, whereas Rosenbaum's first book is a book primarily about loss, his debut novel is primarily about the rage that accompanies such loss and, even more specifically, about the destructive power of this rage.

Although Duncan seeks as an adult to extricate himself from his mother and her toxic influence, he finds that he cannot escape her painful psychic legacy: "The Holocaust shaped those who were survivors of survivors. Inexorably, cruelly, and unfairly so" (2). Duncan can escape Miami Beach for Washington, D.C., but as a survivor of survivors, he nonetheless psychically inherits his mother's rage, a rage that manifests itself in several small ways in the novel: Duncan's viciousness as a linebacker at Yale, his manic weight lifting, his street brawls that continue into his adulthood, his mangling of an unfortunate Mercedes, his aggressive rather than affectionate coupling with a supermodel (narratively juxtaposed, interestingly, against one of his street fights). More significantly, the obsessive desire for vengeance—rather than justice alone—motivates Duncan to accept a job out of law school as a Nazi hunter for the federal government: "Many of his colleagues were similarly fanatical, unafraid of initiative, even on a government salary. . . . What set him apart was the endless procession of demons. . . . He was savage and relentless in peeling off their masks. Duncan's hands clamped the witness box, the railing nearly coming unhinged. The accused were not safe there. They would have to tell the truth; otherwise they might simply not get out alive" (20–21). Duncan's unchecked anger unsurprisingly pushes him to investigate one suspected concentration camp guard with unwarranted and illegal zeal, which leads to his ouster at the Office of Special Investigations and to the gradual dissolution of his marriage to Sharon. She initially attempts to cure her husband of his demons but eventually abandons him, taking their daughter with her: "While Duncan was preparing briefs on the prosecution of Nazis, she was marshaling all the psychological data on what had, in actuality, become the Nazis' purest victory. . . . But finally she gave up, reshifted her focus and strategy, and decided that the results would be better if she worked on saving Milan rather than her husband" (83).

The novel reaches its denouement as Rosebaum's protagonist travels to Warsaw to find Isaac, a sort of Zen master, who helps him to eschew the self-destructive rage that has defined his existence. Only through Duncan's releasing his anger can Rosenbaum glimpse the possibility of a restored, albeit revised Jewish continuity. As Isaac instructively explains, "'I'm not going to lash out and fight back. I could do that. . . . But if I do that, I will be spending my life energy for nothing other than to fight back and cry out, and it will go into the void like everything else. But instead, I will surrender my rage and anger, and let it open up into a higher energy, something more deeply spiritual and life-affirming" (213–14).

In *Second Hand Smoke,* Rosenbaum espouses these convictions but, above all, never underestimates the difficulty of actually living by them. Perhaps the most poignant image in the novel, the rusted set of swings in Warsaw's old Jewish District, illustrates this dilemma. Duncan observes the twelve swings "moving forward and backward—noisily, unrhythmically, and unoccupied" (216). The ghosts of Jewish children at unfinished play, Rosenbaum suggests, rattle the rusted chains of these twelve swings. (He clearly means to evoke the twelve Jewish tribes, all of which are tragically lost in his midrash.) What is more, Rosenbaum's narrative insists that through the cacophony of competing contemporary influences, we must continue to listen to these ghosts. To ignore them would be to desecrate the memory of the six million. Alas, anguish, mourning, and, yes, rage are just baby steps away from such memories, especially for children of Holocaust survivors like Duncan, for whom "the staggering reality of the cattle cars, the gas chambers, and the crematoria did not feel remote" (1–2). All of which is a tremendous burden for the child of survivors, but also the muse that I suspect will keep Thane Rosenbaum writing novels for quite some time.

5

Rebecca Goldstein's Feminist/Jewish Problem

In September 1992, *Commentary* published an essay by Rebecca Goldstein entitled "Looking Back at Lot's Wife." In the essay—collected some months later in *Out of the Garden: Women Writers on the Bible* (1994), edited by Celina Spiegel and Christina Buchmann—Goldstein meditates on the biblical story of Lot's wife that frightened her as a child in Hebrew school and that continues to preoccupy her today. In the terse biblical account of Sodom's annihilation, Lot's wife is transformed into a pillar of salt after she disobediently looks back at the accursed city. Goldstein, the daughter of Orthodox Jewish parents, felt an immediate affinity for Lot's wife, for she, too, found it difficult to resist the temptation to look on the forbidden, whether it be the Kohanim during the Priestly Blessing on Rosh Hashanah or, later, the secular teachings of the great Western philosophers: "At my very Orthodox, all-girls high school, those of us who were making plans to continue on to college were warned of the dangers of secular education. . . . Above all, we were admonished, stay away from philosophy, a most dangerous discipline that systematically subjects every article of faith and belief to corrosive analysis and doubt. . . . Don't even look, the teachers said" (Goldstein, "Looking Back" 39). Goldstein, of course, "looked." She received her Ph.D. in philosophy from Princeton University and taught the subject at Barnard College for ten years before becoming a full-time novelist. This is not to say that Goldstein, who acknowledges her "close ties to Orthodoxy," eschewed Adonai for Socrates (Fishman 80). Indeed, her exegesis of the story of Lot's wife represents her attempt, in the midrashic mode, to grapple with this disturbing episode in Genesis.

Goldstein ultimately takes solace in a midrash that she discovered as an adult. The writer of the midrash, citing textual evidence, maintains that all of the people of Sodom were turned into pillars of salt. Consequently, Lot's wife was not, as Goldstein reflects, "the spectacular aberration I always thought her. Her fate was continuous with those who had been left behind" ("Looking Back" 41). That Lot's wife shares the fate of the doomed Sodomites opens up the possibility that God acted out of mercy (or *rachmones*) rather than out of vengeance in turning her into a pillar of salt. "Irit," Goldstein extrapolates, "looked back to see if her two first-born daughters were following, and she saw that they weren't and what had become of them. . . . In such a moment of grief one knows only one desire: to follow after one's child. . . . And it was for this desire that Irit was turned into a pillar of salt. She was turned into salt either because God couldn't forgive her this desire . . . or because He could" (41).

I belabor "Looking Back at Lot's Wife" because I believe it offers valuable insight into Goldstein's artistic imagination. Specifically, it illuminates the tension between Orthodox Judaism and secular feminism that has preoccupied Goldstein throughout her career. Above all, her painstaking and eloquent meditation on the story of Lot's wife illustrates that despite Goldstein's ambivalence regarding Orthodoxy, Jewish scripture and practice continues to inform her life in palpable ways. It should come as little surprise, then, that she explores the rifts between Orthodoxy and feminism through several of her protagonists. Sylvia Barack Fishman, to her credit, has recognized this predominant theme in Goldstein's fiction. However, I believe she exaggerates the even-handedness of Goldstein's approach in her early work. "Within Goldstein's fiction," she contends, "religious environments are depicted unselfconsciously and with a balanced awareness of their strengths and weaknesses" (82). This depiction of religious environments, I would argue, has hardly been so consistent. As I hope to demonstrate, Goldstein's debut novel, *The Mind-Body Problem* (1983), represents a notably hostile view of Orthodox Jewish life. Without abandoning her feminist precepts, Goldstein imagines traditional Jewish environments with far greater subtlety in subsequent stories collected in *Strange Attractors* (1993) and, most notably, in her dazzling fourth novel, *Mazel* (1995), which was published after Fishman's essay appeared. To explore Goldstein's dynamic treatment of the tension between feminism and Orthodox Judaism is to gain a glimpse of one Jewish American woman's ongoing struggle to reconcile through her fiction two essential, but often conflictive elements of her identity.

Goldstein burst on the literary scene in 1983 with the publication of *The*

Mind-Body Problem, her powerful debut novel in which she explores the tension between Orthodox Jewish ritual and the feminist precepts of her cerebral and sensual protagonist, the Princeton graduate student Renee Feuer (fire). Caroline Seebohm of the *New York Times Book Review* praised Goldstein for her entertaining and thoughtful treatment of "a classic dilemma of highly educated females—how to reconcile the dichotomy . . . between 'the outer place of bodies and the inner private one of minds,' which in more basic language might be interpreted as sex versus cerebration" (14). Similarly, the *Harper's* reviewer opined, "I know no other novel of the feminist era that not only anatomizes the dilemma of the intellectual woman in an anti-intellectual society, but also leads the reader into the experience of an intellectual woman's *thinking*" (Taliaferro 74). Most recently, Sven Birkets singled out Goldstein as one of the more promising contemporary American writers given her first two novels and observed that her work "shows that it is possible for lofty, even abstruse thought to elbow its way into fiction" (110). Goldstein wrote her first novel during a summer as a young philosophy professor who, as she put it, "was *supposed* to be . . . writing some massive scholarly study that would guarantee me tenure" (Goldstein, "Writing" 43), making her achievement in *The Mind-Body Problem* all the more impressive. Writing scholarly articles suppressed her true voice, Goldstein more recently reflected, whereas writing her first novel allowed her to create "something that was distinctly mine" (qtd. in Brawarsky 48).

Thus far, *The Mind-Body Problem* and Goldstein's work generally have received limited critical attention. Susanne Klingenstein's exploration of the Holocaust themes that emerge in Renee's visit to Germany represents the most significant scholarly treatment of the novel. In her overview of the work, Klingenstein instructively limns Renee's fractured identity: "She grew up Orthodox but discarded observance while studying philosophy at Barnard; hence she can make sense of orthodox Lakewood as well as goyish Princeton, although she is not at home in either world" ("Visits to Germany" 554). What interests me here is how Renee negotiates this rift in her ethos and, moreover, what this tortured negotiation reveals about Goldstein's early artistic vision.

As I have suggested, a narrative hostility toward Orthodoxy manifests itself in Renee's plight in *The Mind-Body Problem.* Renee, the retrospective narrator, begins her story at the moment that she meets her future husband,

Noam Himmel, a brilliant mathematics professor at Princeton, renowned for his discovery of the "supernaturals" at age twelve. Renee, for her part, is a foundering second-year graduate student in philosophy: "The field had made the 'linguistic turn' and I . . . had not. . . . Instead of wrestling with the large, messy questions that have occupied previous centuries of ethicists, for example, one should examine the rules that govern words like 'good' and 'ought' " (*TMBP* 22). The petty sophistry of her field disillusions her. She thus becomes promiscuous with an uninspired assortment of academic types to salvage a modicum of self-worth: "What I was after was the feeling that I existed, that I mattered. . . . If these men desired me, then surely I counted for something in their worlds" (28). Or, as she more subtly reflects later, "What tied me to my body was not so much its desires as the desires it aroused in others. . . . Through it (my matter, so to speak) I mattered to others, and thus mattered" (104). To be sure, sex empowers Renee. Although she cannot inspire herself to compete intellectually against her male counterparts in the philosophy department, who busily hammer out respectable dissertations, she can exert her dominance through sexual intercourse. "Through sex," she reflects, "a woman gains control over a man's body that he himself lacks; she can move him in ways that he cannot move himself" (111). Still, this empowerment evidently proves fleeting, for by the time she meets Noam Himmel she feels more than ready to "follow the venerably old feminine tradition of being saved by marriage" (20).

The rub, of course, is that Goldstein's protagonist discovers that she is *not* prepared to allow her husband's formidable identity to define (or subsume, rather) her own. Renee is far too intelligent and independent to derive any lasting satisfaction from such an arrangement. More to the point of this essay, her growth as a character depends on her rejection of this acquiescence to a marginal status encouraged and even prescribed by her Orthodox Jewish upbringing. Early in the novel, Goldstein assiduously describes her protagonist's religious childhood and her general disaffection for it. On her first date with Noam, Renee orders crabs (a nonkosher food) and describes her special delight in consuming them because "they're seasoned in sin" (45). Moreover, the meager opportunities afforded to women within the Orthodox fold are what specifically provoke her enthusiastic rebellion against Orthodox practice. As Renee describes her childhood to Noam (a nominal Jew), she mentions that her brother, "being male" (45), received priority to go to a private, religious school; to save money, her parents enrolled her in public school up until the time that non-Jewish boys began calling her for dates. Such sardonic accounts, laced with venom, of her Orthodox upbringing pervade the novel.

Through Renee's reflections, Goldstein meticulously describes and bemoans the marginal status of the woman living within the Orthodox fold. The Orthodox woman's predicament resembles the African American woman's historic plight, perhaps, more so than it does that of the upper-middle-class secular white woman in that although the Orthodox woman is not confined to the home, she is forced to support the family, while the traditional Orthodox husband devotes his life to religious study. Far from a liberated existence in the work force, "Hers is still the indisputably inferior position in those matters that matter in this society: the spiritual and intellectual, which are one and the same" (*TMBP* 77). Hungry for spiritual nourishment, Renee learns from her pious mother that the ritual bath, or *mikvah,* represents one of the few spiritual avenues available for the *ayshes chayul* (woman of worth). The rules of *niddah* (menstrual purity) mandate that Jewish women cleanse themselves monthly in the *mikvah* (see Plaskow 178–85). Renee, of course, bristles against the inextricable sexism perpetuated by such well-defined gender roles. She reflects bitterly, "(For the men: Talmud and logic, while the women try to clean up their bloody messes)" (*TMBP* 77).

Goldstein's intimate knowledge of the Orthodox setting manifests itself through her incisive portrait of the insidious misogyny that dogs Renee as a child. Renee recalls, for example, that her mother "prayed for nine months for the blessing of a male firstborn" (80), only to be disappointed by her birth instead. Further, her mother conditions her as an adolescent to be ashamed of her developing body. When boys begin to stare at her in synagogue, Renee's mother admonishes her to "be a modest, clean Jewish girl who doesn't attract any dirty thoughts" (81). After Renee outshines her younger brother socially at a Shabbat dinner with guests, her mother attempts to silence her by hissing, "'You're just a girl. . . . You're pretty enough. Why are you always trying to show off how smart you are?'" (190). What is more, in case one might suspect that gender roles may relax with a younger generation, Goldstein paints a thoroughly unflattering portrait of Renee's younger brother. As a pious adult, he chastises his sister any chance he gets for her pagan lifestyle and refuses to participate in his own wife's Lamaze childbirth. Through Renee's perspective, Goldstein offers the most cynical take she can muster on his decision: "It was *weibeszachen,* woman's business. (Not surprisingly, the Yiddish term has a pejorative connotation)" (185).

True, there are scattered moments in *The Mind-Body Problem* when Renee recalls the warmth and love that enveloped her as a child in an Orthodox Jewish family. In a particularly nostalgic moment, she longs for the special aura of a Jewish Sabbath: "I stared out at the winter-stripped elms and remembered Shabbos at home. I could hear my father's singing, the sweet warm tenor rising up in his love. Beside it the secular chatter of the Jewish *goyim* I had surrounded myself with, circumcised by doctors and not knowing what it is to yearn for the coming of the Messiah, sounded insignificant and despicable" (277). At an earlier point in the novel, she goes so far as to acknowledge that Judaism's inviolable rules (many of which oppress her in ways I presently discuss) are what imbue the Sabbath with its special meaning. Through her imagination, she takes herself back to the warmth of the Sabbath, "back inside its space, enfolded by its distances, feeling the *enforced but real sense of serenity, bounded round by prohibitions*" (141, emphasis mine). To be sure, these moments in the text are the ones that Fishman has in mind when she lauds Goldstein's "balanced awareness" of the "strengths and weaknesses" of the religious environment (82).

That said, these isolated moments of nostalgia do not add up to a balanced portrait of Orthodox Jewish life. Interestingly, Goldstein challenges Renee's few moments of nostalgia for Orthodox Jewish life with more compelling narrative counterpoints. A scene in which Renee ardently affirms her Jewish identity culminates in extramarital sex during her menstruation (a double taboo, if you will). Goldstein, importantly, depicts this moment as a triumph for Renee as she overcomes the physical self-hatred conditioned into her by Orthodox ritual: "My eyes were oozing tears, my womb blood, and he was embracing it all. And when we finally parted and I saw my blood on his body, I felt clean" (280). Additionally, Goldstein challenges Renee's nostalgia for the comfort of Orthodox rules with the depiction of her protagonist's visit to a childhood friend, Fruma, who, indeed, follows the rules, having never left the Orthodox Jewish community of Lakewood. Goldstein takes pains to emphasize that leading such a pious or *frum* life stunts Fruma's development as a human being. As Fruma herself reflects, "I feel like I'm not really an adult yet, that I haven't reached maturity, because I've never decided for myself how I want to live my life. Someone just handed me the script and I started reading" (198).

Granted, the secular academic environment that Goldstein depicts smacks of sexism in its own unique ways. Intelligent female professors feel obliged to mask any traces of their femininity lest they be taken for bimbos, to put it plainly. "[F]eminine is dumb" (216), as a female professor and friend of Renee observes. On the domestic front, the thoroughly secular Noam Himmel, who refuses even to learn where the house napkins are kept, proves nearly as obnoxious in his chauvinism as Renee's pious brother, and an eery tentativeness surrounds Renee and Noam's reconciliation toward the end of the novel. All of which is to say that Goldstein's female protagonist never quite finds a hospitable American niche for the intellectual woman who refuses to suppress her femininity.

Clearly, however, Goldstein presents Orthodox Judaism as an unpalatable option for Renee and for contemporary American women generally. Through the porous filter of her narrator, one discerns a palpable hostility toward the Orthodox way of life. I realize, of course, that I risk obfuscating the working space between Goldstein, the author, and her protagonist, so let me assure readers that T. S. Eliot's eloquent case for narrative distance in "Tradition and the Individual Talent" remains firmly embedded in my critical consciousness. In a recent interview, Goldstein, for her own part, insisted on the distance between herself and her protagonist in *The Mind-Body Problem*: "Despite similarities on the surface, she and her character 'couldn't be more different,' [Goldstein] insists, asserting that she's too private a person to 'splatter' her own inner life across the page" (Brawarsky 48). Through Renee, who seeks to distinguish her voice from the "great chorus of sexual lamentation being sung by women throughout the land, in first novel (the autobiographical one, right?) after first novel" (214), Goldstein in fact (defensively?) mocks the proclivity of critics to read first novels as autobiographical. So let me be clear: the parallels (some superficial, some not so superficial) between Goldstein and her protagonist are really off point of the argument at hand. Regardless of the arguable autobiographical content of the novel, Goldstein does implicitly espouse the anti-Orthodox views of her protagonist, for she constructs no persuasive voices to counterbalance Renee's decidedly antagonistic view of Orthodox life, nor does she challenge Renee's perspective through other narrative devices (e.g., irony or humor).

To her credit, Goldstein does not join the banal chorus of sexual lamentation in her debut novel; rather, through Renee's eminently plausible perspective, she joins a chorus of contemporary Jewish women who have begun increasingly, in both fiction and nonfiction genres, to challenge the rigid gender roles that continue to define Jewish existence within traditional environments. For example, in "If Only I'd Been Born a Kosher Chicken," Jyl Lynn Felman meditates on the suppression of the Jewish woman's body that encourages her self-hatred as a child. She, indeed, feels a disconcerting affinity with a kosher chicken: "I weigh more than the chicken, but as far as I'm concerned we're identical, the chicken and I. . . . Lots of body hair on this nice Jewish girl that my mother will religiously teach me to pluck and to shave until my adolescent body resembles a perfectly plucked, pale young bird" (83–84). Felman later bemoans, "*Shema Yisrael adonai echad* [Hear, Israel, the Lord is one], I love my people Israel, but I loathe my female self" (85). Other powerful examples of such works abound, including Letty Cottin Pogrebin's *Deborah, Golda, and Me: Being Female and Jewish in America* (1991), Anne Roiphe's *Generation Without Memory: A Jewish Journey in Christian America* (1989), Sylvia Barack Fishman's *A Breath of Life: Feminism in the American Jewish Community* (1993), and several powerful poems, stories, and essays in *The Tribe of Dina: A Jewish Women's Anthology* (1989), edited by Melanie Kaye/Kantrowitz and Irena Klepfisz.

That Goldstein narratively stacks the deck against her Orthodox Jewish characters in *The Mind-Body Problem* does not weaken the novel from an artistic standpoint. Those who look to novels for balanced depictions of religious, ethnic, or racial groups are looking in the wrong place. As Philip Roth argued in defense of his own artistic imagination when it came to Jewish characters, "To confuse a 'balanced portrayal' with a novel is finally to be led into absurdities. . . . The concerns of fiction are not those of a statistician—or of a public relations firm" ("Writing about Jews" 212). True enough. However, the often elusive narrative perspective of a work does yield valuable insights regarding the writer's artistic agenda. To read, for example, Roth's *Goodbye, Columbus* (1959) is at least in part to read a harsh critique of the postwar mores of newly affluent suburban Jews in America. *The Mind-Body Problem* similarly gives us a clear sense of Goldstein's early artistic preoccupations.

I do not wish to suggest here that Goldstein's work subsequent to her debut novel represents a complete turnabout in her artistic vision, for there exist marked parallels between *The Mind-Body Problem* and that subsequent work, which includes three additional novels and a collection of stories. Her second novel, *The Late Summer Passion of a Woman of Mind* (1989), revolves around a cerebral philosophy professor embroiled in a passionate affair with a student against her better intellectual judgment; in *The Dark Sister* (1991), her third novel, Goldstein creates a highly intelligent Jewish woman who must suppress aspects of her inner self to get by in America. Broadly speaking, then, her oeuvre reveals her pervasive interest in "'women of tremendous vitality in settings in which they're not allowed to express themselves'" (qtd. in Brawarsky 48). That said, however, Goldstein's artistic output since her debut collection also betrays a pronounced concern over the cultural dissolution of Judaism as she ventures ever more subtle evocations of traditional Jewish characters and environments.

To glean as much, one need only contrast Goldstein's debut novel with her recent and most impressive work to date, *Mazel*. First, however, I would like to explore briefly some of the stories collected in *Strange Attractors*, for these stories, written over a ten-year period beginning immediately after the publication of *The Mind-Body Problem*, herald a transition in Goldstein's approach toward traditional Jewish life. In *Strange Attractors*, she experiments with a wide variety of voices—not all Jewish or female or contemporary, for that matter. As one reviewer has suggested, the collection smacks of a young writer cutting her teeth on the tools of her medium (see Crittenden). The stories in which Goldstein engages Jewish milieus, however, contrast strikingly with her approach in *The Mind-Body Problem* as she meditates on the fate of Judaism in a post-Holocaust America rife with competing influences.

"The Legacy of Raizel Kaidish" represents the only story of the collection that has received serious critical attention (see Klingenstein, "Destructive Intimacy" 169–72, and Berger, "American Jewish" 230). To Goldstein's credit, it ranks among the most powerful stories written to date that focuses on the legacy of the Holocaust for the children of survivors. Unfortunately, the sheer force of "The Legacy of Raizel Kaidish" has overshadowed two other powerful stories in the collection, "Mindel Gittel" and "Rabbinical Eyes," which bear more directly on Goldstein's increasing concern over Jewish continuity. In "Mindel Gittel," Goldstein charts the rapid assimilation of the Zweigel family and of American Jews generally through the retrospection of the narrator, who befriended the Zweigels many years prior to events of the story. The narrator, Sol, first meets the Zweigels after he coaxes the affluent, assimilated Jews of his Connecticut exurb into renting a rabbi to lead High Holy Day services. Sol, a refugee from the Holocaust, feels an immediate affinity for Reuven Zweigel, an applicant for the position, whose "skin had still the grayness of over there" (*SA* 135). Thus, in addition to offering Reuven the temporary rabbi position, he helps the Zweigels escape their impoverished life in New York by securing a luncheonette for them to run full-time in his lush Connecticut town. In Connecticut, the sickly Zweigels raise a conspicuously attractive daughter, Mindel Gittel, who takes the next step toward complete assimilation when she marries not only a gentile but the son of a blue-blooded U.S. congressman.

Although Sol does not regret encouraging Zweigel to give up his impoverished existence as a rabbi for a more comfortable secular life, his role in the Zweigels' assimilation provokes him to reflect on what they (and, Goldstein suggests, countless other Jewish Americans who plotted a similar course) have lost. When a customer in Zweigel's restaurant acts rudely, Sol thinks, "Here is the son and grandson and the great-grandson of rabbis, and now he stands behind a counter in a white apron, and he spreads carefully mayonnaise on white bread, and answers with such humility to any rudeness" (142). The rift that grows between the Zweigels and their daughter exemplifies most profoundly the cultural dissolution of Judaism that Sol sets in motion. To shield Mindel Gittel from her painful legacy, the Zweigels raise her to be just like any other "American" child in Connecticut. They call her by her "English name," Melody, and do not tell her that her grandmother and namesake, Mindel Gittel, was a victim of the Holocaust (143). Ignorant of her family's past, Mindel Gittel/Melody grows increasingly estranged from her parents and vice versa.

The Zweigel episode convinces Sol to reclaim his Jewish identity by making aliyah to Israel: "So, after I lost my Surala, and then my two dear friends, I found that the roots I had put down in Connecticut they weren't *taka* so deep after all" (157). At the end of the story, he takes a small measure of comfort in the possibility that a subsequent generation of Jewish Americans might follow his lead to achieve a spiritual return, or *t'shuvah*. "Who knows," Sol ponders, "if it won't happen some day a little golden grandchild or great-grandchild or even great-great-grandchild of my friends the Zweigels should maybe know to quote a little something from the Zohar?" (159). Despite such clinging optimism, Sol's earlier reflections on a fairy tale he read as a child resonate more profoundly in this poignant story. In the fairy tale, two reclusive dwarfs raise a normal son who abandons them for the outside world of regular-size people, while they return to their old life without sorrow. Goldstein's story of the Zweigels reaffirms Sol's early critique of the fairy tale: that "[n]o matter how different the generations may be, one to the other, yet they cannot be sliced away from each other and it happens nobody suffers" (129). "Mindel Gittel" is, above all, a lamentation on intergenerational rupture and cultural loss.

Goldstein depicts this rupture and loss in *The Mind-Body Problem* as well, but one does not bemoan this rupture in that novel, given the pernicious and downright debilitating Orthodox rituals and mores that Renee Feuer eschews. By contrast, "Mindel Gittel" and "Rabbinical Eyes" (which I discuss below) condition the reader to respond more thoughtfully to the intergenerational rifts that beset her characters and the concomitant rupture in Jewish continuity; herein, Goldstein challenges her earlier narrative perspective in *The Mind-Body Problem.* This shift in narrative perspective is particularly striking in "Rabbinical Eyes" because its narrator resembles Renee of *The Mind-Body Problem* so closely on the surface. Like Renee, this narrator is a formidably intelligent daughter of Orthodox Jewish parents, a student of philosophy, who drifts away from traditional Jewish practice. Goldstein, however, devotes little space in the story to any unsavory depictions of traditional Jewish life. The narrator's egalitarian upbringing contrasts intriguingly with Renee's childhood. Although the narrator has read the "angry literature" by "Jewish feminists" (Goldstein's first novel, perhaps?), she weighs in contrariwise because "the kind of mindless dismissal of girls that seems to typify certain parts of the Orthodox Jewish world simply wasn't my experience at all" (207). Indeed, a powerful nostalgia for the Jewish world left behind permeates "Rabbinical Eyes." For example, the narrator waxes on the hours she spent studying Talmud with her father, a scholarly, albeit uncharismatic rabbi.

Readers may wonder why the narrator ever left the Orthodox Jewish fold to begin with until they stumble across the abrupt lines, "I was disowned by them all two years ago, when I married Luke, who is a Gentile. My father, my mother, and my brother sat *shiva* for me, as if I were dead" (190). Through this narrative interruption, Goldstein artistically dramatizes the abrupt and utter rupture between two Jewish American generations. Importantly, however, the narrative emphasis in the story does not bear down overtly on the implacable rigidity of the narrator's Orthodox family; rather, Goldstein devotes her artistic energies to dramatizing the narrator's despondency in and of itself. Upon the birth of her severely impaired daughter, the narrator needs and sorely lacks her father's spiritual guidance. At story's close, she dreams of a reconciliation: "I saw my father together with Luke. . . . when he turned around I saw he was holding the baby" (216). Like "Mindel Gittel," then, "Rabbinical Eyes" concludes with a desperate vision of Jewish continuity.

Before we move on to *Mazel,* it is worth noting that Goldstein created the novel's principal characters—Sasha, a former star of the Warsaw's Yiddish theater; her daughter, Chloe, a classics professor; and Chloe's daughter, Phoebe, a mathematics professor—in two stories collected in *Strange Attractors,* "The Geometry of Soap Bubbles and Impossible Love" and "Strange Attractors," the title story. In these stories, Goldstein explores the subtle ebb and flow of Jewish identity in America through three generations of Jewish women. She pithily evokes the rifts between the generations as the third-person narrator of "The Geometry of Soap Bubbles and Impossible Love" reflects, "Chloe and Phoebe don't speak Yiddish, Sasha and Phoebe don't speak ancient Greek, and Sasha and Chloe don't speak mathematics" (178). Goldstein evidently realized that she had far from exhausted the creative potential of these three characters in *Strange Attractors.* They kept "'jabbering away'" she recalled recently (qtd. in Brawarsky 48), so in *Mazel,* she returned to explore their interrelationships and the disparate cultural influences that give shape to their Jewish identities.

Mazel, which won the National Jewish Book Award and the 1995 Edward Lewis Wallant Award for the year's best work of Jewish American fiction, might be seen as a culmination of Goldstein's most pressing artistic concerns. In it, she revisits the feminist arguments of her first novel but counterbalances these arguments with a more nuanced depiction of Orthodox Jewish life; she does not limit her attention to the contemporary *tsores* (troubles) of the young intellectual woman in America, but dramatizes the continuity of the female experience within the Orthodox Jewish tradition through three generations and brings her artistic imagination to bear on the old country in Eastern Europe as well as on the new country in that adopted suburban homeland of the American Jew, New Jersey.

In the broadest sense, *Mazel* challenges Mark Krupnick's recent assertion that "secular mindedness remains the norm" among young Jewish American women writers (305). For example, in the chapter "Counting the Omer" (referring to the forty-nine-day period between the Jewish holidays of Passover and Shavuot), Goldstein assiduously charts the religious observances of her Jewish characters in Shluftchev, Galicia. The chapter reminds us that several Jewish Americans still anxiously anticipate the significant Jewish months of Tishrei and Nissan rather than the English months of December and April. More specifically, *Mazel* represents Goldstein's ambitious attempt to test out the viability of Orthodox Judaism in three representative Jewish milieus of the twentieth century: the prewar Galician shtetl of Schluftchev, the cosmopolitan prewar Warsaw, and the contemporary Orthodox Jewish suburb of Lipton, New Jersey.

In setting her sights on the European Diaspora, Goldstein partakes of a recent trend in Jewish American fiction that Ruth Wisse anticipated in her 1976 essay "American Jewish Writing, Act II." As I explored in some depth in chapter 3, Wisse predicted that writers who took their Judaism seriously would have to explore the issue of Jewish identity as it played itself out beyond the American border. Goldstein's *Mazel* affirms Wisse's observations but also, interestingly, qualifies them. As Wisse cannily anticipated, Goldstein ships her characters to the European shtetl to explore the vexing issue of female Jewish identity. However, they carry with them round-trip tickets to wind up stateside in an Orthodox Jewish suburb. Phoebe, who represents the new Jewish American woman, embraces the Orthodox rituals that her mother and grandmother reject (Goldstein does not envision Phoebe's *t'shuvah* in the two stories in *Strange Attractors*), thereby dramatizing the sociocultural resurgence of Orthodoxy, a revitalized resistance to the lure of secular mainstream America. Wisse, writing some twenty-odd years ago, never anticipated this religious renaissance or Goldstein's concomitant imagining of an Orthodox Jewish enclave amid an increasingly assimilated American Jewish population. Goldstein's Lipton, New Jersey, where the novel begins and ends, is a far cry from the secular New Jersey suburbs of Philip Roth's fiction (suburbs that, Wisse bemoaned, "lent [themselves] to the production of satire, but not so far to any nobler art" ["American" 45]).

Although the resurgence of Orthodoxy in America emerges as the novel's predominant theme, Goldstein takes great pains in dramatizing its earlier decline. Her portrait of 1920s Shluftchev, the Galician shtetl of Sasha's youth, suggests convincingly why Sasha embraces at her first opportunity the "enlightened" secular city of Warsaw and, later, New York. Through the tragic story of Sasha's sister, Fraydel, Goldstein examines the origins of

Renee Feurer's feminist plight in *The Mind-Body Problem.* Fraydel possesses a hunger for books and a creative imagination, qualities that her insular shtetl does not extol even in men, much less women:

> one must beware of books, even if they're beautiful—especially if they're beautiful—resisting the pull of the pagan fascination. . . . Only Fraydel, somehow, didn't seem to know this. Any book on which she could get her hands had the power to absorb her entirely. Give her a book on the constellations of the stars in the sky, or the adventures of Marco Polo in China, a silly sentimental tale of love by Shomer, or homilies on the modesty appropriate to Jewish girls: if it was printed, Fraydel would devour it. The words she drank from the page seemed, more than the food at which she barely nibbled on her plate, to give her the little nourishment sustaining her. (*Mazel* 68)

A girl in Shluftchev might read from the few books especially designed to spoon feed them bits and pieces of Torah, but "[b]eyond that, what did a girl need from books?" (69). So it goes in Schluftchev. Alas, one senses early on that Fraydel's sheer individuality will doom her in the pious shtetl, where, as Sasha reflects, "the girls were all supposed to be pressed out from the same cookie cutter, anything extra trimmed away" (18). Fraydel cannot conform to Shluftchev's rigid codes of conduct, based on roughly equal doses of halakah (Jewish law) and local custom; the other children ostracize her and torment her with the Yiddish chant, *"Fraydel, Fraydel, da meshuggena maydel!"* (Fraydel, Fraydel, the crazy girl!) (56).

The freedoms of the pagan world prove tempting, indeed, and Fraydel nearly runs off with the Gypsies, but Leiba, her mother, thwarts her escape and arranges for her prompt marriage to a "presentable," albeit crippled bridegroom. Leiba believes that "[w]hen Fraydel had, God willing, a husband and children of her own, then she would be bound through her heart to the ordinary and simple" (128). Fraydel predictably cannot embrace the rewards of domesticity laid out before her and demonstrates as much when she violates the rules of the Sabbath by picking and carrying flowers (see the *Mishnah Shabbat* 7:2). As Sasha observes at the time, Fraydel, flowers in hand, adopts the libidinous codes of the pagan realm: "Fraydel wasn't walking like Fraydel either, not like any Jewish girl or woman walked. She was barefoot—where were her shoes?—and was rolling her hips in the loose and easy motions of the Gypsy women" (148). One can almost hear the collective groan "enough is enough" emanate from Shluftchev's shanties. The shtetl will simply not tolerate Fraydel's paganism as her fiancée's family predictably calls off the wedding. Because Fraydel, for her part, cannot embrace Shluftchev's piety, she sews rocks into the bottom of her skirt and—à la Shakespeare's Ophelia—drowns herself.

The battle between the pagan and the Hebraic, between Pan and Moses, has also been Cynthia Ozick's muse from the start of her career. "Great Pan Lives," Rabbi Isaac Kornfield ecstatically declares in Ozick's landmark story, "The Pagan Rabbi" (17); he thus blurs the Creator with the created. Learning only too late that his soul belongs to Torah, not to the trees—that one cannot be both a pagan and a rabbi—Kornfeld hangs himself from a tree by his prayer shawl. To be sure, Ozick's influence on Goldstein manifests itself clearly as the pagan and Hebraic realms vie for Fraydel's soul (as I explore below, Ozick's thumbprint can be seen elsewhere in *Mazel*). Goldstein, however, gives the Ozickean theme a decidedly feminist twist through Fraydel's tragic story.

Warsaw affords Sasha the pagan opportunities that remained just out of her sister's reach in "sleepy" Shluftchev (*shluf* means "sleep" in Yiddish). In this cosmopolitan city, Sasha learns to speak Polish, Russian, German, and English, and yields to the widespread assimilatory urgings of her generation: "All across the former Pale were Jewish parents having their Jewish hearts broken, as sons and daughters broke away from the old ways, made a blind run for the light" (*Mazel* 201). Sasha leaves the pious, provincial world of the shtetl behind most forcefully by becoming an actress. After all, "[o]f all the arts—music, letters, painting—drama is the only one that receives absolutely no recognition within rabbinical sources" (177). To Sasha's father, Nachum, a theater "smelled unpleasantly from Hellenistic corruption. . . . a Jewish play was a paradox in itself" (180). Nachum's pious sensibilities aside, one can readily appreciate Sasha's attraction to the theater. While on stage, she can give free rein to the creative energies that she and her sisters, in a seemingly former lifetime in Shluftchev, could unleash only behind the closed door of their cramped bedroom via their collaborative storytelling.

Moreover, the theater offers Sasha and her Jewish cohorts in the Bilbul Art Theater a communicative power within mainstream Warsaw society—an opportunity to partake of and contribute to mainstream culture. Whereas Sasha's parents' generation struggled to maintain a pious existence despite material hardship, more heady possibilities preoccupy Sasha's generation:

> How could there be time enough to touch it all, absorb it all, and then—yes—contribute something of one's own? A piece of the melody, an equation, a theory, a canvas—something of one's own that will make a difference. It doesn't have to be big, though all the better if it is. But *something* to show that one is there, *there,* inhabiting the text itself, no longer stranded in the despair of those despicably narrow margins. (202)

To Sasha's generation, Jewish piety (or, rather, Judaism itself) seems a hopeless anachronism in Warsaw, the seat of high European culture. As Sasha's friend Jascha Saunders reflects, "there was no reason to keep oneself separate and cut off any longer. The world at large, or at least enough of it, had freed itself from the steel-trap dogmas and pieties of the past, so that there was room at last to enter" (222). In Jascha's eyes, those Jews intent on clinging to the particularity of the Jewish experience and to the collective destiny of Jews everywhere (the Yiddishists, Bundists, and Zionists, most conspicuously) were "stalled halfway on their path to clear thinking, overcome by the centuries-weighted pull from the past" (222). An aspiring composer, Jascha claims Bach, Beethoven, and Brahms as his mentors and feels only a remote affinity for Abraham, Yitzchak, and Yaakov. (Jascha's passionate embrace of a mainstream rather than a Jewish cultural heritage evokes the sentiments of Philip Roth's familiar protagonist, Nathan Zuckerman in *The Counterlife* [1986, see especially 58–59].) Sasha, no doubt, would express roughly the same detachment from her matriarchs: Sarah, Rebecca, Rachel, and Leah.

Small wonder that Sasha, who roundly admonishes those who mistakenly attach a "Mrs." rather than a "Dr." to her daughter's and granddaughter's names, can scarcely locate any redeeming qualities in Phoebe's adopted 1990s community of Lipton, New Jersey. One must remember that "Sasha hated shtetl life: close and narrow, shut off from that great wide world with which Sasha has been, ever after, carrying on her impassioned love affair" (336). Right down to its foul-smelling brook, Lipton reminds her of Shluftchev and its stinking puddle, of all that was provincial and sordid about her childhood shtetl. Even more significantly, Lipton upholds and perpetuates Shluftchev's rigid Jewish codes of conduct, which proved too much for Fraydel to bear. When, for example, Sasha dares to don pants on the Jewish Sabbath in Lipton, Phoebe's future mother-in-law warns her that "women simply don't wear pants here on Shabbes," to which Sasha replies, "So *stone* me, Beatrice" (323, emphasis in original). Sasha cannot fathom why her contemporary, educated granddaughter would subject herself to the indignities of Orthodox Jewish life. "You're an educated woman!" she berates Phoebe. "'A *professor!* Why would you want to start up all over again with those *old ways?*'" (338). When friends of Phoebe's in-laws press Sasha to share her impressions of their town, she peppers her response with the most provocative dramatic pauses she can muster: "'Lipton, New Jersey . . . is Shluftchev . . . with a designer label'" (333).

Through Phoebe's *t'shuvah*—despite Sasha's antagonism toward Lipton and its values—Goldstein affirms, with something of a vengeance, Sol's optimistic vision of Jewish continuity in "Mindel Gittel." That Phoebe adopts Orthodox Jewish values represents, perhaps, Goldstein's greatest imaginative leap in *Mazel;* however, it should be noted that Goldstein might have drawn from any number of real-life models to envision Phoebe's religious ardor. As I suggested earlier, an unprecedented number of young Jewish Americans, raised largely ignorant of Judaism, have become part of the *baal t'shuvah* (returnee) phenomenon.

What accounts for the growing appeal of the "old ways," as Sasha puts it, to Phoebe's generation? The answer in *Mazel* is somewhat nebulous, which seems appropriate given the often ineffable nature of spiritual inspiration. Still, Goldstein engages the issue of Jewish particularity in several memorable scenes that shed light on Phoebe's religious ardor. A fairy tale told by Hershel Blau, the director of the Bilbul Art Theater, resonates throughout the novel. In the tale, a peasant suddenly knows all the answers to the profound questions that have been vexing him for his entire life. He owes his burst of knowledge, he realizes, to the *shmutz* (dirt) on the bottom of his sandals. During a recent storm, a leaf from the tree of knowledge adhered to the dirt on his sandals. The moral of the story is clear enough. Though it may be the Jews' destiny to trudge in their sandals through the muck of history, their singular experience contains hidden virtues and rewards.

The assimilationist, Jascha, refuses to take the story's message to heart and instead borrows from its symbolism to predict the imminent decline of Judaism: "In a few generations, three or four at the most, nobody will even remember who was a sandal-wearer and who wasn't" (269). The looming Holocaust, of course, will prove Jascha wrong, but external pressures notwithstanding, Hershel believes in his story's message, as evidenced in the precepts of the Bilbul Art Theater. Rather than produce "Yiddishized" versions of the Western classics (Goldstein treats us to one Yiddish troupe's hilarious version of *King Lear,* a popular play in the Yiddish theater), Hershel and his group produce only works from their distinctively Jewish imaginations. The play that finally makes a name for the Bilbul Art Theater is *The Bridegroom,* Sasha's adaptation of one of Fraydel's dazzling stories. The Bilbul Art Theater, then, makes its contribution to culture by transmitting Fraydel's Jewish Shluftchev voice, "a voice like no other" (227). Schmaltzed-up Jewish versions of Shakespeare, Goldstein suggests, will not carry the day, nor will Jascha's parallel artistic attempts to build a musical masterpiece on the mainstream foundations of Bach, Beethoven, and Brahms. The score that finally earns Jascha a reputation is the thoroughly Jewish music he reluctantly agrees to write for *The Bridegroom,* "music that went against all he believed" (282). Through the success of *The Bridegroom* and its music, Goldstein affirms the lesson of Hershel's fairy tale: the Jewish identity is one that is worth both preserving through ritual and transmitting through art.

The shofar metaphor in Cynthia Ozick's important essay "Toward a New Yiddish" resonates in the success of *The Bridegroom*. Ozick exhorts her Jewish readers, "If we blow into the narrow end of the *shofar,* we will be heard far. But if we choose to be Mankind rather than Jewish and blow into the wider part, we will not be heard at all" (177). The lesson, of course, is that Jewish artists must not suppress but rather engage their Jewish particularism in their work.

It is curious that Sasha and Jascha, so integral to the production of *The Bridegroom*, seem impervious to the lesson of its success. Phoebe, at any rate, recognizes the importance of nurturing a distinct Jewish identity; thus, "Lipton, New Jersey, seems to be the very place in which [she] feels quite entirely at home" (*Mazel* 8). Mainstream American culture offers its share of material rewards, to be sure, but it offers only thin fare for the soul. By contrast, abiding by Orthodox ritual in Lipton satisfies Phoebe's spiritual yearnings. Even Chloe, a thoroughly pagan classics professor, recognizes these spiritual yearnings within herself. At Lipton's synagogue, she feels a "spine-tingling awe, the sense that one was tapping into rituals that, despite any modern accretions along the way . . . reached far back into something authentically ancient and therefore thrilling" (330). To ask that Orthodox Judaism abide by the contemporary secular ideals of scientific rationalism and gender equality is to miss the point (and the beauty) behind its ancient and inviolable rituals. Phoebe realizes this, and so does her mother. At the conclusion of the novel, even the implacable Sasha must concede that her grandchild wears the Jewish sandals of Hershel's story not because the Christian world has forced them onto her feet, but because she believes in their magic.

Curiously, Goldstein has downplayed the particularism of *Mazel* to emphasize its "universal" significance, "the nuances of mother-daughter relationships, assimilation and the meaning of America for immigrants" (qtd. in Brawarsky 49). "My feeling," Goldstein has stated, "is that if you are very true to whatever particularity, that's where the universal comes in" (49). Here, she echoes Chaim Potok's comments concerning his truly "particular" corpus of work: "I am writing about my world precisely the same way Faulkner wrote about Yoknapatawpha County. And nobody in a million years will convince me that Yoknapatawpha County is more American than the world I am writing about" ("Conversation" 87). The Orthodox Jewish world that his characters inhabit "can be any world," he reflected more recently, "Christian, Muslim, Native-American, African-American, Hispanic, secular, Australian aborigine, others" ("Invisible Map" 30).

What I find intriguing is not so much the eminently valid universalist argument that Goldstein, like Potok before her, articulates, but rather the defensiveness that manifests itself in the argument. This defensiveness bespeaks, I believe, the nagging sense on the part of contemporary Jewish American writers that their culturally specific experiences are perceived both as less "American" than the experiences of mainstream writers and less "strange" than the experiences of other minority writers (i.e., Asian American, Hispanic, Native American, and African American) who currently command our rapt attention in our multicultural zeitgeist. As Ted Solatoroff recently noted, "Jews today, rightly or wrongly, are perceived to be part of the white mainstream. Their formerly marginal position is now occupied by the people of color. . . . The multicultural movement passes them by and anti-Semitism is mostly a demagogic way of attacking the power structure" ("Open" xx). Indeed, as I suggested in the introduction to this volume, a double bind plagues the contemporary Jewish American writer. Pigeonholed somewhere between the mainstream and the marginal, writers such as Goldstein must constantly affirm both the culturally specific and universal validity of their work.

In this light, Goldstein's choice of a conspicuously "particular" title for her most recent novel, *Mazel,* emerges as a daring and meaningful act. The title, I believe, appropriately exemplifies her increasing artistic absorption in the Jewish realm. Whereas she seems to bid a good riddance to the traditional Jewish environment in her debut novel, she sets out to retrieve this world in *Mazel.* "Too Jewish," I can only imagine an endless string of Viking Penguin editors proclaiming when they glanced at Goldstein's title on their page proofs. In writing *Mazel* and in clinging to the Yiddish title, Goldstein has dared once again to "look back," like Lot's wife. That looking back for Goldstein in 1995 entailed looking upon the traditional Jewish realm gives us a sense of where Jewish American women's writing has been over the past several years and where we might expect it to go in the future.

6

Toward an Ethical (Re)Definition of Jewish Literature

The Fiction of Robert Cohen; or, It's American, but Is It Jewish?

> [M]y heart was consumed with the demand I have mentioned—*I want, I want!*
>
> —Eugene Henderson, in Saul Bellow's *Henderson the Rain King*

> *[S]omewhere deep within, where I expected to find stillness, there remained these jabs of restlessness and yearning. The heart, the bladder, the mind. They will not keep still. And why should they have to?*
>
> —Hesh Freeman, in Robert Cohen's *The Organ Builder*

If the bulk of contemporary literary criticism tells us anything, it tells us that we have undergone a sea change from the time earlier in this century when one could unabashedly explore, as Alfred Kazin recently put it, "the raw hurting power that a book could have" (18). Put simply, we have lost the conviction that fiction and poetry (i.e., primary texts) can and should move us, that the best works will simply not stand to *be* read but, instead, will read us. Moreover, I am certainly not the first critic to note that literature itself seems to have moved from the center to the margins of our critical attention.

Amid such a zeitgeist, one runs the risk of appearing downright unscholarly, even sentimental, if one dares to display a poem prominently in one's academic office. Indeed, I suppose it might qualify as a small expression of academic rebellion that the now faded copy of Gerald Stern's poem, "Behaving Like a Jew," has enjoyed for several months now a conspicuous perch just beside my computer screen. Each and every day (as I type these very words, in fact) it faces, challenges, and inspires me. The poem is beautiful to me because it does exactly what Alfred Kazin insists that literature, at its most powerful, does: it "reclaim[s] the world that is constantly receding from us" (12). Briefly: the poet comes across a familiar scene in the country, a dead opossum on the road. Although he realizes that he should be inured to the common sight of roadkill, he resolves to fight off numbness: "I am going to be unappeased at the opossum's death. / I am going to behave like a Jew / and touch his face, and stare into his eyes, / and pull him off the road" (55). In the face of death, the poet seeks not relief from an intense emotional response; rather, he actively courts grief. What Gerald Stern "reclaims" here, then, is an appropriate moral response to the death of an individual, a response that has almost irrevocably receded as we focus instead on the good of the masses; we "praise the beauty and the balance" of the "immortal lifestream" (55). In refusing to revel in the "immortal lifestream," in rejecting numbness, Stern affirms the sanctity of life.

The poem raises the following question: What, exactly, is so Jewish about the poet's behavior? After all, Judaism is certainly not the only religion that extols the sanctity of life. In fact, one would be hard-pressed, I suspect, to find a religion in which the celebration of life does not figure prominently in its rituals. That Jews possess no monopoly on the issues of morality Stern engages has led several scholars of Jewish literature to reject the ethical imperative as even a partial definition of this body of writing. Hana Wirth-Nesher, for example, has done so with considerable aplomb: "Some critics of Jewish literature have argued that theme determines Jewishness, and have then proposed that such universal topics as conflict between generations or ethical commitment are signs of Jewish texts. The latent moral imperialism implied by such an approach is as dismaying as its intellectual shabbiness" ("Defining" 4; see also Alter, "Jewish Voice" 40). Presumably, a thematic definition of Jewish literature would not rankle Wirth-Nesher if it were predicated on a particularly Jewish rather than a universal topic. Cynthia Ozick's take on the thematic approach to Jewish literature—"if Jewish fiction articulates ideas that are not duplicatable outside of Jewish tradition, then you might be justified in calling that fiction thematically Jewish" ("Interview" 378)—would, no doubt, sit well with Wirth-Nesher. Interestingly, however, Ozick is not so quick to dismiss the ethical imperative from the Jewish particular. She identifies "the imposition of moral structure in natural life and on nature itself" as a distinctively Jewish principle (378). Under Ozick's and Wirth-Nesher's exclusivist paradigm, then, one might feasibly make a case for the Jewishness of a work based on its moral content.

This possibility notwithstanding, I believe that our definition of Jewish literature need not be so exclusively bound to Judaic principles. It seems to me, for example, that Wirth-Nesher unnecessarily conflates literary definitions with religious definitions when she frets over the "moral imperialism" of scholars who have observed a characteristic "ethical commitment" in Jewish texts, for to claim that Jewish writers have exhibited a conspicuous concern with ethical issues is not to deny the morality of other religious faiths, nor is it necessarily to espouse the morality of Judaism. Rather, when, say, Ted Solotaroff argues that "Jewish material can be as intractable morally as it is imaginatively" ("Philip Roth" 87), he describes one unifying characteristic of the Jewish texts he has encountered. In the essay from which I have just quoted, "Philip Roth and the Jewish Moralists," Solatoroff could not ignore the parallels that stared him directly in the face as he studied the fiction of Philip Roth, Bernard Malamud, and other noteworthy Jewish American writers:

> both Roth and Malamud seem involved in a similar effort to feel and think with their Jewishness and to use the thick concreteness of Jewish moral experience to get at the dilemmas and decisions of the heart generally. Writing from the struggle to illuminate and assess and extend the fading meaning of being a Jew, they write from their hearts—sophisticated, witty, tough-minded as they may be—and usually it is back to the heart that their work leads us: to its suffering and its trials and, particularly, to its deep moral potency. (90–91)

One probably has already intuited where I stand on the conundrum of morality and Jewish writing. It has always seemed to me a characteristic of this body of writing that serious ethical issues (the sanctity of human life, the inexorable responsibility to one's family and to the larger human community) bear down on the most resonant protagonists in Jewish American fiction—a characteristic too prominent to be ignored, regardless of the arguable universal nature of these precepts. What is more, the protagonists of this body of writing (and here I am admittedly speaking mainly about post–World War II male protagonists in Jewish American fiction) often curiously resemble one another and consequently plot similar courses for engaging the deep moral issues. They are often highly intelligent but impassive, disaffected, and estranged from their families. At the beginning of a novel, they appear to plod mechanically through life, often holed up in an office where they pursue professional but meaningless careers. To restore meaning into their lives, they often must eschew their intellectual impulses, as Solotaroff suggests in "Philip Roth and the Jewish Moralists," and embrace the deeper truths that lie in the human heart. More often than not, these truths are to be realized only once the protagonists revisit their childhoods or reckon with their family's history generally. To be sure, as Solotaroff argued recently, "what Walden pond is to Thoreau or the West End of London to Henry James, a family situation is to the Jewish writer" ("Open" xxiv). Jewish writers' moral vision, then, is often bound up in their often shadowy recollections of childhood.

Saul Bellow's fiction, perhaps, stands out as the most representative model of this Jewish American theme. His eminent historian, Moses Herzog, for example, discovers that braininess gets one only so far in the wake of a marital collapse. To regain his sanity, he must rediscover the Herzog heart by revisiting his materially (although not emotionally) impoverished childhood on Napolean Street. "Here," Bellow writes, "was a wider range of human feelings than he had ever again been able to find" (*Herzog* 140). Only after revisiting his childhood does Herzog achieve a modicum of spiritual peace. *"Hineni!"* (310), he cries in Hebrew to God toward the end of the novel—"Here I am!" Most of Bellow's protagonists (e.g., Asa Leventhal, Augie March, Tommy Wilhelm, Artur Sammler) must awaken their slumbering souls if they are to understand the human contract (i.e., covenant) between themselves and God. Even Bellow's gentile protagonist, Eugene Henderson, seeks to burst his spirit's sleep and does so not so much through his imaginary adventures in Africa, but through his reminiscences of childhood and the common bond of despair that he shared with his coworker at a carnival, a trained bear. For Bellow—as for Philip Roth or for Bernard Malamud or, I would argue, for Gerald Stern—to heed the heart's moral instruction over the dizzying pedantries of the high-I.Q. head is to "behave like a Jew."

At this point, I would like to turn my attention to a contemporary Jewish American writer, Robert Cohen. More profoundly than the work of his contemporaries, Cohen's fiction embodies this prevalent vision of his Jewish American predecessors. The protagonists of his first two novels, *The Organ*

Builder (1988) and *The Here and Now* (1996), must awaken from an etherized existence. In the Bellovian tradition, they must burst their spirit's sleep. Moreover, to engage the big, often ethical questions and to realize a meaningful future, they must pursue the mysteries of the past, specifically their family's past.

Exceedingly few reviewers of Cohen's first novel identified it as a distinctively Jewish American work, which suggests that Hana Wirth-Nesher's rejection of the ethical definition of Jewish literature apparently holds sway. Allow me to entertain one significant reason why this might be so. Since the 1980s, we have enjoyed a surge of Jewish American fiction on distinctively Jewish themes such as the Holocaust, Israel, and *t'shuvah* (spiritual return). "Collectively, Jewish novels," as Alan Berger observes, "are increasingly exploring the meaning of being Jewish from within rather than from the perspective of American culture" ("American Jewish" 222). Thus, scholars of Jewish American literature need not bother these days with the more polemical definitions of this body of writing or with those writers whose work falls into these definitions. Hence, in his entry "Jewish American Literature" in a multicultural sourcebook, Mark Krupnick focuses on those contemporary Jewish American writers (e.g., Cynthia Ozick, Rebecca Goldstein, Allegra Goodman) who engage the irrefutably Jewish themes I have named, but he neglects to list Robert Cohen's name in his "Selected Primary Bibliography" (see Krupnick). The former fiction editor for *Tikkun,* Rosellen Brown, however, instructively casts her net a good bit wider when it comes to defining Jewish works. She makes no bones about defining *The Organ Builder* as a Jewish novel: "Does it matter that Heshie is Jewish, even though he gives no specific thought to his religion? Of course it does: his father became the man he was—a scientist who finally abandoned his work on the atomic bomb for reasons of conscience—within a *moral* and historical conscience in which his background played a decisive part. He was a Jew in American history" (83, emphasis mine).

The protagonist in Cohen's second novel, *The Here and Now* (1996), however, *does* give specific thought to his religion (as I presently explore), which goes a long way toward confirming, once and for all, Cohen's Jewishness as a writer. All the same, I embrace Brown's criteria for identifying works of the Jewish American imagination, which are decidedly less rigid than Wirth-Nesher's or Ozick's. Interestingly, the moral and historical conscience of Cohen's characters merit Brown's special attention, earmarking even *The*

Organ Builder as a Jewish work in her eyes. It is precisely this moral and historical conscience, I would contend, that secures Cohen's position along the continuum of the Jewish American literary tradition.

The Organ Builder revolves around Hesh Freeman, an eighth-year associate at a blue-chip New York law firm. We meet the lugubrious Freeman in the midst of a foundering career and home life. The first few pages of the novel, in fact, reveal his disaffection with both his immediate family and the law office of Pinsker & Lem. He and his wife, Joanne, have separated, and a conspicuous lack of feeling rather than outright hostility defines their relationship. Some blockage in Freeman, one senses, precludes intimacy. Even the birth of their son, Solly, failed to rally them together behind a shared sense of purpose: "A certain seriousness of purpose was required of us, and it wasn't present. Fundamentally, we lost respect for each other, and made our retreats. . . . I'm fairly sure neither of us had affairs, though I'm not at all sure why not" (*TOB* 13–14). It comes as little surprise that Freeman cannot muster up the enthusiasm for copyright law, either: "Somehow my energies had atrophied and gone sour. Perhaps they had been worn down by the pressure, or dulled by the relentless triviality and avarice of corporate litigation. I didn't know. All I knew was that I had come to embody a certain waste that leaked from the firm like a toxin" (7). At the beginning of the novel, then, Hesh Freeman emerges as a character treading water both at home and at work, and, if I might belabor this metaphor, he has been treading water for a long enough time to realize that he must either discover a way to swim or succumb to drowning.

Like so many Jewish American protagonists, Freeman does not wish to drown just yet; he desperately wishes to imbue his life with meaning. His very disillusionment with his current workaday existence indicates as much. In the novel's prologue, written in the form of a letter to Abby Gordon, Freeman exclaims, *"I am out to make an attempt. I've been drifting backward through the chamber of my self for as long as you've known me, and now I am going to put some work into changing direction"* (xi). The fervent convictions of Bellow's Moses Herzog—*Survival! . . . Till we figure out what's what. Till the chance comes to exert a positive influence"* (*Herzog* 128)—resonate in Freeman's protestations. Both characters wish to heal their wounded souls so that they might transcend their self-absorption and exert a positive influence in the larger human community. Freeman wishes, for example, to connect with the "Oriental fellow" whom, from his window each day, he sees working industriously in an office across the street

(*TOB* 11). Also, the revelation that he will, most likely, never again see an acquaintance at a poker game disturbs him profoundly (*TOB* 34). Something in Freeman doesn't like the emotional fence that blocks his relationships with others.

As Hesh's letter in the prologue suggests, his (non)relationship with his father, Eli Freidmann, stands at the center of Hesh's contemporary burdens. Eli Friedmann, we learn, was one of the younger physicists at Los Alamos working on the Manhattan Project during World War II. He became estranged from his wife, Ruth, during this period and eventually disappeared altogether. In an attempt to extricate himself from his father's legacy, Hesh changed his surname to Freeman. "There was a lot of protest going on at the time," he explains to a colleague late in the novel, and continues, "I wanted to make something clear" (232). By changing his name, then, he wished to free himself from the sins of his father.

Of course, the emotionally embattled Hesh is anything but a "free man" at the beginning of the novel, and there is no dearth of reality instructors on hand who attempt to lead him back on course. A corpulent, epicurean senior partner at his firm, Charlie Goldwyn, seeks to inspire the spiritless Hesh by encouraging him to adopt his own crude, materialistic motivations. Goldwyn, interestingly, has had to reckon with his own Jewish father. Resentful of the material impoverishment of his childhood, his family's "grubby little apartment," he strives and succeeds in escaping the world of his father, an "Old World dreamer" (74). What is more, by prospering financially, Goldwyn "had erased him, supplanted him. He made himself into his own father, became a man of force" (74). To erase his father, of course, is exactly what Hesh had hoped to accomplish by changing his name. Small wonder that Goldwyn, despite his downright grotesque appetites (both carnal and culinary), appeals to him.

Hesh, however, cannot erase his father as easily as Goldwyn can his, for he is dogged by the deep ethical and moral implications of his father's work on the Manhattan Project. Indeed, Hesh's numbness at the beginning of the novel illustrates that a blithe, Goldwyn-like renunciation of his past cannot carry the day. He will not burst his spirit's sleep until he looks squarely down the maw of his family's past. Two rather propitious events spur on the equivocal Hesh. First, Arthur Gordon, a filmmaker hoping to retrieve the story of Eli Friedmann, locates Hesh; with the help of his enchanting wife, Abby, he lures Hesh into the project. Both Arthur and Abby Gordon—their own ulterior professional and personal motives aside—prove themselves far more attuned than Goldwyn to the realities that bear down on Hesh. Arthur Gordon advises him that he must confront his past before he can hope to realize any meaningful future: "the only thing that keeps you from spinning off the planet is your past. It's heavy at times. I won't deny it can get oppressive. But it's all you've got, dammit. Without it you think you can fly, but you can't even move" (44–45). Abby Gordon suggests, "You can't go somewhere from nowhere, Hesh" (69). Then, Goldwyn recruits Hesh to assist him on a mineral rights case against the Navajo in (where else?) New Mexico, just minutes from his childhood home at Los Alamos. Hesh, despite his inclinations toward stasis, takes flight in search of his past.

Through this journey into his past, Cohen engages not only the deeply personal childhood traumas of his protagonist, but also the larger ethical dilemmas at the root of the Friedmann family's disintegration. As one reviewer of the novel observed, "This is a most serious novel, serious in the sense that it pivots not alone on dour Hersh Freeman . . . [who] undertakes a search for the values he can live with in a sleazy world, but with values themselves, their necessity as a sane foundation that makes life livable (Review of *The Organ Builder* 115). Rather than depict Eli Friedmann solely through the shadowy recollections and discoveries of his protagonist, Cohen narrates several chapters of the novel through Eli's perspective as a young physicist at Los Alamos. Interestingly, he also interrupts Hesh's first-person narration with a chapter that he devotes to the perspective of Eli's mother, Ruth, and with a separate chapter that he devotes to Charles Goldwyn's perspective. Cohen thus gathers a variety of Jewish viewpoints from the margins of the narrative and resituates them, if only momentarily, at the center.

This ingathering of distinct and often clashing Jewish voices recalls Philip Roth's *The Counterlife* (1986). True, Roth plunges head first into the ocean of experimentalism with his narrative, whereas Cohen dips only a toe. The five chapters of Roth's novel contradict one another in essential ways. Still, Mark Shechner's astute interpretation of the underlying purpose of Roth's narrative structure in *The Counterlife*—that the narrative maze evokes the mazelike experience of the Jew in the twentieth century ("Zuckerman's Travels" 229)—also obtains for Cohen's novel. By continually shifting its narrative perspective—and thereby challenging the centrality of Hesh's experiences—Cohen's narrative embodies the manifold and contrastive destinies of the Jew during this tumultuous century. One marvels at the cunning of historical forces that produce a Jewish physicist working on the atomic bomb in one generation and a pacifist Jewish attorney in the next.

Their surface disparities aside, the affinities between Eli and Hesh are striking. Both men are intelligent and analytical; both struggle to communicate with others, especially with their spouses; both misguidedly begin families (and both have sons) to repair their wounded marriages; and, perhaps most significantly, both Friedmann and Freeman are beset by angst as they each yearn to tap into the redemptive possibilities just beyond their grasp. Our first glimpse of a twenty-three-year-old Eli shows him as a man of conscience. Just as Hesh wishes to achieve a "connection" with fellow human beings, his father wonders, "What is the glue" that holds America together (*TOB* 20)? Eli pursues such spiritual issues through his scientific research. Indeed, what his parents discover in socialism and his wife's parents find in their fastidious observance of Jewish ritual (in a word, redemption), Eli seeks in scientific knowledge. Thus, he must square his participation in the Manhattan Project with his redemptive pursuits. Initially, the biblical symbolism implicit in the work appeals to him. He reflects, "There is a rightness to it, something at work beneath the surface, bringing Jews to the desert in a kind of reverse-Biblical journey, an Exodus to yield a Genesis" (20). Lamentably, one senses that an imminent moral crisis awaits the young, even naïve physicist. Cohen foreshadows this crisis through the perspective of Eli's talented colleague Max Baker, who, unlike Eli, does not attempt to reckon his work on atomic fission with any moral or redemptive framework. Rather, he curiously obfuscates the significance of their work at Los Alamos:

> You seem to be laboring under the impression that you're a scientist. But you're not. None of us are, really. See, the science part, as you should know, is over. . . . what this is, see, is a very well-endowed factory. . . . We're no different, really, from those slobs who built the pyramids, or the Chinks that built the railroads. We're just your run-of-the-mill engineers, working on a bigger scale. Clerks and coolies in white coats. (22)

Baker's cavalier attitude suggests that he has glimpsed beyond the symbolism of their desert project and that what he sees frightens him. His vehemence serves as a defense mechanism to fight off his moral demons. *"We're only a phase"* (23), he scrawls on sheet of paper that he hands to Eli, thus attempting to eschew responsibility for the human devastation that their work engenders. To cope, Baker adopts a rather mercenary approach to his scientific research. Singly engaged by his search for scientific truth, he refuses to acknowledge the inextricable connection between his work on atomic fission and the human consequences of that work.

Through the sections of the novel devoted to Eli's perspective, Cohen largely dramatizes the young physicist's struggle to adopt Baker's philosophy. After all, from a strictly scientific outlook, their work on atomic fission is pretty heady stuff. Naturally, Eli would like to embrace a philosophical framework that would allow him to pursue such research unfettered by ethical issues. Ultimately, however, he cannot ignore the "human variable" (104) at play in each and every scientific discovery. True, he is intoxicated by the scientific discoveries in which he partakes at Los Alamos, but his work also horrifies him enough to cause his emotional withdrawal from his wife and eventually from the scientific community. As the title of the novel suggests, he becomes an organ builder.

Eli and Ruth Friedmann's becoming estranged from one another at Los Alamos is perhaps the greatest tragedy of the novel, for in the chapter devoted to her perspective, Ruth emerges as a human being beset by the same moral and ethical dilemmas that burden her husband. They appear remarkably well suited to one another. Like Eli, Ruth is a human being of deep conscience, one who cringes, for instance, at the racist epithets written into a song that she and the other scientists' wives perform. She feels alienated from the other wives at Los Alamos because "[t]hey were frivolous people, filling their hours with gossip in the commissary, while half the world away people were being blown apart and gassed. Around them she felt so clogged, so heavy, so . . . *Jewish*" (56, emphasis in original). Ruth, like her husband, clings to the ethical component of the Manhattan Project. Thus, she must assimilate her husband's work on "'the gadget'" (58) into her Jewish moral vision, which renounces murder. Problematically, she senses early on that the mysterious device that her husband works on embodies a force that cannot be reconciled with her Jewish conscience. As she gazes through the fence toward the technical area where the gadget lies, she focuses on "the single blue unblinking light of what she has always assumed is a water boiler. But now it does not look like a water boiler, nor does it really sound like one. . . . It is something else. . . . A chill runs through her" (63). Although Ruth and Eli suffer similar chills, they fail to communicate with one another and suffer their torments alone.

Cohen suggests that the rigid divide between the male and female realm in traditional Judaism accounts, at least in part, for the barrier between Eli and Ruth Freidmann. The fence that stands between Ruth and the technical area where the gadget lies interestingly parallels the fence that restricted her from the male realm during her Orthodox upbringing:

> As a girl she was fenced off from the boys at *shul,* consigned to the balcony with the bald women, the widows—the meek serfs in the rigid feudalism of the Orthodox. Very well, that was tradition. But later she was fenced off from going to college. . . . And now the fences are proliferating, and there is one between her and Eli, and one between her and the other girls, and another between her and the mountains, and another, it is beginning to seem, between her and something larger than any of those things, something inside herself.(62)

The gender roles to which Ruth must conform as an Orthodox Jewish child, then, plague her throughout her adulthood. The expectations placed on the Ashkenazi Jewish woman force her to adopt a persona utterly at odds with her inmost yearnings. Lamentably, Eli cannot fathom that Ruth might be burdened by the same ethical dilemmas that torment him. He thus does little to engage his wife on any intimate level. He assumes that she possesses an "affinity for loneliness" (100), and Ruth, for her part, comes to fear her uncommunicative husband. Although they could be a source of great comfort to one another, the Friedmanns become strangers instead. As the passage above suggests, Ruth ultimately loses her own sense of identity and becomes something of a stranger to herself. In New Mexico, Hesh locates his feeble and disoriented mother, not yet sixty years old, in a convalescent home.

Gradually, Hesh manages to retrieve essential details of his family's past at Los Alamos. Through the Gordons' interviews with aging Los Alamos physicists, he learns of and even vicariously experiences his father's ethical quandaries. One scientist, for example, articulates Max Baker's scientific philosophy with which Hesh, like his father before him, must grapple. When Abby Gordon asks the physicist whether the ethical implications of his work bother him, he replies, "Was it unethical of the apple to hit Newton on the head? Who says science grows from ethics? The thing was technically sweet. . . . We were—are—scientists. It's our duty, and our passion, to find out how the world works" (130). The phrase "technically sweet" sticks in Hesh's throat. He recoils at the scientist's myopia in celebrating the technical sweetness of a device without any apparent concern over the use to which the device was put.

Hesh gradually begins to understand what his father came to realize more than twenty years earlier—that his actions (and even inactions) reverberate to affect others in the human community of which he, like it or not, is a part. A guilt-ridden colleague in New Mexico leads Hesh to this epiphany by forcing him to recognize that he has unwittingly duplicated his father's sins:

> First our great-grandparents steal this land from the Pueblos and Zunis and Navajos, all the old Anasazi types. Now, where'd they come from? Asia. Then our old men come out here and build this thing in the forties. What for? To fry thousands of Japanese. Now it's thirty years later, and you and me help the oil companies snatch what's left out from under those assholes on the reservation, and for what? It's so perfect it's gotta be divinely ordained. *Uranium.* A closed circle. (232)

Importantly, Eli did what he could to keep the circle from enclosing his son. His rejection of physics for organ building suggests that he accepts his culpability for the human devastation—the "frying" of thousands of Japanese—that arose from his research at Los Alamos. The organ represents a device that he can make "technically sweet" and that sings of rather than decimates humanity. The composition Eli writes and that Hesh hears toward the end of the novel has overtones of both classical music and the Kol Nidre (a haunting prayer intoned on the eve of Yom Kippur); it "was so thoroughly human a sound, so much a part of things, that it must, I thought, have always been with us" (283). Through organ building, then, Eli pursues the Jewish vision of *tikkun olam,* the repair of the world. He seeks to restore the humanity almost torn asunder by his own hand.

Just as Eli Friedmann acknowledges his culpability for the devastation in Japan (even though he did not drop the bomb himself), Hesh comes to accept his culpability for the exploitation of New Mexico's Native Americans (even though his mineral rights victory against the Navajo represents only a small contribution to their victimization) and for the collapse of his own family. "What is life, after all," he reflects, "but a game of connect-the-dots. . . . Every act was a stone I'd thrown, a moment that rippled through space and time like a seiche, rippled outward to nudge something or someone that would itself nudge something or someone else, ad infinitum" (239). Hesh recognizes that his solipsism has wounded not only himself but those whom he most loves: his parents, his wife, and his son. He resolves to locate his father, and Cohen suggests that he just might repair his relationship with his wife and son. The final pages of the novel sizzle with the electric potential of Hesh's humanity. Through his reconstruction of the past, Hesh glimpses a more hopeful future. In the Bellovian sense, he bursts his spirit's sleep.

In his second novel, *The Here and Now* (1996), Cohen revisits his primary concerns. In fact, the protagonist, Samuel Karnish, strikingly resembles Hesh Freeman in a number of ways. He is a brooding, disaffected Jew struggling to locate some meaning in what appears to be his half-baked existence. Cohen belabors the "halfness" of his protagonist's condition. In addition to being only half-Jewish (strictly speaking, he is not even that because he derives his Jewish heritage from his father, not his mother), he has "half-completed master's degrees" (*THAN* 156), writes desultory articles that the middlebrow magazine he works for as an editor refuses to publish—his boss describes his writing as a "grab bag of halfheartedness" (31)—and, perhaps most significantly, his twin brother, his "stillborn other half" (306), does not survive their delivery. Indeed, one gathers pretty early on in the novel that Karnish is only half a man. Still, like Hesh Freeman, he broods over the right questions, what we might call the Big Questions, not least of which is: Can one affirm the sanctity of human life in an increasingly prosaic world wherein nothing appears sacred? Karnish echoes Freeman's (as well as Eli Friedmann's and Gerald Stern's protagonist's) sentiments when he laments the seemingly random human losses in his own family and wonders, "Can these things be explained to anyone's satisfaction? Does it matter, does it affect the outcome, whether we understand them or not?" (82).

Additional elements of *The Here and Now* harken back to *The Organ Builder.* Most significantly, Karnish, like Freeman, becomes entangled in the life of an infertile Jewish couple who facilitate his journey into his own family's history, and it is through this journey that he manages to awaken from his etherized existence. Cohen's two novels might seem nearly identical in the broad strokes, but the details of *The Here and Now* more convincingly distinguish Cohen as a prominent contemporary Jewish American voice. Through Karnish's journey into his past, Cohen squarely rather than tangentially engages the vexed issue of contemporary Jewish identity. Karnish need not reconstruct any particular event in his father's life connected to the father's Judaism (like, for example, Eli Friedmann's participation in the Manhattan Project and his subsequent withdrawal from the scientific community); rather, he must confront his father's Jewish identity in and of itself, and recognize his own place along the continuum of Jewish history.

A combination of factors stir the complacent Karnish from his stupor. First, the very heat of the New York summer bears down on him: "It turned out to be somewhat hotter in New York that August than even the most hard-core global-warming alarmists had anticipated. The sun was a kind of comic book version of its usual self, orange and bloated beyond recognition; even after it quit for the night the heat did not diminish, the haze refused to lift" (197). In his influential study, *City Scriptures: Modern Jewish Writing* (1982), Murray Baumgarten noted the Jewish American writer's proclivity for urban fictional terrain. Although we have lately enjoyed a surge in the number of Jewish American writers who evoke regions beyond the city (e.g., Allegra Goodman, Benjamin Taylor, Tova Reich, Steve Stern, Rebecca Goldstein, and Enid Shomer, to name but a few), Baumgarten, writing in 1982, could aptly describe Jewish American fiction largely as an "urban phenomenon," to borrow the title of his first chapter (1). In passages like the one I just quoted from *The Here and Now*, Cohen, like his Jewish American predecessors, dramatizes convincingly the urban claustrophobia that burdens his protagonist. This passage, specifically, evokes once again the work of Saul Bellow (a writer who figures prominently in Baumgarten's study). One might turn to the first lines of Saul Bellow's own second novel, *The Victim* (1947): "On some nights New York is as hot as Bangkok. The whole continent seems to have moved from its place and slid nearer the equator" (3). Cohen, like Bellow, fleshes out New York as fully as any character. The stifling heat of the city exacerbates the spiritual and emotional angst of his protagonist, forcing the moment to a crisis. Something must give.

No one realizes this as profoundly as does Karnish himself. We catch our first glimpse of him en route from his home in New York to a friend's wedding in Houston, brooding over his squandered twenties and "preoccupied by affairs left half-completed" behind him (*THAN* 15). On the plane to Houston, Karnish meets a Hasidic Jewish couple who—like the Gordon's in *The Organ Builder*—encourage Cohen's protagonist to rediscover his identity. Unlike the Gordons, however, Aaron and Magda Brenner force Karnish to reckon with his Jewish identity specifically. At first, they are merely a curiosity to Karnish; he feels no affinity for them. "All I knew of Hasids," he reflects, "was that they were old pious Jews you saw on television, or in sentimental plays on Broadway" (19–20). Although he recoils when he hears a fellow passenger mock Aaron Brenner, Karnish must admit to himself that they make him, too, feel uncomfortable. That said, something about the Brenners (besides his physical attraction to the twenty-something Magda) draws him inexorably into their lives. Against his better judgment, he accepts Aaron's invitation to join them for Sabbath dinner at their home back in Crown Heights. While there, he learns that he has more in common with Aaron Brenner than he suspected. Brenner reveals that his upbringing was every bit as secular as Karnish's own, right down to the drugs and rock and roll. Brenner is a *Baal T'shuvah,* one who has come back. Heading for a "nice secular nervous breakdown," he divorced his secular wife and embraced Hasidic Judaism (104).

Thus, Cohen, as he did in *The Organ Builder,* engages the contrastive and multiform possibilities for Jewish existence in the twentieth century. Through his depiction of the Brenners, however, he entertains the possibility of an ultra-Orthodox existence in an overwhelmingly secular America. That Aaron Brenner is a *Baal T'shuvah* reinforces Cohen's suggestion in both novels that one's Jewish identity is not predetermined or fixed, but dynamic—incessantly challenged by the cunning of historical and sociological forces, and thus constantly subject to improvisation and revision.

Perhaps Karnish should adopt Aaron Brenner's model of spiritual return? Several events in the novel conspire to draw him closer to the Jewish identity he has suppressed and encourage him to ponder the possibilities of an ultra-Orthodox Jewish American identity. First, he encounters anti-Semitism firsthand when a group of teenagers accost him along a path at Riverside Park. Cohen depicts the scene with scrupulous artistic care to dramatize Karnish's gradual and reluctant recognition of his Jewish identity. Importantly, at the time of the verbal assault, Karnish hears but does not recognize its anti-Semitic content: "a couple of the larger boys, as if in afterthought, yelled a few taunts in my direction, and another one—tall, thin, and ravaged by acne—called me a name. I was aware of being afraid, but not very much" (72). He feels little threat because he empathizes with the teenagers, "restless and bored, wired with hormones they were unable to channel—*as I had been at their age*" (72, emphasis mine). Only moments (and a few pages) later does Karnish taste the bitterness of the specific word the boy calls him, *"Hebe"* (74).

Upon reflection, he recognizes that the teenagers targeted him, just as they might have targeted his father or his long dead grandfather who wore a caftan, as the locus toward which to vent their anti-Semitic rage. Karnish, ultimately, recognizes his affinity for his Jewish father and grandfather. Cohen sardonically suggests here that contemporary secularized American Jews enjoy a luxury denied their counterparts of a generation or two ago: they must *learn* to take offense at the pervasive anti-Semitism in mainstream America, as innocuous as it might appear.

The manifestation of anti-Semitism in the park provokes Karnish's memory of the time during his childhood when someone painted a giant red swastika on his family's garage. Illustrative of the uncanny durability of anti-Semitism, the swastika proved difficult for his father to remove; he labored deep into the night over the thing that "would not go away" (81). Subsequent to his reflections on this childhood encounter with anti-Semitism, Karnish visits his mother's house and sees a portrait he has never seen before of his religious grandfather donning a caftan and fringes, "something raw and aggrieved in his gaze" (207). We can see what is happening here. Karnish begins to feel an affinity for Jewish suffering. Later, when he accompanies Magda Brenner to her nephew's *bris*, he notices a concentration camp tattoo on the baby's grandfather and envisions a curious link between circumcision and the tattoo: "This first must be endured. This first is who you are. Today the flesh is cut; tomorrow maybe a number is tattooed upon your arm. The brand of the people" (244). Karnish thus experiences an epiphany. He faints, and when he recovers, he feels the years "flake off me in layers, like old skin. . . . I felt like *I* was the one who had just been born" (253).

It comes as little surprise that Karnish, something of a professional sufferer, identifies strongly with Jewish persecution, which he now (erroneously) believes defines one's Jewish identity. The prayers and rituals of the Jews remain alien to him, but one thing is for certain—he feels their pain. An affinity with Judaism rooted in such negative stuff cannot carry the day, of course. It does little justice to the beauty of the religion, to its sacred history and liturgy. Magda Brenner realizes this and admonishes Karnish:

> Here you don't know the first thing about Judaism, not even the basic prayers. But put a number on a man's arm and suddenly you know all about them. You're their best friend. . . . Thousands of years of history mean nothing to you, but five years of gas chambers, that means everything. It's perverse, no?

> The side that suffers and chokes and is defeated, that's the side that feels like a Jew. The healthy part is out playing with the *goyim.* (257)

There is nothing anomalous, of course, in Karnish's identification with Jewish suffering. Arthur Hertzberg and other eminent observers have noted that Holocaust remembrance and a concomitant secular Zionism *became* the religion of the Jews in America after Israel's Six-Day War in 1967 (see Hertzberg 375). Magda Brenner joins a chorus of contemporary Jewish American voices who have recognized the insufficiency of Holocaust remembrance (and of its resultant secular Zionism) as the sole ingredient of Jewish identity. In their influential study *Saving Remnants: Feeling Jewish in America* (1992), Sara Bershtel and Allen Graubard, after acknowledging that "the Holocaust exerts a strong emotional force for Jewish identification," reaffirm Magda Brenner's essential concerns:

> What is so poignant for those who actually knew and loved the culture that was destroyed is that there is so little positive interest in and knowledge of what the *Yiddishkeit* of that world meant. . . . What cultural meaning can the Holocaust have? Jewish classes on the Holocaust get a more active response from students than traditional classes on the Bible or Jewish history. But what is learned is not anything about Jewishness. What is transmitted is a message of victimhood and an idea of the Jews as the most special victims ever.(120)

Although Bershtel and Graubard critique Karnish-like identification with Jewish victimhood (rather than with Judaism per se) in a rather scholarly fashion, American Jews can sound every bit as truculent as Magda Brenner herself. In a recent *Commentary* symposium, "What do American Jews Believe?" David Klinghoffer, the literary editor of the *National Review,* goes so far as to identify Holocaust remembrance and Zionism as contemporary false idols luring American Jews away from Judaism. He admonishes rabbis who "feel compelled to give congregants what they seem to want: less about Torah and more about Israeli politics and the Holocaust," and he encourages American Jews to make "Judaism itself the principal object of organized Jewish life" (56). Magda Brenner—like Klinghoffer, Bershtel, and Graubard—realizes that a meaningful Jewish identity must be rooted in Judaism.

The romantic affair that transpires (only to expire quickly) between Karnish and Magda Brenner represents the least plausible element of the novel.

One reviewer's critique of Cohen's depiction of the affair between Abby Gordon and Hesh Freeman in *The Organ Builder*—"her dialogues with Hesh never quite ring true" (Sonenberg 30)—also obtains for Cohen's treatment of Magda and Karnish in *The Here and Now.* Magda, even more so than Abby Gordon, remains too nebulous a character. One gropes to discern what Magda sees in him beyond his physiological virtues (i.e., healthy sperm). That said, Karnish's attraction to Magda is clear enough. It represents a projection of his attraction to their observant, Hasidic life. Through her, Karnish seeks to retrieve a meaningful Jewish identity that has eluded him. The Brenners possess some of the things that he sorely lacks: family, community, and identity. The sparse appointments in his apartment—a toaster, a blender, two director's chairs, an empty fish tank—betray the emptiness of his life. His existence has been defined, he realizes, largely through negatives. He is an unmarried nonsmoker, he reflects at one point in the novel. Magda tells Karnish, "With you, everthing is parts" (284), and thus prods him into recognizing that he only partly lives. Alternatively, by embracing the covenant, the Brenners have affirmed life. The hopelessly impassive Karnish desperately wishes to say "yes" to something, as well.

Karnish escapes New York and flies to Israel, ostensibly to search for a fleeing Magda, but actually to search for himself. Atop Mount Sinai he spreads his arms and thinks, *"here I am"* (350) echoing Abraham's and Moses's cry in Hebrew, *Hineni,* and Saul Bellow's own Moses, Moses Herzog, who also cries *Hineni* in the final pages of *Herzog*. It is significant that Karnish recognizes that he may or may not stand perched atop the *real* Mount Sinai, for spiritual illumination, like Mount Sinai itself, remains elusive to him. Ultimately, he cannot say yes to the covenant. Such an affirmation so soon for Karnish would strain credulity. Like Hesh Freeman, he triumphs by overcoming paralysis. Cocooned for too long underground in the New York subways and behind their office desks, both protagonists take flight in search of their Jewish souls.

Robert Cohen's first two novels raise provocative questions for scholars of Jewish American literature, perhaps more questions than answers. Specifically, although few scholars would dispute the "Jewish" status of Cohen's second novel, several would question the Jewishness of *The Organ Builder,* thus forcing us to address intertextual critical issues. As I hope I have suggested, I embrace *The Organ Builder* as a Jewish American novel in and of itself. That said, *The Here and Now* challenges more exclusivist scholars to reconsider the arguable Jewish content of Cohen's ethical vision in his first novel. The novels, after all, are too similar in too many ways for us not to undertake such considerations. Although Judaism per se seems scarcely a peripheral interest for Cohen in *The Organ Builder* as Hesh Freeman retrieves his family's past and engages concomitant ethical quandaries, he does address substantive Jewish ideas through Sam Karnish's retrieval of his own family's past and through his subsequent moral vision. Cohen's second novel, it seems to me, implicitly suggests that Freeman's journey (and Cohen's artistic vision in his first novel generally) is more "Jewishly" informed than it superficially appears.

The inexorable urge to affirm the sanctity of human life amid countervailing influences, the mining out of redemptive possibilities across a seemingly irredeemable terrain, the search for the big answers through filial, often emotive memory rather than through book knowledge—these convictions and concerns, I would argue, are quintessentially Jewish. *The Organ Builder* suggests as much; *The Here and Now* affirms it in thunder.

Allow me to conclude this chapter with the plea that we broaden rather than narrow our vision concerning what might qualify a given work by a Jewish American writer as a Jewish American work. Perhaps the slipperiness of the Jewish element in Cohen's artistic vision (and the slipperiness of our definition of a Jewish artistic vision generally) appropriately reflects the manifold possibilities for realizing a Jewish identity in America. As Bershtel and Graubard's study suggests in its very title, contemporary Jewish Americans go about being and "feeling Jewish" in a plethora of ways. Robert Cohen's fiction challenges us, above all, to recognize that even the most secular Jewish American may possess an irrepressible and ever emergent Jewish soul.

7

The Jewish American Writer, Emergent Israel, and Allegra Goodman's *The Family Markowitz*

It is a perspicacious literary critic who can gauge the pulse of the zeitgeist and usher in a new wave of literary productivity, who can anticipate those first creative glimmerings in the eyes of imaginative writers. In the realm of Jewish American fiction, Robert Alter has proven himself a perspicacious critic, indeed. In 1966, he bemoaned the dearth of Jewish American imaginings of the Holocaust: "With all the restless probing into the implications of the Holocaust that continues to go on in Jewish intellectual forums . . . it gives one pause to note how rarely American Jewish fiction has attempted to come to terms . . . with the European catastrophe" ("Confronting" 67). As if on cue, Jewish American writers (such as Saul Bellow, Cynthia Ozick, Chaim Potok, Edward Lewis Wallant, and Arthur A. Cohen, to name but a few) began to explore the Holocaust overtly in their work, and since the 1960s, we have enjoyed a rather steady outcropping of Jewish American fiction on the Holocaust—enough novels and short stories to merit book-length studies on them, most notably Alan Berger's *Crisis and Covenant: The Holocaust in American Jewish Fiction* (1985) and S. Lillian Kremer's *Witness Through the Imagination: Jewish American Holocaust Literature* (1989) and *Women's Holocaust Writing: Memory and Imagination* (1999).

Some twenty-one years after Alter's tacit prodding of Jewish American novelists to take on the Holocaust in their fiction, he lodged a complaint over the concomitant dearth of Jewish American imaginings of Israel. It seemed suspect to him that Jewish American writers "should so regularly imagine a world in which Israel was scarcely even a presence on a distant horizon" ("Defenders" 55). "Israel," Alter observed, "represented a fundamental alteration in the facts of Jewish existence, so that a fiction that simultaneously ignored the momentous challenge of renewed Jewish autonomy could scarcely be thought to probe the problematic of modern Jewish identity" ("Defenders" 55). One would have been hard-pressed, in 1987, to challenge Alter's contentions. A few notable exceptions aside (e.g., Meyer Levin, Leon Uris, E. M. Broner, and Hugh Nissenson), Jewish American writers seemed perfectly content to leave Israel to the Israeli writers. Several scholars of Jewish American fiction have noted this dearth of Jewish American imaginings of Israel. Naomi Sokoloff, for example, observed in 1991 that "[g]iven the importance of Israel for American Jewish identity and communal self-expression, considering the quantities of ink spilled on polemics about relations between the two cultures, and taking into account the increasing familiarity of each with the other, not much imaginative writing has addressed the topic in a substantive way" (65). Bernard Malamud offered perhaps the most significant reason for this dearth when he suggested that he would write about Israel if he knew about it, but because he did not, he would leave it to the Israeli writers (Field 50). Most writers, Jews included, tend to write about the communities in which they live, whether it be Dublin, Lafayette County (a.k.a. Yoknapatawpha), or Newark.

Still, given Alter's track record, it probably should have surprised no one that a surge of Jewish American novels on Israel followed hard on his comments and continues apace today. (Ted Solotaroff, it should be noted, also anticipated this surge when he asserted in 1988 that "[i]n the overlapping area of consciousness that Israeli and American-Jewish writers share, the seeds of a new fiction are waiting to sprout" ["American-Jewish" 33].) I am thinking primarily of novels such as Anne Roiphe's *Lovingkindness* (1987), Philip Roth's *Operation Shylock: A Confession* (1993), Carol Magun's *Circling Eden: A Novel of Israel* (1995), Deena Metzger's *What Dinah Thought* (1989), and Tova Reich's *Master of the Return* (1988) and *The Jewish War* (1995). Ted Solotaroff and Nessa Rapoport's recent anthology of Jewish American fiction, *Writing Our Way Home: Contemporary Stories by American Jewish Writers* (1992), and a special issue of *Response* titled "Post-Zionism" (summer–fall 1996) also contain several stories set in Israel. Indeed, as a graduate student in English cutting my teeth primarily on Jewish American fiction writers, I felt that there was only one thing to do given this new wealth of Jewish American fiction on Israel: devote my doctoral dissertation to the exciting development.

Having decided to write the first book-length study of Jewish American fiction on Israel, I was intent on devoting my energies primarily to those works in which Israel emerged as the dominant presence or idea of the work. Thus, I devoted my chapters to the writers who, I felt, had engaged Israel with the most focus and intensity in their work: Meyer Levin, Leon Uris, Saul Bellow, Hugh Nissenson, Chaim Potok, Philip Roth, Anne Roiphe, and Tova Reich. Although I do not regret the path that I chose (at least not at this point), it occurred to me more than once during my preparation of the manuscript that there was at least one more entirely separate book to be written about Jewish American fiction and Israel, a book that would focus not so much on those (dare I say it?) obvious texts that I had explored, but on those novels and stories in which Israel or Middle East issues generally emerge more subtly. These works, perhaps, betray most accurately the role that the Jewish state continues to play in forging the Jewish American ethos.

Jewish Americans, to be sure, grapple daily with distinctively American concerns, concerns ranging from the viability of traditional Judaism in an increasingly secular milieu to rising tensions between African Americans and Jewish Americans. Israel, however, remains the foremost preoccupation of the American Jew. "All Jewish rivers," as one Jewish American writer has suggested, "run toward Israel. . . . The safety of Israel is of intense mythic and realistic proportions to all American Jews" (Roiphe 31, 53). It is for this reason that so many Jewish Americans flock to Israel during times of crisis or, less extraordinarily, scan their local newspapers first thing for any news concerning the Middle East. Indeed, Arthur Hertzberg observed aptly that an "identification with Israel" became the "religion" of many Jewish Americans after Israel's victory in the 1967 Six-Day War (375). More to the point of this essay, it is for this reason that Israel emerges so forcefully, if often tangentially, in contemporary Jewish American fiction.

At this point, allow me to turn my attention to one of our more promising emergent Jewish American fiction writers, Allegra Goodman. Her latest collection of stories, *The Family Markowitz* (1996), bespeaks the essential, albeit often overshadowed space that Israel occupies both in the lives of contemporary Jewish Americans and in the imagination of contemporary Jewish American writers. Allegra Goodman burst onto the literary scene in 1989 with the publication of her first collection of stories, *Total Immersion.* Scholars and critics were quick to hail her (then twenty-one years old) as one of the more promising Jewish American writers to appear in quite some time. Most notably, perhaps, Ted Solotaroff singled Goodman out along with Nessa

Rapoport and Daphne Merkin as one of the young Jewish American writers on whose shoulders the future of Jewish American fiction rested ("American-Jewish" 33). What impressed critics most, Goodman's youth aside, was the sharpness of her satire (see Krupnick, "New Writers"; Moskowitz; and Pinsker, "Jews, Jewish Traditions"). That most of Goodman's stories revolved around Jewish characters living in Hawaii (where Goodman grew up) added a distinct flavor to *Total Immersion.* Finally, if Goodman engaged several of the concerns that have dogged Jewish American writers for years—"struggles between generations, problems with rabbis, styles of fund raising, progressive Orthodox day school conflicts, and the never-ending struggle between tradition and acculturation" (Rothchild 16)—she did so in a voice thoroughly her own.

Still, there lingered a nagging sense that Goodman would make an indelible mark on Jewish American fiction only once she ventured beyond the well-trod path of Jewish American assimilation and its burdens. Israel represents one of the more fruitful recent themes in Jewish American fiction, one that Goodman scarcely broached in her first collection, and it appears more and more each day that, as Nessa Rapoport has mused, "No one can be a serious Jewish writer here [in America] and not turn east" ("Text" 43). Interestingly, Sanford Pinsker, in a most favorable assessment of Goodman's early work, found it a shortcoming that she "has yet to explore the impact of Israel on the Jewish American consciousness" ("Satire" 184).

Judging by the reviews of Goodman's recent collection, *The Family Markowitz,* one would suppose that Goodman had decided merely to stick to those tried and true themes that had earned her such kudos before. Michiko Kakutani, for example, noting her "satiric eye for the absurdities of modern existence," lauded the collection as "a book that builds upon the considerable achievement of Ms. Goodman's first book of stories" ("Through Life" B2). What reviewers failed to note is the pervasiveness of Goodman's Middle East concerns in the collection. To Goodman's credit, she engages Israel with considerable intensity in these stories to illustrate how prominently Middle East concerns bear down on Jewish American consciousness.

The opening story of *The Family Markowitz,* "Fannie Mae," exemplifies the subtle emergence of Israel in contemporary Jewish American fiction. On the surface, the story has little to do with Israel or the Middle East. Rather, Goodman focuses on the matriarch of the Markowitz family, Rose, and her struggle to cope with the physical decline of her second husband, Maury Rosenberg. Rose must also grapple with a visit by Maury's estranged daughter, Dorothy, whom she believes hastens Maury's decline with her relentless barrage of questions. "You've sapped his strength; you've bled him dry" (*TFM* 16), Rose explains to Dorothy and finally convinces her to pack her bags for home. Lamentably, Maury passes away regardless, whereupon Rose must oversee the funeral arrangements and play referee as her two sons, Edward and Henry, wrangle over their conflicting strategies concerning their mother's financial portfolio. In a bold (even obdurate) act of will, Rose ignores the advice of both her sons and invests in a single stock, Fannie Mae. What is more, in a will that she hastily prepares, she stipulates that all of her money go to charity upon her death. Her sons do not need her money and, besides, have offered her precious little comfort in her golden years: "As for whether they'll approve of her will, she cannot worry about that now; it is hers to write, and they won't know about it for years and years. She won't say a word" (27). With considerable empathy, Goodman thus explores in "Fannie Mae" the contemporary pressures that bear down on the American family and the ties that bind. This, one might explain to the prospective reader, is what the story is about.

But this is not *all* that the story is about, for I have omitted several crucial details. Rose does not leave her money to just any charity, but to the "Girls' Orphanage in Jerusalem" (5), to which she has donated modest sums of money for years. She has donated money to an orphanage primarily because she was once something of an orphan herself (her Viennese parents sent her to London when she was seven years old to escape the ravages of the First World War), and she has always wanted a little girl of her own. That she chooses to support an Israeli orphanage is significant, however, for it betrays her spiritual bond to the Jewish state. Goodman takes pains to emphasize that the girls in the Israeli orphanage "'are instructed strictly according to the precepts of Torah'" (6). Moreover Rose's small annual donations (and, one presumes, the monies from her estate once she dies) "support the schools, the woodworking shop and sewing classes, the dowry fund for brides—'*to help them build a Jewish home*'" (6, emphasis mine). In "Fannie Mae," then, Israel emerges as the primary locus at which one American Jew envisions the continuity of Jewish existence; it remains the spiritual homeland for Rose in *galut* (exile), who wishes "to see Jerusalem" (22) before she dies.

Of course, the actual relationship between American and Israeli Jews has never been as harmonious as one might presume. A good many Israeli Jews find American Jewish "support" of Israel (i.e., philanthropy of Rose Markowitz's ilk) to be patronizing at best. At a recent conference between American and Israeli Jews, one participant summed up the feelings of several of his fellow Israelis when he cried, "'We're tired of being treated like the younger brother with a runny nose. . . . We come with 45 years of resentment at being considered a charity case" (qtd. in Marcus A4). In his influential book *From Beirut to Jerusalem* (1989), Thomas Friedman interestingly documents an episode during which an Israeli Jew accosted him with just such resentment (462). That American Jews claim a proprietary interest in the Jewish state but simultaneously refuse to give up the luxury of living in the United States exacerbates tensions as well. As one American Jew has noted, "I have heard American Zionism called 'air conditioned Zionism' . . . Just as American Jews have developed Judaism without the yoke of Torah, so they also have Zionism without the yoke of aliya" (Feingold 22). An almost insurmountable barrier exists between Israeli and American Jews because Israeli Jews are the ones who put their lives on the line daily to ensure the survival of the Jewish state, while American Jews (whatever their professed spiritual connection to the land) eschew this burden.

This Israeli Jewish resentment toward Jewish Americans emerges forcefully in Matti Golan's *With Friends Like You: What Israelis Really Think about American Jews* (1992). At one point in the book, written in the form of a dialogue between a typical Israeli Jew and a typical American Jew, the Israeli excoriates his American counterpart:

> Jews like you . . . are the heart of the problem. You're someone with what's known as a "deep personal commitment to Israel." You do all the right things. You give to the United Jewish Appeal. You visit Israel every couple of years and never forget to bring back a souvenir from the Wailing Wall and a painting from the artists' colony in Safed. . . . How can there be a partnership between someone who sends his son to fight in Lebanon or the Occupied Territories and someone who sends his son to college? (6, 9)

All of which confirms Irving Howe's earlier suspicions concerning what several Israeli Jews were itching to tell Jewish Americans like himself: "'Look here, *chaverim,* come live with us or stop calling yourself Zionists; and if you choose not to come, then good-bye and good-luck'" ("American Jews" 73).

To Goodman's credit, she engages the rift between American and Israeli Jews in "Fannie Mae." An additional element of the story that I intentionally neglected to mention in my gloss above is that Maury Rosenberg's estranged middle-age daughter, Dorothy, is an Israeli. Although Rose feels an almost ineffable, spiritual bond to the Israeli orphans, she and Maury scarcely know a thing about Dorothy's life in Israel. Rose knows only that Dorothy "simply grew up in greenhouses, raising tomatoes" (*TFM* 7). That they know so little about Dorothy's life (evidently on an Israeli kibbutz or moshav) suggests, on one level, how foreign the Israeli experience remains to most American Jews. Whatever feelings of connectedness American Jews might harbor for their Israeli counterparts, most possess only the vaguest sense of contemporary daily Israeli existence. Instead, American Jews cling to stereotypical images of heroic Israeli soldiers and settlers. Rose's impressions of Dorothy's life certainly seem informed by the settler stereotype. Recent efforts by Israeli tourist guides to emphasize the less glamorous nature of Israeli life have been received less than enthusiastically by Jewish American tourists. In a recent *Wall Street Journal* article, Amy Dockser Marcus describes the disheartening experiences of one Israeli tour guide, Andrea Katz:

> Ms. Katz isn't certain how interested American Jews really are in getting a more realistic view [of Israel]. The few times she has tried to forgo the usual trip to an army base, the tour groups have complained. "They want to see heroic Israel, Israel facing the odds," says Ms. Katz, as a group of American Jews standing on the Golan Heights are told about the battle that took place there with the Syrians. "If I told them we're hard-working Joes, my biggest problem is fighting the city to get a permit to build a porch . . . I can almost guarantee that no one would want to come." (A4)

The Jewish American thirst for stereotypical images of Israeli life notwithstanding, the language difference represents a tangible barrier between the two groups. Goodman dramatizes the strength of this barrier as Esther, Rose's friend, attempts unsuccessfully to communicate in Hebrew with Dorothy: "'*At garah bimoshav? Osah tapuzim baboker? Ovedet maher?*' What she means to say is, It must be terribly difficult to raise tomatoes on a farm and live the life of a farmer, getting up before dawn. What comes out is: Do you live on a farm in the morning? Do you make oranges? Do you work fast?" (13). Esther's desire to communicate with an Israeli Jew in Hebrew unravels in a comic mess. That Goodman herself mistranslates the Hebrew in the passage (which means, "Do you live on a farm? Do you make oranges in the morning? Do you work fast?") also betrays, somewhat ironically, the strength of the language barrier. (Goodman also dramatizes the Hebrew illiteracy of the American Jew in "The Wedding of Henry Markowitz," wherein Henry traces his disaffection for Judaism to the lackadaisical Hebrew language training he received in Hebrew school as a child: "[Henry] didn't have the vocabulary. He told Susan how they made him practice for his bar mitzvah and he had to memorize the Hebrew and pretend he understood it" [88].)

Dorothy, for her part, seeks to achieve a connection with an American Jew, her father. In a "dark" and "smoky" Israeli accent, she tells Maury, "'I have come here to be with you. . . . I have wanted to come and talk to you, so that you and I would know each other just once. I have wanted to tell you about my life'" (8). However, she never gets the chance to tell her father much about her life in Israel. He interrupts her because he cannot hear, and, frankly, he does not have the strength to listen to his daughter's story; he nods off repeatedly. Dorothy finally leaves at Rose's prodding. That Dorothy begrudgingly accepts a check Rose makes out to her suggests the reluctance with which Israeli Jews accept Jewish American financial support. One sees this reluctance, for example, in Haim Chertok's recent assurance to his Jewish American readers that, without their financial support, "You could bet your sweet VISA that Israel surely would survive" (189). In "Fannie Mae," then—a story in which Israel emerges only peripherally—Goodman manages to evoke the spiritual centrality of Israel to American Jews, the ardent longing for connection between American and Israeli Jews, and the seemingly insurmountable barriers between them.

Goodman further dramatizes the complex interweaving of American and Israeli Jewish lives in the second story of the collection, "The Art Biz." More specifically, the Israeli citizenship of Amalya Ben Ami and her son, Eitan, functions on two important levels. First, it offers Goodman the opportunity to explore the Jewish American predilection to exoticize Israelis. Second, it adds a significant dimension to Goodman's modern midrash on a biblical story from 1 Kings.

"The Art Biz" revolves principally around Rose Markowitz's son, Henry. Having been denied tenure as an art history professor, Henry finds himself managing Michael Spivitz Fine Art Gallery in Venice Beach, California. A foundering career, however, is the least of Henry's troubles, for he must come to terms with the moral wantonness that pervades the "art biz" in Los Angeles. His boss, Michael Spivitz, embodies this salaciousness in his affair with a sixteen-year-old boy who has fled his mother and moved into Spivitz's home. As in "Fannie Mae," the details in the story are important. The adolescent boy in question and his frantic mother are the Israelis named above who have just recently arrived in Los Angeles from Haifa. Henry learns sketchily about Eitan's situation after the boy's mother, Amalya Ben Ami, bursts into the gallery and, "with a heavy Israeli accent," accuses Spivitz of kidnaping him: "Your employer has got my son. . . . He is keeping him" (31). Later, Henry's Jewish dermatologist informs him that the Jewish Federation has decided to support Amalya Ben Ami financially and to provide her with legal assistance as she attempts to extricate Eitan from Spivitz's home.

Spivitz's actions, so far beyond the pale of the ethical, would seem to offer little dramatic tension to the story. Henry's sexual ambivalence, however, fuels the nagging guilt with which he must reckon. Although Henry stands foursquare against Spivitz's behavior, he cannot suppress his own attraction to the Israeli boy. He recoils, for example, at Spivitz's lavish party—replete with "erotic ice sculptures" (40)—when the Israeli child blasts out of an enormous cake wearing only a G-string, but the image of the child's "perfect, hairless little body" haunts him (43).

As I have suggested, in making the object of Spivitz's (and Henry's) desire Israeli, Goodman addresses the tendency of Jewish Americans to exoticize Israeli Jews. Eitan, a "tanned teenager with dark eyes" (31), represents an exotic Other to the "fair-haired" Spivitz (39). Although the attraction may run both ways, Spivitz exploits the child by offering his dark Israeli body up for public display at the party. In this disturbing scene, the exotic Israeli body becomes the object of visual consumption for a roomful of Americans. In a passage worth quoting in some length, Nessa Rapoport evocatively describes the sexual allure of the Israeli Jew and of Israel itself to Diaspora Jews:

> We Diaspora Jews who made our first trips to Israel in the early seventies certainly know how Israel changed our bodies: To arrive, as I did then, in April

> and descend from an airplane into the redolent air, shocking in its potency, was to identify the land forever with youth and sensuality and a tactile freedom undreamed of by our sincere Zionist parents. Has anyone fully described the eros of Israel to the *galut* Jew, the beautiful dark men, the profusion of flowers, the tropical landscape so alien, so ours. ("Afterword" 146)

Although Henry does not think overtly in these erotic terms, he nonetheless feels complicit in the whole sordid affair given his immersion in Spivitz's hedonistic realm. Henry, we learn, once lived with Spivitz, and it took him "[a] year to give up Michael's house, his cars, his sleek kitchen, his beautiful things, his quick glances, sure touch, his sweet voice with just the faintest tang of sarcasm" (35). Thus, Henry cannot quite bring himself to admonish Spivitz outright: "He looks at Michael and feels indignation mixed with guilt. If only he could tell him off. If he could speak to him with some authority and say, This is wrong, this is foolish. But he is too close to pass judgment. Confounded, compromised. He has been in the past a little like Michael and a little more like this boy. He has felt them both within himself, the tiger and the lamb" (37–38).

Henry's ambivalence is rooted in his amorphous, catch-as-catch-can moral code. Goodman takes pains to emphasize that Judaism and its implacable ethical code (or Covenant) play only a marginal role in Henry's life. For example, he begrudgingly attends Yom Kippur services, one of the High Holy Days of Judaism, with his mother. Goodman chooses an apt holiday to dramatize Henry's disaffection for Judaism not only because of Yom Kippur's sheer importance, but also because the communal nature of Judaism manifests itself strongly during the Yom Kippur service and challenges Henry's antithetical inclinations. During his sermon in "The Art Biz," the rabbi emphasizes that "we beat our breasts as a community. This is our tradition. One of communal, rather than personal, guilt, and one of communal redemption" (41). The sermon Goodman imagines, one should note, is eminently plausible. As Rabbi Morris Kertzer has noted, "Jewish confessions [on Yom Kippur] are communal, not private; they are liturgical staples that everyone says together, rather than personal soul-searching shared only by a single solitary soul with God" (216).

The very idea of community lies at the heart of Judaism. The expression one often hears in Orthodox circles, "We were at Sinai together," bespeaks the Jewish belief that all Jews were spiritually present as God handed down the Law to Moses atop Mount Sinai. Through adhering to their Covenant with God, Jews of every epoch sustain a relationship with one another; they form links in a chain of Jewish continuity. Indeed, as Cynthia Ozick has expressed, "In Jewish thought there *are* no latecomers" ("Literature" 194). So prevalent is community in Jewish thought and ritual that an African American character in Gloria Naylor's recent novel *Bailey's Cafe* (1992) feels an affinity for Judaism because "nothing important can happen unless they're all in it together as a community" (227).

Sadly, Henry Markowitz cannot embrace the communal nature of Judaism and succumbs to solipsism near the conclusion of the story: "He does not want to be sitting there in that congregation, does not want to be connected to that mass of people, or, in fact, to anyone. He wants to go home. Back to his bed. He wants to be absolutely alone except for his books" (*TFM* 43). Henry cannot bear the communal burden of Spivitz's sins, nor does he wish to shoulder the burden of Amalya Ben Ami's transgressions (he spots her caressing the hand of her married Jewish benefactor in synagogue). He sees Los Angeles as a modern-day Sodom and resolves to escape the city and to "rededicate himself to beauty" (44). Thus, Goodman engages the tension between Hellenism and Hebraism—between Pan and Moses—that Cynthia Ozick has so powerfully addressed in such works as *The Pagan Rabbi and Other Stories* (1971) and *The Cannibal Galaxy* (1983). In "The Art Biz," the Hellenistic realm of aestheticism wins Henry's soul. (This triumph of the Hellenistic realm in the battle for Henry's soul manifests itself even more concretely in "The Wedding of Henry Markowitz," wherein Henry reflects that he had planned his escape from Judaism "ever since he'd learned to read, when he uncovered Arabian caverns and climbed Scottish citadels and read Keats's odes in the bathroom" [87].)

Finally, Amalya and Eitan Ben Ami's Israeli citizenship adds depth to the modern midrash embedded in "The Art Biz." Goodman alludes briefly to King Solomon's most famous dispensation of justice as Henry passes a mural at his temple "depicting Solomon sitting in judgment of the two women, the great king dressed in what looks like Masonic robes, holding a saber over the head of the innocent babe" (41). Of course, in the biblical story (1 Kings, 3:16–28) the baby's true mother saves her child's life and simultaneously proves that she is its mother by insisting that Solomon give the child to her antagonist. (This other woman, for her part, proclaims, "'It shall be neither mine nor thine; divide it.'") In "The Art Biz," Eitan Ben Ami—to whom Henry alternately refers as a "child" (35), a "little one" (36), and a "very young boy" (36)—might be seen as the "innocent babe" of the Solomon story. That sinfulness besmirches not one but both the parent figures in Goodman's story—one Israeli, one American—casts an ominous shadow over her midrash. The innocent child of Israel may not be spared in modern-day Los Angeles. Neither Jewish Americans like Spivitz nor Israeli Jews like Amalya Ben Ami adhere to a covenant that proscribes their illicit behavior. Moreover, King Solomon's authoritative Jewish voice is conspicuously absent in the story. The dispersion of the Jews throughout the Diaspora and in a largely secular Israel, Goodman suggests, has resulted in a moral degeneration.

I have, thus far, concentrated on two stories in *The Family Markowitz* in which Israel emerges peripherally, though intriguingly. The Middle East figures more prominently, however, in the several stories that feature Henry Markowitz's brother, Edward. Through Edward Markowitz, a history professor at Georgetown University, Goodman simultaneously satirizes the foibles of academics and addresses the myriad of dilemmas that beset the Middle East and bear down heavily on American Jews. That is, she mocks his leftist academic perspectives but also uses them to dislodge comfortable Jewish American pieties regarding the Middle East. Edward's chosen specialty, the Middle East conflict, illustrates foremost the absorption of one American Jew in the fate of Israel. Edward hardly emerges as an indomitable moral presence, though. C. Beth Burch describes Edward as a "straight-ahead and egocentric academic" (90), and, indeed, that well-worn cliche about academics and ivory towers often comes to mind in the stories featuring him. Goodman, who holds a Ph.D. in Renaissance literature from Stanford, cannily depicts how wide of the mark the latest academic theory often lands, however earnestly applied, when issues of life and death are at stake. One can be fairly sure that Goodman means to poke fun at that special myopia of academics via Edward, who assiduously attends West Bank conferences in London (*TFM* 98) and Intifada conferences at Berkeley (101), where he delivers papers such as "The Terrorist as Other" (162). He also has at the ready a "popular" paper on "terrorism, tolerance, double standards" (106).

In Henry's eyes, Edward represents everything that has gone wrong in the American academy. Henry lives for "texture and artistry," laments the intrusion of "political textual agendas" in the humanities, and recognizes (in "The Wedding of Henry Markowitz") that Edward "has become a shaper himself of the tawdry yellow thing they sell now as the humanities. The cheapening of craft and light, intuition and sensibility, into the social sciences. Edward had begun as a Near Eastern historian and now is nothing more than a political expert. Another cog in the grant-getting, TV-interview machine" (76).

That Edward abandoned long ago his book on Arabic thought and art for the "political thing" (84) grates against Henry's aesthetic sensibilities. But aesthetic issues aside, Goodman questions in several stories whether scholarly academics, like Edward, are really cut out to do the "political thing" in the first place. In "Mosquitoes," for example, she dramatizes the chasm between the Jewish American academic who purports to know about the Middle East and the felt life of the Israeli Jew. In the story, Edward finds himself at a remote midwestern ecumenical institute for a conference on Christians and Jews after the honorarium proves too generous to pass up. He gets more than he bargains for, however; he learns that the conference discourages panels and papers, and instead encourages the participants (five Christians and three Jews) to "speak from the heart, talk with total honesty and sincerity" (107). The curmudgeonly Edward squirms in his chair as the participants, one by one, unburden themselves of their inmost thoughts: "It's agonizing sitting here like this, forced into this kind of voyeurism" (113). We sympathize and cringe along with Edward for most of Goodman's rendering of this New Age conference—as a rabbi discusses his alcoholism and divorce, as Brother Marcus Goldwater describes how his immediate supervisor at Sears and Roebuck "courted" him to Catholicism (113), as Sister Elaine describes only nebulously her epiphany in the "mother house" (111).

However, toward the conclusion of the story, Goodman thwarts our expectations. Suddenly, Edward's cool, detached academic professionalism seems suspect as the Israeli Jewish scholar, Avner Rabinovitch, enlists our sympathies. Rabinovitch relates how the death of his son in Lebanon influenced his scholarship as it forced him to reinterpret the binding of Isaac story (the Akedah) in the Bible: "'The true scholar must consider the texts with his own experience. What can my colleagues gain, counting words? I take up Scriptures in the dark night of my soul. I demand it—speak!'" (132). Edward, as one might expect, recoils at Rabinovitch's perspective, which smacks of the downright unscholarly to him. To the Israeli's critique of academics who "only look at minutiae," Edward blasts back, "I am a scholar! . . . That means every once in a while I stop picking my nose and focus on something outside myself and my own pain. I work on achieving some distance. I work on some objectivity. . . . It's about discipline! You're sitting here massaging each other with Cheez Whiz, and I'm sick of watching!" (133).

To be sure, Edward's arguments might ring true for several readers who, like Goodman's professional academic, would rather not mix business with "the dark night of the soul" (134). Still, Edward protests here a bit too much for his own good. The vehemence of his assault against his Israeli counterpart's experiential scholarly approach betrays a defensiveness that suggests the shortcomings of Edward's academic approach to the Middle East. All the erudition in the world, one suspects, cannot trump the experience that the Israeli Jew, Rabinovitch, brings to bear on the Middle East.

Goodman alludes here to a central argument that Israeli Jews launch against American Jews who weigh in on Middle East issues: from the smug safety of the United States, the American Jew cannot understand Israel's actions, nor should he or she judge them. The following anecdote, which more than one Israeli saw fit to tell me during my visit to the Jewish state, bespeaks this sentiment on the Israeli side. A toad on the bank of a river finds itself face to face with a scorpion, its mortal enemy. The toad has escape on its mind, but then the scorpion asks its would-be prey, "Will you take me across the river on your back, for I cannot swim." The toad naturally replies, "Do you take me for a fool? You are my mortal enemy. If I let you on my back, you'll sting me and I'll die." The scorpion reasons with the toad, "Now why would I do such a foolish thing? If I sting you, you'll drown, and I'll surely drown with you." Convinced by such sound reasoning, the toad allows the scorpion to crawl onto its back and begins swimming across the river. Halfway across, the toad feels the scorpion's fatal sting penetrate its soft flesh. The toad cries out, "How could you do such a stupid thing? Now we're both going to die!" As they begin to drown, the scorpion answers, "Welcome to the Middle East."

The story, told one way, amusingly informs the American Jew that the "civilized" logic of the West does not apply to the Middle East. Told in a sterner tone, the Israeli storyteller conveys a not so subtle admonishment to the American listener: "If you refuse to sacrifice the luxury of living in the United States, that's fine, but don't feel entitled to judge the moral standards of my country!" Such logic still enjoys an undeniable currency within the

Jewish American community. For example, after a talk that I delivered for a charitable Jewish group in which I discussed some of the tensions between feminism and the halakic laws that remain the order of the day in Israel, a member of the audience courteously expressed her belief that Israel had enough problems without having to deal with external pressures from American Jews like me. Nonetheless, an increasing number of American Jews these days believe that they might best express their Zionism through speaking up against the Israeli government.

Significant Jewish American criticism of Israeli policy began to emerge from the political left only after the Intifada began in 1987. Woody Allen's op-ed piece in the *New York Times* exemplified the thrust of this criticism. "I am appalled beyond measure by the treatment of the rioting Palestinians by Jews," Allen wrote (A27). Interestingly, after the signing of the Declaration of Principles between Israel and the Palestine Liberation Organization (PLO) in 1993, Jewish Americans on the political right began to speak out against the Israeli government as well, but for the sake of Israeli security rather than for Palestinian rights. Norman Podhoretz, writing as editor of *Commentary* at the time, retracted his former position that "American Jews had no moral right to criticize Israel's security policies" and roundly criticized Israel's peace accord with the PLO in three separate articles (see *Commentary,* April 1993, 19; June 1993; and December 1994). Jewish American criticism of Israeli policy currently can be found in both the progressive pages of *Tikkun* and the conservative pages of *Commentary.*

Goodman's Edward Markowitz, of course, represents one of these American Jews none too shy about throwing his hat into the Middle East ring. The left-leaning nature of his politics offers Goodman the opportunity to address the divisiveness within the Jewish American community concerning the present course of the Middle East peace process. In "The Wedding of Henry Markowitz," for example, Henry derides his brother as "some sort of apologist to the media for the PLO or the Arab League" (84). Goodman explores the tensions within the Jewish American community most forcefully, however, in "The Persians" and "One Down."

"The Persians" takes place in the wake of the World Trade Center bombing. These are heady times for Edward Markowitz, who is in heavy demand on radio and television as a "terrorism expert" (160). Moreover, Edward's preshow interview with the solicitous producer of his forthcoming public radio stint fuels his optimism that his balanced scholarly approach to the

Middle East crisis—a "more enlightened, more cosmopolitan view of the world" (178)—might just be gaining a foothold in the public realm. To Edward's delight, the producer has actually read his work and listens thirstily as he extemporizes on the nature of terrorism:

> It is vital for us to examine the "Other" in order to understand ourselves. But at the same time, we have to remember that the terrorist really is alien to us—his otherness is real, and his world is different from ours—and here's my point: if we can learn about ourselves from great, generous liberal minds like Tocqueville or Crevecoeur, then we can learn from the terrorist as well. And if we have trouble with the parallel, then that says a great deal about us, and what we are willing to find in the mirror the Other presents to us. (165)

One anticipates that Edward's academic jargon will not likely appeal to the listeners of *Talk of the Times.* Indeed, a dream that Edward has before the show foreshadows some of the problems that he will encounter. In the dream, he works in an exquisite Islamic garden. Other than a couple of peacocks, he is entirely alone. When he attempts to leave the garden, he cannot find his way out and wanders from one garden to the next. The dream suggests the isolation of Goodman's scholar who, like Voltaire's Candide, reclusively tends his own garden.

At the beginning of Edward's radio show, Goodman dramatizes the real life rift between Edward's scholarly concerns and the more pragmatic concerns of the show's listeners. Whereas Edward wishes to elaborate on terrorism as a "complex phenomenon with many facets" (175), the first caller wishes to know only whether it is safe to fly to the Middle East. The second caller blathers on about Hollywood's latest movie on a woman's plight in Iran (Edward must inform her that Iranians are Persians, not Arabs). Edward's patience with the unsophisticated nature of the questions begins to run thin. However, a call from a man named Hasan, who espouses radical anti-Israel views, betrays the limits of Edward's cool, professional approach to the Middle East. The caller accuses Edward of being part of Israel's propaganda apparatus and launches into a by now familiar anti-Israel diatribe: "'Israel is a U.S. colony dedicated to a racist ideology. It is occupying land and holding indigenous peoples in concentration camps and building up weapons arsenals'" (177). Such anti-Israel attacks from the radical left crop up these days even in English graduate seminars (like the one at Penn State

University that I myself endured) because "postcolonialism" is currently the rage in English departments across the country. More specifically, one hears more and more in our public discourse those on the radical left appropriating the language of the Holocaust, à la Hasan, to describe the plight of the Palestinians. Given their perception of Israel's brutality in the Middle East, these individuals self-consciously use the language of the Holocaust against the Jewish state to challenge the Jewish claim of an ethos of persecution. For example, in 1994, a leader of the progressive organization New Jewish Agenda published an essay provocatively entitled "Palestinian Holocaust Memorial?" (Silverman 4). Edward's scholarly detachment falls by the wayside as he defends Israel from Hasan's scurrilous charges and challenges him, "'Let's hear who's paying you, Hasan'" (*TFM* 178). The exchange becomes so heated that the show's host passes Edward a note pleading with him not to antagonize the callers.

Edward later regrets his outburst on the show. He believes that he made "a perfect fool of himself" (178). At a bat mitzvah, however, several friends and acquaintances approach and congratulate him for defending Israel so vehemently. One friend applauds his efforts thus: "You took out that Arab from Oklahoma City" (179). Edward, who never wished to champion an unreflective Zionism on the show, realizes that he gave his friends the "Arab-baiting performance they were looking for" (179).

By forcing her Middle East scholar into dialogue with the wider populace—either on a radio show or at a bat mitzvah—Goodman means to satirize that special brand of academic obstinance and blindness. One critic's take on Edward in Goodman's earlier collection of stories as an "out-of-it" academic "so committed to cultural relativism that he sees a forest without specific trees" (Pinsker, "Satire" 186–87) would certainly seem to apply to the Edward in several of the stories in *The Family Markowitz.* Goodman, however, does not content herself with merely satirizing Edward's perspective as "academic" and, perforce, as naïve. Although she encourages the reader to scoff at his self-importance, his semantic quibbling, she is not glibly dismissive of the progressive agenda hidden beneath his esoteric jargon. With Edward's progressive political views, she manages to dramatize with both levity and considerable seriousness the Jewish infighting over the current Middle East crisis.

Jewish infighting, generally, has long served as a rich source of Jewish humor. As one quip has it, if three Jews founded a town, two would establish rival synagogues, and the third would spit on both their houses. Small wonder that on matters regarding Israel, specifically, Jewish Americans find themselves divided today as Israel warily pursues peace with the Palestinians and its other Arab neighbors. In the years since Israel's signing of the Declaration of Principles with the Palestinians, I have noticed a conspicuous reluctance among new Jewish acquaintances even to broach the issue of the Middle East. The reason for this reluctance, I believe, is that although Israel remains a foremost preoccupation of American Jews, Jews can rarely be sure these days where other Jews stand on the Middle East crisis. One's political party affiliation—Republican, Democrat, or Independent—proves, at best, an unreliable gauge of one's hawkish or dovish inclinations. Thus, Jewish American acquaintances often cat-foot around the Middle East issue until friendship has been solidly established, for where one stands on Israel (within the Jewish American community at least) has slowly evolved into one of those hot-button issues—like abortion or, to a lesser extent, affirmative action—on which friendships can either be readily established or irretrievably dissolved.

In the final story of *The Family Markowitz,* "One Down," Goodman humorously depicts this rift within the Jewish American community. The wedding between Edward and Sarah's daughter, Miriam, and Jon Schwartz serves as the dramatic vehicle for this depiction of the collision between two antithetical Jewish American perspectives regarding the Middle East. Just before the wedding, Edward reads a letter to the editor in the *New York Times*—written by the father of his future son-in-law—that both shocks and enrages him: "The Palestinian will hate Israel no matter what Israel does. Give land for peace and you will give up all the security Israel has won in previous wars. A Palestinian state will be a launching pad and a suicide. . . . The solution to the problem was simple, but it was not followed in the past. Give the Palestinians a one-way ticket out of Israel" (236).

Edward can hardly bear the thought of the imminent union between his daughter and the son of someone who would publish such "crap" (237), to use Edward's descriptor. "'Sarah, he's a reactionary, a maniac'" (238), he cries. Zaev Schwartz's implacable stance on the Middle East brings to mind Nathan Zuckerman's Uncle Shimmy in Philip Roth's novel *The Counterlife* (1986). In Shimmy, who opines, "'bomb the Arab bastards till they cry uncle'" (42), Roth depicts as caricature the hawkish Jewish American perspective of the Middle East. Zuckerman (and perhaps thus Roth) dismisses

Shimmy as "neanderthal" and "arguably the family's stupidest relative" (41–42). Goodman, however, treats Zaev Schwartz's hard-line Zionism more seriously. That is, her narrative does not dismiss Schwartz's perspective out of hand. At the rehearsal dinner, we learn that Schwartz lived in Israel as a child, raising chickens when he was thirteen. His mother, Ilse, fled to Palestine to escape the Holocaust. (One of her sisters perished at the concentration camp, Dachau.) Schwartz, like the Israeli scholar in "Mosquitoes," just may possess a keener understanding than Edward of what is at stake in the current deliberations over the Middle East map. He, in fact, tells Edward as much after Edward criticizes his letter to the *New York Times.* Schwartz disparagingly calls Edward an "academic" and challenges the validity of mere book knowledge of the Middle East crisis: "'You have to live in *Eretz Yisrael*—on the land. . . . You have to walk through the hills and valleys. Then you see how small it is and you have a better idea what this land-for-peace means. The country is a splinter" (*TFM* 253).

Interestingly, Goodman's perspective concerning Israel's policy in the Middle East remains nebulous. The debate between Edward Markowitz and Zaev Schwartz ends in something of a stalemate after the two fathers use their respective wedding toasts to challenge one another's wrongheaded views. Goodman hilariously dramatizes the clash of their voices but refuses to tilt her own hand when it comes to the Middle East. This narrative stalemate, I would contend, parallels the equivocal Middle East position of the Jewish American community as a whole. Moreover, it illustrates the streak of antididacticism that pervades Goodman's work. Burch has observed of Goodman's fiction that it "does not suggest solutions; rather, it offers accommodation and an intimation of redemption" (90). As Burch suggests, Goodman does not propose, tacitly or explicitly, a solution to the Middle East crisis in "One Down," nor does she champion any particular position. Rather, she offers an intimation of redemption through the wedding itself, the culminating scene of *The Family Markowitz.* The marriage between Miriam Markowitz and Jon Schwartz suggests that the ties that bind Jews to one another far outweigh the Middle East tensions that threaten to rip apart the community. The fathers' feud over Israel will not escalate into one of Shepherdson and Grangerford proportions.

An intimation of redemption—a fitting place at which to bring this essay to a conclusion. As several scholars have argued, intimations of redemption have earmarked Jewish American fiction from the start. Nessa Rapoport, for example, recently argued that "To be a Jewish writer is to do what Jews have always done: fashion text and language in the hope of redemption" ("Text" 44). Allegra Goodman, then, situates herself along the continuum of Jewish American literary history in *The Family Markowitz.*

As Robert Alter has argued, the birth of a Jewish state fundamentally altered the consciousness of modern Jews ("Defenders" 55). In *The Family Markowitz,* Goodman joins the ranks of other powerful contemporary Jewish American writers such as Philip Roth and Tova Reich (one thinks of Roth's *The Counterlife* [1987] and *Operation Shylock: A Confession* [1993], and of Reich's *Master of the Return* [1988] and *The Jewish War* [1995]) in exploring just how Israel figures into the Jewish American consciousness. Like Roth and Reich, and to her credit, Goodman engages the vexing Middle East concerns that bear down on the contemporary Jewish American community as Israel outgrows its role as the "transcendent object," to coin Solotaroff's phrase ("Open" xv), on which Jewish Americans project their fantasies of Jewish heroism and religious piety. Although Israel emerges in *The Family Markowitz* as the spiritual homeland for Jewish Americans, Goodman also explores the rifts between American and Israeli Jews; although Israel emerges as a refuge for Jews in the aftermath of the Holocaust, Goodman also explores the tangled conflict between the Israelis and the Palestinians that currently divides the Jewish American community. All of which is to say that *The Family Markowitz* shows just how far Jewish American fiction on Israel has come since, say, Leon Uris's exploitation of Israeli and Arab stereotypes in *Exodus* (1958), and it serves as a hopeful harbinger of future Jewish American imaginings of the Jewish state.

8

Steve Stern's Magical Fiction of *Tikkun*

> When the great Chasid, Baal Shem Tov, the Master of the Good Name, had a problem, it was his custom to go to a certain part of the forest. There he would light a fire and say a certain prayer, and find wisdom. A generation later, a son of one of his disciples was in the same position. He went to that same place in the forest and lit the fire, but he could not remember the prayer. But he asked for wisdom and it was sufficient. He found what he needed. A generation after that, his son had a problem like the others. He also went to the forest, but he could not even light the fire. "Lord of the Universe," he prayed, "I could not remember the prayer, and I cannot get the fire started. But I am in the forest. That will have to be sufficient." And it was.
>
> —Steve Stern, recounting the Hasidic parable

Although it was Allegra Goodman's good fortune to discover her voice and achieve literary success early (she began publishing stories in *Commentary* while she was an undergraduate at Harvard), Steve Stern experienced the protracted agonies more typical of fiction writers before finally carving out a niche for his work in the literary marketplace. For more than ten years, he struggled to hammer out stories that agents and publishers only scoffed at. Despondent, he returned to his hometown of Memphis in the early 1980s at age thirty-five to wallow in self-pity, by his own account. Luckily for him, an old friend hired him to conduct an oral-history project on the waning Jewish ghetto in Memphis called the Pinch for the Center for Southern Folklore. Stern found himself immediately drawn to the place and to the stories that the aging Jews eagerly shared with him: "The voices on the tapes—oral history interviews with salty old musicians, promoters, legendary figures from the heyday of fabled Beale Street—turned out to be regular siren songs. . . . I was a captive audience, a *hazer* for their cockamamy tales" ("Brief Account" 87).

What is more, Stern adopted the Pinch—its streets and its inhabitants—as his Yoknapatawpha. "The Pinch," he remembers, "rose up like the Lost Continent of Atlantis for me and began to look like a home for my stories" (qtd. in Pinsker, "Jewish Novelists" 64). He proceeded to tell the stories of his postage stamp of nonnative soil in a flurry of creative work, which to date includes two novels, *The Moon and Ruben Shein* (1984) and *Harry Kaplan's Adventures Underground* (1991); three collections of stories, *Isaac and the Undertaker's Daughter* (1983), the acclaimed *Lazar Malkin Enters Heaven* (1986), and *The Wedding Jester* (1999); a collection of novellas, *A Plague of Dreamers* (1994); and two children's books.

Given the Jewish American writer's predilection for the gritty, urban environment (Murray Baumgarten instructively titled his study of modern Jewish novelists *City Scriptures* [1982]), Stern's vivid and often surreal evocations of the Pinch struck many readers as a refreshing departure from the likes of Philip Roth, Saul Bellow, and Bernard Malamud. Small wonder that articles and book reviews of Stern's work sported such titles as "Dybbuks in Dixie" and "Ashkenaz on the Mississippi." Stern, however, departs from his most immediate predecessors in more significant ways than in his choice of settings.

The writers who brought Jewish American fiction to prominence in the 1950s and 1960s (Bellow, Roth, Malamud, and so on) achieved success by engaging primarily the postimmigrant burdens of their Jewish protagonists. The inexorable tug-of-war between the rituals and values of the Old World and the conflictive exigencies of the New World provided the dramatic tension they needed to fashion such complex characters as Moses Herzog, Morris Bober, and Eli Peck. As Irving Howe suggested in his introduction to *Jewish American Stories* (1977), our most celebrated Jewish American writers enjoyed the advantage (artistically, if not sociologically) of an "inescapable subject: the judgment, affection and hatred they bring to bear upon the remembered world of their youth, and the costs extracted by their struggle to tear themselves away" (3).

The postimmigrant experience of alienation and marginality looms as only the memory of a memory for Stern, a generation or so removed from this eminent cohort of Jewish American fictionists. Accepting the Edward Lewis Wallant Award for his dazzling collection of stories *Lazar Malkin Enters*

Heaven, he reflected wistfully on his latecomer status as a Jewish American writer: "the first indication I had that my Jewish birthright mattered at all to me was an intense pang of jealousy. Born too late, I'd been cheated out of what I had coming: oppression and persecution you say, wretched poverty and nightmares amok in broad daylight I grant you, but also a vitality beyond anything I'd known" ("Brief Account" 85). Faced with a thinning of the resources that fueled the work of his most immediate predecessors, Stern arrived at a bold decision. Rather than forage "for crumbs on a table that Bernard Malamud, Saul Bellow and Philip Roth had wiped clean," as Morris Dickstein put it (11), Stern chose largely to bypass in his fiction the experiences of the postwar Jewish American generation. Despite the allure of this angst-ridden locus of Jewish American existence—"I'm of the generation," Stern writes, "that honors Philip Roth for his savaging of Jewish suburban philistinism, his exploration of the terminal identity crisis among American Jews" ("Stern Un Ikh" 94)—he has taken it upon himself to reach *further* back into the collective memory of Jewish Americans. That is, he focuses primarily on the motley assortment of Jewish characters living in the Pinch prior to the Holocaust and World War II, the generation he learned so much about as the director of the Center for Southern Folklore's Ethnic Heritage Program in 1983.

Above all, Stern endeavors in his fiction to reclaim and thereby redeem a Jewish world rapidly vanishing from our collective memory. By reinscribing the world of the Pinch into our collective memory, he repairs essential links in the chain of Jewish continuity. As Mark Shechner argues, "the act of entering into their conception of life is an act of solidarity with their world, their life, and the visions that animated and gave purpose to their existence. It is an act of *yizkor* or memory" ("Steve Stern" 418). Stern has claimed, interestingly, that an alter ego ambushed him into this literary project of *tikkun:* "He [Stern's alter ego] believes he must journey there [to the Jewish past] like a hero journeys to the underworld to redeem what's lost. The idea being that this act of '*tikkun,*' as he calls it, after the kabbalistic practice of gathering the scattered sparks of righteousness—he's acquired quite a vocabulary in recent years—that this act sanctifies history" ("Shtern un Ikh" 51). Stern's construction of a literary alter ego eerily evokes Philip Roth's own yen for constructing alter egos in his fiction (Roth has lately taken to the protagonist "Philip Roth") and his nonfiction (the real Philip Roth never seems to stand up in his memoir, *The Facts: A Novelist's Autobiography* [1988]). However, whereas Roth constructs counterlives to probe the enigmatic, fragmented nature of the postmodern ethos, Stern's own construction of a literary alter ego betrays not his absorption in postmodern aesthetics or precepts but rather his defensive attempt to distance himself from what he perceives as his *chutzpahdik* artistic undertaking.

Eschewing perhaps the most essential lesson of the modernist masters (e.g., Isaac Babel, James Joyce, Sherwood Anderson, William Faulkner), Stern consciously decided *not* to write about what was in front of his nose; dogging him, then, is the nagging suspicion that he is, in his own words, "the thief of an experience that did not belong to me" ("Brief Account" 86). He declares, "It's pretty presumptious of me, I suppose, a third-generation Jew plunking my characters down in a place that had virtually vanished before I was even born, but I can't help it!" (Ross 404). In the most ambitious study of Stern's artistic vision to date, Janet Hadda explores how his work, specifically "The Ghost and Saul Bozoff," embodies the discomfort that accompanies the author's resolution to appropriate and transmit stories not his own. In "The Ghost and Saul Bozoff," Stern's struggling writer-protagonist wishes to write the story of a turn-of-the-century female writer, Leah Rosenthal, whose ghost visits him and urges him to do so. Though drawn to the project, Saul Bozoff fears that the story is not really his to write, that "the few fragments of Leah that he had to put in it weren't enough from which to assemble a palpable woman" (*LMEH* 198). To her credit, Hadda recognizes Bozoff's quandary as analogous to Stern's own: "At issue is Saul's right to appropriate the Eastern European and American immigrant vision of his collective past when he has not personally experienced it. . . . Saul, and, one suspects, Steve Stern as well, worries about the question of mimetic reproduction" (98).

Although Hadda focuses on "The Ghost and Saul Bozoff" to examine Stern's anxiety, one should note that Stern addresses the enigmatic issue of retrieving and transmitting the collective (rather than personal) experience of the Pinch in an earlier story, "The Book of Mordecai," which was collected in *Isaac and the Undertaker's Daughter* and reprinted in *Lazar Malkin Enters Heaven.* In "The Book of Mordecai," the narrator's aging and feeble Uncle Mordecai remains alive owing only to the urgency he feels to transcribe his memoirs. The narrator observes that his uncle, holed away in an inconspicuous corner of their living room, "was writing now with a cumulative fury, seldom eating, frequently drinking, stalking his own biography toward its source" (*LMEH* 179). Upon finishing the memoir, Mordecai predictably expires. Importantly, the narrator salvages the memoirs (overlooked by the rest of his family) and considers them, for better or for worse, his legacy: "I can't say that the book of Mordecai has been any particular blessing. My own life has been for the most part beneath contempt. . . . Nevertheless, the book is by gift, and I live in constant fear of losing it" (181). He, as one might have already gleaned, resembles Stern himself; with characteristic self-effacement, he finds he must redeem stories two generations removed.

It is both Stern's good fortune and ours that he has overcome his anxiety regarding mimetic reproduction by making it his occasional muse, for his work, as I have suggested, represents a radical departure from his most immediate predecessors while harkening back to the vision of more distant literary forebears. Indeed, if Stern introduces his carnival hucksters, Mississippi river-boat workers, and Klu Klux Klan members (who, incidentally, purchase their white sheets wholesale at Zimmerman's Emporium) to the canon of Jewish American fiction, the dybbuks, golems, and angels that crop up harken back to the Yiddish masters such as I. B. Singer, I. L. Peretz, and Moishe Kulbak. Like these predecessors, Stern constructs "stories in which this world," Shechner aptly observes, "collides with 'yene velt' (the other world)" ("Steve Stern" 416). It is the role that the *yene velt* plays in Stern's fiction that I would like to explore for the balance of this chapter. Interestingly, the phrase that Walter Allen revived to elucidate David Schearl's predicament in Henry Roth's *Call It Sleep* (1934)—"The Semites are like to a man sitting in a cloaca to the eyes, and whose brows touch heaven" (443)—might be dusted off again to illustrate the predicaments of Stern's most memorable protagonists Indeed, if Stern's overarching goal has been to retrieve and redeem the Jewish world of the prewar Pinch, what draws one to these characters are their own redemptive urges amid the quotidian muck of their Memphis environs.

In "Shimmele Fly-by-Night," collected in *Lazar Malkin Enters Heaven,* Stern poignantly evokes the special predicament of the Pinch Jews through the agonies of its kosher butcher, Red Dubrovner. More specifically, through the reflections of Dubrovner's son, Shimmele, Stern situates the Pinch Jews within their culturally specific immigrant milieu. Red Dubrovner, we learn, fled the town of Byelorussia for America (to avoid military conscription in the czar's army) just before Cossacks invaded the town and murdered his entire family. Shimmele recalls that the root of his father's implacable rage lies in his disappointment with his adopted country: "'Some golden land!' he would groan, slapping his barrel chest. Then he would count on his fingers the ways that we were persecuted: by the infernal heat and the crooked politicians, the high water at Pesach, the diseases that followed the floods, the yokels in their white sheets that they bought wholesale at Zimmerman's Emporium" (90). These external pressures on the Pinch Jews, Stern suggests, provoke their spiritual descent, which more profoundly wounds the irascible but perspicacious Dubrovner. He recognizes and laments their spiritually impoverished lives, ranting about his fellow Jews, "They are shaving off their beards and peddling corsets on Shobbos, they are stuffing themselves with chazzerai [pig]. They are running away to join the vaudeville. They are forgetting their mama-loshen [mother tongue]" (91). Dubrovner, then, lives a life of double exile insofar as he has been exiled from a more spiritually rich (albeit more physically perilous) existence in the European Diaspora.

Importantly, the narrator, Shimmele, rather than Dubrovner himself, remains the focal point of the story. Through Shimmele's reminiscences as an adult, Stern explores the young Shimmele's unusual capacity to see beyond the surface of his father's rage—a fury that drives away Shimmele's sister and mother—to its soft underbelly. Indeed, Stern charts in the story not primarily the spiritual decline of the Pinch Jews, but Shimmele's gradual recognition of this decline that so wounds his father. Consider, for example, the vivid moment that Shimmele recalls after his sister ran off with the profligate bootlegger Nutty: "On the crippled table in front of him [Shimmele's father] were his open *Shulchan Aruch* and three empty bottles of kiddush wine. In his mouth was a piece of melting ice; an ice pack was perched atop his bald and swollen head, fastened there by his blue-striped tallis. . . . The Saturday night hullaballo started up outside the window, nearly drowning out the voice of my father lisping a kaddish for his daughter Fagie" (102). The mourner's kaddish Dubrovner intones, I would argue, might as well be for an entire generation. Revelry and licentiousness has usurped the role of study and law among the younger generation of Jews in the Pinch. What is more, Shimmele understands the gravity of the historical moment. It is for this reason that he, and he alone apparently, empathizes with his father. He tellingly hurries to his father's side after his sister and her bawdy friends mock him during a confrontation.

In "Shimmele Fly-by-Night," one hears echoes of Reb Pankower's lament in Henry Roth's landmark novel of the Jewish American immigrant experience, *Call It Sleep* (1934): "What was going to become of Yiddish youth? What would become of this new breed? These Americans? This sidewalk-and-gutter generation?" (374). However, because "Shimmele Fly-by-Night" is a story by Steve Stern, magical possibilities lie just a baby step away from the sordid realities of the immigrant experience. The story culminates in a transcendent moment as a drunken flock of pigeons carries Shimmele aloft. Stern leaves us with a vision of Shimmele "over the rooftops, the neighborhood diminishing to a huddle of tenements" (112).

These magical possibilities in Stern's fiction, which generally overshadow the more mundane realities of life in the Pinch, tie Stern's artistic vision more closely to that of the Yiddish masters of the nineteenth century than to that of either the immigrant Jewish American writers (whose historical terrain Stern revisits) such as Abraham Cahan, Anzia Yezierska, and Michael Gold or to that of his more immediate predecessors, Saul Bellow, Philip Roth, and Bernard Malamud, who write primarily in the social realist vein. A recent story written by Stern, "The Tale of a Kite," collected in *The Wedding Jester,* might be considered his declaration of artistic independence from his immediate predecessors. The story, I would argue, resembles "Eli, the Fanatic," one of Roth's earliest and most powerful stories, too closely for Stern not to have been aware of it, which makes the essential contrasts between the stories especially relevant. As one might recall, Roth's story revolves around the thoroughly assimilated Jews of suburban Woodenton, who live "in amity" with their hosts (the Woodenton Gentiles) by eschewing their "extreme practices" ("Eli" 189). Consequently, when a yeshiva opens in Woodenton replete with eighteen (a number that signifies life according to Gematria) young Holocaust survivors and a Hasidic instructor (also a survivor), Woodenton's secular Jews worry that such a flagrant display of Jewishness might encourage the Gentiles to reconsider their tolerance toward the Jews in their midst. Thus, they leave it to the lawyer among them, Eli Peck, to convince the principle of the yeshiva to close the school. As one of Woodenton's citizens explains to Eli, "There's going to be no pogroms in Woodenton. Right? 'Cause there's no fanatics, no crazy people" (200). The story culminates as Eli's moral obligations toward the yeshiva's Holocaust survivors get the better of his pragmatic, assimilationist impulses.

In "The Tale of a Kite," Stern's Jacob Zipper faces a quandary strikingly similar to Eli Peck's. Consider, for example, Zipper's perspective of Rabbi Shmelke's Hasidim, who have recently settled in the Pinch: "Recently transplanted from Shpink, some godforsaken Old World backwater that no doubt sent them packing, Shmelke and his band are a royal embarrassment to our community. . . . Like I say, we citizens of Hebrew extraction set great store by our friendly relations with our Gentile neighbors. One thing we don't need is religious zealots poisoning the peaceable atmosphere" ("Tale" 69–70). Like the Jews of Woodenton, Zipper and his fellow Jews on the North Main Street Improvement Committee fear that the Hasidic "fanatics" might provoke the town's Gentiles. "Let the Gentiles see . . . Shpinkers wrapped in their paraphernalia," Zipper worriedly reflects, "mumbling hocus-pocus instead of being gainfully employed, and right away the rumors start. The yids are poisoning the water, pishing on communion wafers, murdering Christian children for their blood" (72). Zipper and his largely assimilated cohorts, again like Woodenton's Jews, plan to put the kibosh one way or the other on the rapidly growing Hasidic community.

What distinguishes Stern's story from Roth's is the narrative awe in the transcendent powers of the holy, which, although present in "Eli, the Fanatic," is subordinated by Roth's satire on the moral decay of Woodenton's secular Jews. Specifically, in "The Tale of a Kite," Rabbi Shmelke can fly. Stern hereby infuses the Hasidim with a magical quality, unexplored by Roth, that gradually wins over the secular Jews of the Pinch. First, the adolescents begin to rebel against the thin Jewish content of their upbringing by adopting Hasidic customs and rituals. "Some adopt muskrat caps (out of season)," Zipper observes, "to approximate the Chasid's fur *shtreimel.* Milton Rosen wears a mackintosh that doubles for a caftan; the dumb Herman Wolf uses alphabet blocks for phylacteries. My own Ziggy has taken to picking his shirttails into ritual tassels" (74).

Stern's story reaches a climax as Zipper (and Stern, I would argue) revels in the transcendent possibilities brought on by Rabbi Shmelke's holiness. Zipper and his fellow committee members raid Shmelke's *shtibl* (a small Hasidic prayer house) to cut the ropes that keep Shmelke earthbound. They wish, simply, to get rid of him and his followers, who will assuredly abandon the Pinch once their rabbi is gone. Upon bursting into the *shtibl,* however, Zipper, hedge shears in hand, remains frozen, "struck with the wonder of having seen [Shmelke] rise" (74). Gaining his senses, he manages to sever the ropes, whereupon hordes of Shmelke's followers, including Zipper's son, cling to the ropes and head skyward to Paradise with Shmelke. Though Zipper pleads with his son to come back, he succumbs to his own fantasies of transcendence. "I grab hold," he imagines, "and am carried aloft with the kids. . . . Across the river the sunset is more radiant than a red flare over a herring barrel, dripping sparks—all the brighter as it's soon to be extinguished by dark clouds swollen with history rolling in from the east" (75).

Roth's Eli never achieves any such transcendent vision. He triumphs by means of the moral stand he takes on behalf of the Hasidic yeshiva instructor. True, he adopts Hasidic clothing and strolls down Woodenton's streets, but he does so primarily to reject the ruthlessness of Woodenton's assimilated Jews; the clothes, to be sure, do not make the man in Roth's story. Engaging a newly affluent post-Holocaust milieu, Roth offers an unsparing glimpse of Jewish Woodenton's moral bankruptcy. Stern, by contrast, engages a Jewish community at a more tenuous historical place and moment (a Jewish ghetto in the American South just prior to the Holocaust) and shifts the focus from the mean impulses of the assimilated Jewish community to the magical possibilities that quell these impulses. Stern's protagonist triumphs not by taking any token moral stand, but by actually seeing what the Hasidim see, by participating in the magical realm.

In the opening story of *Lazar Malkin Enters Heaven,* "Moishe the Just," Stern offers a more detailed portrait of the Jews' historical moment in the Pinch, which teems with sordid characters and run-down buildings, but, yes, magical possibilities as well. Consider, first, the adolescent narrator's account early in the story of how he and his cohorts wheedle away the long, steamy hours of a Memphis summer:

> We would kneel on the sticky tarpaper, our chins propped on top of a low parapet encrusted with bird droppings. In this way we watched the clumsy progress of the courtship of Billy Rubin and the shoemaker's daughter. We saw, like a puppet play in silhouette, Old Man Crow beating his wife behind drawn shades. Through their open windows we saw the noisy family Pinkus gesticulating over their hysterical evening meal. We saw Eddie Kid Katz sparring with shadows and the amply endowed Widow Taubenblatt in her bath, but even with her we got bored. (*LMEH* 3)

Stern thus paints a decidedly unlovely portrait of the Pinch. One can almost smell the encrusted pigeon feces in the steamy air of the Memphis summer. Moreover, the Jews we encounter through the narrator's eyes range from the despicable (a wife beater) to the pathetic (sheepish lovers). The narrator and his peers, for that matter, seem little more than mischievous rogues. In the hands of several contemporary writers, the Pinch no doubt would serve as the ideal place through which to explore the bankruptcy of the American dream, the squalor of the immigrant existence in a southern backwater. After reading the opening lines given above, those unfamiliar with Stern's work might expect just that in the pages to follow.

Stern, however, pulls the rug out from under these unsuspecting readers after scarcely a page when the narrator abruptly recalls the question one of his peers asked, "'What if Moishe Purim was a *lamed vovnik?*'" (4). It is with this line, I would argue, that readers are suddenly immersed in the magical realm of Stern's imagination. The Pinch, they soon discover, is not a locale where nihilism (so au courant in much contemporary fiction) reigns, but a place where a *lamed vovnik*—according to the talmudic Rabbi Abbaye and to Jewish folk belief, one of the thirty-six righteous men whose goodness precludes God's destruction of the earth—just might exist (see *Sanhedrin* 97b and *Sukkah* 45b). Despite or maybe even because of the squalor of the Pinch, mystical things can and do happen.

Moreover, Stern's characters redeem their humanity, despite their often macabre cruelties, through their headlong pursuit of the holy as they attempt to transcend the rot of their surroundings. In "Moishe the Just," the narrator and his group of pranksters set out to determine whether or not the pious junk collector, Moishe Purim, is a *lamed vovnik* by testing his carnal restraint and, finally, his physical invincibility. They booby-trap his room with a strategically placed anvil. As they wait on the roof for Moishe Purim to meet his fate, the narrator observes that "[i]n the west the setting sun, like a broken yolk, was running an angry red all over the sky, spilling into the river. Somewhere in the east, beyond the ocean, a storm—as our parents liked to remind us—was brewing. And there we were on a roof above our crummy neighborhood, feeling particularly exposed to the elements, like we might be marooned" (20). Through this shimmering prose, Stern situates his protagonist in a tumultuous historical moment that he seeks to transcend. Stranded in a Jewish ghetto in the American South far from his brethren to the north (New York) or east (Europe), the imminent Holocaust looming as a storm on the horizon, Stern's protagonist and his peers crane their necks toward the realm of the holy. Put simply, they need this realm.

Although Jay Rogoff accurately enough characterized this yearning as an "obsession with the forbidden" (xxx), it must be emphasized that, rather than their downfall, this obsession turns out to be the means by which

Stern's characters triumph. In the titular story of *Lazar Malkin Enters Heaven,* for example, the narrator, Julius, redeems himself by overcoming his hard-boiled rejection of the magical possibilities that can occur in the Pinch. Stern once again takes pains to evoke, through his protagonist's eyes, the decrepit state of the neighborhood: "The neighborhood, which was called the Pinch, had been dead since the War. Life and business had moved east, leaving us with our shops falling down around our ears. Myself and the others, we kidded ourselves that North Main Street would come back. Our children would come back again" (28). What mainly distinguishes Stern's middle-age narrator, Julius, from the adolescent pranksters in "Moishe the Just" is that years of hardship have inured him to the magical possibilities in his midst. The Pinch, it seems to him, offers only earthly despair to its residents. All the more reason for him to wonder why his father-in-law, Lazar Malkin, insists on living "far past the age when it was still dignified to be alive" (29). "'[G]o to heaven already. . . . What do you want to hang around this miserable place anyway?'" (33) Julius pleads with Malkin, who has taken up residence in a shed in his daughter and Julius's backyard.

Only after Malkin finally becomes ill does Julius realize how much spiritual stock he and his neighbors have placed in the old man's apparent invincibility. They believe (subconsciously at least) that "if the angel of death can pass over Lazar, he can pass over the whole neighborhood" (35). Faced with the prospect of his own mortality in Malkin's imminent death, the hard Julius acknowledges his own need for the magical, which he has suppressed for so long. Malkin's inexplicable resiliency, he realizes, offered him proof, albeit subliminally, of the magical possibilities amid his otherwise grimy surroundings. With Malkin confined to his shed, "it was like there wasn't a 'beyond' anymore" (35), Julius confides in his wife. By placing the word *beyond* in quotation marks, Stern suggests that Julius means both the physical locations beyond the Pinch, where Malkin roamed on peddling expeditions throughout his long life, and the mythical beyond, the transcendent realm where Malkin, Julius suspects, journeyed as well.

Armed now with the self-knowledge that he believes in a magical realm beyond the Pinch, Julius can finally brush up against this realm. Observing the light of a lamp in Malkin's shed in the middle of the night, he ventures out to examine what is going on because "[w]ho knew but some miracle had taken place and Lazar was up again?" (37). This Julius, who now consciously believes in miracles and seeks them out, is an utterly transformed Julius, I would argue. He has peeled away the scales from his eyes, caked on by years of earthly disillusionment and despair. Upon gazing into the shed's window, Julius sees the Angel of Death—a "poor shnook" (37) with wings "no larger than a chickens" (39)—pleading with Malkin to give up the ghost.

Unremarkable visitors from the *yene velt,* like the angel, have become something of a trademark for Stern. Artistically, their ordinariness lends a measure of credence to one of his major points—that the magical realm and its inhabitants are palpably present if only we, like Julius, would look. Stern recently contended, in fact, that he suffuses his work with fantastical elements to "create a symbiotic relationship between what's generally considered real and what's generally assessed as magic. . . . What hopefully happens when you do that is that you create a world in which magic can happen quite naturally, and it becomes a natural function of what is otherwise a very ordinary environment" (qtd. in Ross 405). As a reward for his insistence on "looking," Julius catches a glimpse of this magical realm beyond the Pinch: "It looked exactly like the yard in back of the shop, only—how should I explain it?—sensitive. It was the same brick wall with glass embedded on top, the same ashes and rusty tin cans, but they were tender and ticklish to look at. Intimate like (excuse me) flesh beneath underwear" (40). Importantly, it is only after he accepts that miracles can and do occur, only after he seeks out this promise in Malkin's kindled lamp, that he sees through the prosaic to the sublime.

Stern intensifies his explorations into the magical realm in his recent collection of novellas, *A Plague of Dreamers.* In several respects, the principle characters of the first two novellas, Zelik Rifkin of "Zelik Rifkin and the Tree of Dreams," and Hyman Weiss of "Hyman the Magnificent," harken back to the saintly schlemiels so prevalent in Yiddish literature (see Pinsker, *The Schlemiel as Metaphor* [1971], and Wisse, *The Schlemiel as Modern Hero* [1971]). Broadly speaking, these characters are foolish bunglers, ostracized and often sadly abused by their neighbors. What endears them to us, however, is their unflappable goodness and their faith in the world beyond—the very attributes that ensure their victimhood in the world at hand. I. L. Peretz's Bontshe Shvayg (more popularly known as Bontshe the Silent), for example, patiently and passively suffers throughout his life and, for his unswerving faith and endurance, receives a hearty greeting in Heaven once he expires. A heavenly judge tenderly tells Bontshe, "'you have suffered all in silence. There is not an unbroken bone in your body, not a corner of your soul that has not bled. And you have kept silent. . . . There in the World of Deceit, your silence went unrewarded. Here, in the World of Truth, it will be given its full due" (Peretz 151). That the humble Bontshe, granted all of Heaven's bounty, can think to ask only for a warm roll with butter every morning merely amplifies his simple goodness. I. B. Singer's most celebrated protagonist, Gimpel the Fool, similarly suffers the cruelties of the World of Deceit. He takes to heart the rabbi's adage, "'better to be a fool all your days than for one hour to be evil'" (Singer 4). Thus, he refuses to abandon his adulterous wife on the slight chance that, say, the perfectly healthy baby born to his wife four months after their wedding might be his. Although less oblivious to his victimization than Bontshe and consequently more tempted to exact revenge against his victimizers, Gimpel triumphs by overcoming such banal emotions and looks forward to the magical world that surely lies ahead: "Whatever may be there, it will be real, without complication, without ridicule, without deception. God be praised: there even Gimpel cannot be deceived" (14).

A cursory reading of Stern's two novellas is enough to reveal that Stern cuts Zelik Rifkin and Hyman Weiss from similar cloth as Singer's Gimpel and Peretz's Bontshe, for in their communities, both Zelik and Hyman are good-hearted pariahs who seek the reward of a kinder, gentler realm of existence beyond the cruel Pinch. Zelik is a diminutive, impassive adolescent who lives only a vicarious existence in the margins of the Pinch: "Famous for his cowardice all along the length and breadth of North Main Street, Zelik Rifkin spied on the other boys at their adventures" (*APOD* 2). Forced cruelly by the Pinch gang to scale an oak tree, Zelik stumbles upon a dream world considerably more appealing. Hyman Weiss of "Hyman the Magnificent" is also a *nebbisheh* (weak) character who endures the petty scorn of his community. By appointing himself as the "successor to the great Houdini," Hyman, like Zelik, seeks to transcend the brutish material world. Escape, then, is the leitmotif of both "Zelik Rifkin and the Tree of Dreams" and "Hyman the Magnificent." Stern, like Singer and Peretz, creates protagonists ill-suited for the harsh realities of their environments—individuals who seek transcendence in an alternative, magical world.

In emphasizing the parallels between Stern's characters and those of two Yiddish masters, I wish to place Stern's vision squarely in this tradition without suggesting that his work is merely derivative, for if it is true that he draws on the themes and characters of these Yiddish writers, it is equally true that he tinkers with the raw materials of this tradition to make it his own. Indeed, his protagonists grapple with the specific burdens of their prewar Pinch milieu; neither their predicaments nor their actions resemble those of Singer's Gimpel or Peretz's Bontshe. In "Zelik Rifkin and the Tree of Dreams," Stern meticulously evokes Zelik's time and place in Jewish history: "All day the population of the Pinch—mostly Jews who liked to call themselves a lost tribe, so far were they scattered from the more kosher habitats of their brethren—kept as much as possible to the shade. Wearing ice bags in place of their yarmulkes they gathered in panting quorums to say prayers invoking rain" (2). Here, Stern depicts a Jewish community grappling to preserve their religious traditions and culture against a hostile environment. The battle, as in "Shimmele Fly-by-Night," appears to be a lost one as scattered as they are from their brethren. Ice bags tellingly have already supplanted their yarmulkes.

In the sentences quoted in the previous paragraph, Stern introduces us to a world in stark contrast to most of the *shtetlach* depicted in Yiddish literature. If the saintly schlemiels and their fellow Jews in Yiddish literature were plagued by the inexorable threat of physical persecution at the hands of Cossacks, their spiritual health was often strong. As Irving Howe and Eliezer Greenberg argue in discussing shtetl life in their indispensable introduction to *A Treasury of Yiddish Stories* (1954), "Because the *shtetl* lived in constant expectation of external attack—and not merely expectation, it was periodically subjected to pogroms—*all the internal tendencies that made for disintegration were kept in check.* The outer world, the world of the gentiles and the worldlings, meant hostility, sacrilege, brute force" (7, emphasis mine). That is, the constant threat of eradication by a hostile world from without galvanized the shtetl Jews from within; their distinct rituals and traditions in the prewar European Diaspora were reinforced *because* rather than in spite of the hostility of the dominant culture. Much of Yiddish literature, as Howe and Greenberg go on to suggest, affirms the spiritual resiliency of the Jews that overcomes both poverty and the barbarousness of the world outside the shtetl:

> Yiddish literature repeatedly turns to the theme that the material poverty of this world is dreadful, yet seldom rests with social description or complaint; it insists that hunger . . . could always be transcended by a people secure in its

> destiny. And so too could the blows of the outer world. In the writings of Peretz and Sholem Asch, the idea, deeply embedded in Jewish psychology, that the spirit of endurance cannot be broken by external attack received repeated expression. (7–8)

By contrast, the cultural dissolution of the Pinch in Stern's "Zelik Rifkin and the Tree of Dreams" seems inevitable owing largely to the Jews' relative safety in America. Whereas assimilation is scarcely an option for the Jews of the shtetl in Yiddish literature, the Jews of the Pinch appear well on their way toward adopting the secular values of the more tolerant (albeit still anti-Semitic) outside world. Indeed, although several adults in the Pinch still cling to their traditions, Stern suggests that Zelik's younger generation of hooligans will not follow suit. His depiction of the lowly status of Aharon Notowitz, the town's Hebrew teacher, goes a long way toward convincing one that the cultural decay of the Pinch is at hand. Although Zelik's mother hires Notowitz to teach Hebrew to her son, Zelik reflects that Notowitz was just a "cut above a common shnorrer [beggar]" (*APOD* 6). Notowitz, as Zelik recalls, laments the spiritual decay of the Pinch and loses faith himself: "Touting himself as a once-celebrated scholar, descended on his mother's side from the archwizard Isaac Luria, Mr. Notowitz had a favorite gripe: he'd lost his faith. 'To this farkokte country are following us the demons.' . . . 'But God,' pointing a finger aloft, 'He stays behind' " (7). Stern also evokes the death of *yiddishkeit* through the persistent mourning of Zelik's mother for dead relatives left behind in Europe. Her life seems utterly empty save for these "commemorative errands" (7). Rather than lead a life-affirming existence in the here and now, rich in Jewish culture and religion, she leads a ghostly existence, scarcely acknowledging the presence of her son. The implication seems to be that a vibrant Jewish existence is not to be had in the Pinch. Such an existence died, apparently, in Europe and is something to be mourned.

Small wonder that Zelik yearns to shed his skin and occupy a new body in a new realm. Fortunately for him, he gains this opportunity once the Pinch gang chases him up the oak tree, the giant tree under which his fellow residents sleep to escape the oppressive heat of their apartments during the summer. Their dreams, Zelik discovers, commingle at the top of the oak tree to create an alternative dream world. Leaving his terrified, earthly body shaking on the oak tree, Zelik strolls through the streets of the dream world in a more confident body. This magical realm, save for a few "random intrusions of the extraordinary" (19), resembles the "real" world of the Pinch, right down to its streets and buildings. Zelik, so passive in the real world, acts in the dream world to repair it and thereby effects change in both realms. For example, he enters Aharon Notowitz's room in the dream world to breathe inspiration into the lugubrious scholar. He addresses Notowitz, "'It is I, your hallowed ancestor Isaac Luria'" (30), and proceeds to chase out the evil spirits plaguing the Hebrew teacher. He also writes "RACHEL RIFKIN'S COMING OUT" (31) in the present day of his mother's calendar in the dream world.

Zelik discovers that his efforts to restore a meaningful Jewish present in the realm of dreams magically take effect in the ordinary world. In Notowitz's bedroom, anticipating another lackluster Hebrew lesson, "Zelik found the teacher poring feverishly over texts" (33). Zelik also discovers his mother finally taking an interest in the here and now: he catches her primping in front of the mirror in her bedroom, "mildly distressed at having nearly forgotten her Cousin (three times removed) Zygmund's yahrzeit, who had died of something someplace far away" (34). What is more, Zelik gains popularity and respect in the real world that he transforms through his activities in the dream realm: "Suddenly the daylight North Main Street was making a bid to compete with its nocturnal counterpart" (40). As in much of Stern's earlier fiction, then, redemptive possibilities exist in the Pinch. One need only tap into the magical possibilities of the *yene velt* nigh at hand.

Curiously, fed up with the capriciousness of his fellow residents in the Pinch (they revert to their mean behavior once winter sets in and the dream world recedes), Zelik abandons the real world for the dream realm once and for all. Some characters, it seems, are ill-suited for the real world no matter how redeemable it might be. Hyman Weiss of "Hyman the Magnificent" seems headed along a similar trajectory as Zelik, but manages to make his peace with the Pinch by the end of the novella. At first glance, the works have little in common. Hyman, unlike Zelik, never discovers a realm of dreams. Rather, as an inept magician, he remains very much mired in the physical demands of the real world, botching one death-defying trick after the other. He suffers terrible burns, lacerations, near suffocation and drowning. In fact, the only thing incredible about his act is the variety of ways in which he maims himself.

Still, the essential theme of transcendence obtains in both novellas. At the root of Hyman's fascination with Houdini—and of his desire to emulate the magician—is the very concept of escape and all that it means to a scrawny Jewish adolescent growing up in the American South. The narrator of the novella, a childhood friend of Hyman, recalls the allure of Houdini's magic: "He threaded needles in his mouth, produced lit candles and miles of silks from his pockets. . . . But most of all he escaped: from every variety of fetter and shackle, from caskets, racks, and iron maidens, police vans and sausage skins and kegs of beer, from the bowels of prisons and the bellies of monsters, from vaults lashed with chains and dropped into the sea" (66). Through the course of the story, one realizes that to Hyman (and to the narrator who gravitates toward the daring of his hapless friend), escape means a good bit more than its surface dazzle. On one level, the prospect of fame and fortune beyond the Pinch appeals to Hyman. To be sure, Stern's depiction of an anti-Semitic Memphis suggests at least one reason why he would want to escape for more illustrious gigs in Atlantic City. Hyman's fellow Jews cannot bear to watch him torture himself, but throngs of anti-Semites in Memphis attend his shows and even "assist" the apparently masochistic Jew. Hyman, for example, does not even need to appoint volunteers to submerge him for his milk-can escape. "A self-appointed committee," the narrator recalls, "had stormed the loading dock in the middle of Hymie's speech, lifting him by the armpits with his legs cycling the air and stuffing him into the milk can" (92).

Of course, several of Hyman's cohorts wish to escape the Pinch for more hospitable American terrain. What makes Hyman special, however, is that like many of Stern's protagonists, he yearns for more than merely a physical escape from the Pinch. The contrast between his efforts at escape and Nathan Zuckerman's in Philip Roth's novels proves instructive. Zuckerman wishes merely to escape the stifling expectations of his Jewish family and the larger Jewish community, who want to rein in his tell-all fiction that is sure to be bad for the Jews. In *The Ghost Writer* (1979), Zuckerman seeks to emulate the reclusive Jewish writer E. I. Lonoff because he sees him as "'the Jew who got away'" (50). More magical possibilities occupy Hyman's imagination. Magic primarily serves as the vehicle through which Hyman seeks to tap into a more sublime realm "far beyond the boundaries of the Pinch" (64). He plans to shout "'Here am I!'" once he reappears after one of his escapes (77). Stern thus evokes the Hebrew *Hineni* (Here am I) intoned by both Abraham and Moses before God (see Genesis 22:1 and Exodus 3:4).

Hyman, like Abraham and Moses, gets his chance to meet his maker in the *yene velt* once he dies during another botched trick. Interestingly, his dead parents on the other side convince him to "escape" back into life. The Pinch apparently seems hospitable to Hyman compared to the "Russians and the diseases and the whole gantseh megillah" (109) that dogged his parents in Europe. The novella ends as Hyman eschews his magic in favor of a happy life of domesticity with the narrator's lovely sister. Everyday life in the Pinch, Stern suggests, just might contain all the magic a Jewish soul needs.

What draws readers interested in contemporary Jewish American literature to the work of Steve Stern, which shares so little in common with his most immediate and illustrious predecessors? Though solid arguments have been made on behalf of his evocation of a fantastical place in Jewish American history—the magical prewar Jewish ghetto of the Pinch—I would argue that his fashioning of recognizable, though thoroughly unique Jewish characters distinguishes his fiction as something special. Whether magic actually exists in the Pinch seems almost beside the point. Winning characters such as Hyman Weiss, Zelik Rifkin, Shimmele Dubrovner, and countless others in Stern's fictional universe indefatigably seek out the magical amid the gritty Memphis streets, betraying Stern's admiration for their endurance and their resiliency, and more precisely for the endurance and resiliency of the real Jewish people of the Pinch who inspired their creation. The sheer linguistic energy that ripples across the pages of Stern's work suggests a narrative urgency to recover, first and foremost, the people of the Pinch rapidly fading from memory.

Which brings me back, finally, to the long epigraph to this chapter that addresses the issue of memory and its tenuousness. Steve Stern revealed his fondness for this Hasidic parable by recounting it at least three times: once as a postscript to his novella "The Annals of the Kabakoffs" (collected in *A Plague of Dreamers*), once to close his reflections on his work in his acceptance speech for the 1987 Edward Lewis Wallant Award for Jewish Fiction, and most recently in his essay "After the Law," which appeared in *Tikkun* as part of a 1997 symposium on the Jewish literary revival. I quote the parable in its entirety because it so vividly evokes both Stern's artistic muse and his special burden as a Jewish American reared in an overwhelmingly secular environment. Too young to remember the Pinch firsthand and reared without an intimate knowledge of the Pinch Jews' religious and folk beliefs, Stern has, regardless, taken it upon himself to reinscribe the Pinch into collective memory: "The solitary custodian of a ghost town, I've had personally to assume a number of North Main Street's outmoded professions, such as matchmaker (*shadchan*) to the marriage of present and past" ("Brief Account" 90). Toward the end of his acceptance speech for the Edward Lewis Wallant Award, he picked up where the Hasidic parable left off to situate his own predicament along the continuum of the Jewish experience. "[L]ook at us now," he pleaded with the Lord of the Universe, "We have forgotten the prayer. The fire is out. We can't find our way back to the place in the forest. We can only remember that there was a fire, a prayer, a place in the forest. So Lord, maybe this will be sufficient?" ("Brief Account" 91). Regarding the hope for redemption, who knows whether Stern's literary project of *tikkun* is sufficient. Regarding his effort to take his place along the hallowed continuum of twentieth-century Jewish American authors, it most assuredly is.

9

Under the Influence

The Schlemiel Revisited in Gerald Shapiro's From Hunger

The schlemiel tradition in Jewish literature has captivated Gerald Shapiro's contemporary imagination even more so than it has captivated Steve Stern's. Let us revisit our terms. The schlemiel, in the broadest sense, is one who "handles a situation in the worst possible manner or is dogged by an ill luck that is more or less due to his own ineptness" (Revel 115). Or, as Sanford Pinsker puts it in his distinction between the schlemiel and the *schlimmazzel,* "'when a *schlimmazzel*'s bread-and-butter accidentally falls on the floor, it always lands butter-side down; with a *schlemiel* it is much the same—except that *he* butters his bread on both sides!'" (*The Schlemiel* 5). The schlemiel has been a popular figure in Jewish culture and literature for hundreds, if not thousands, of years. In *The Schlemiel as Metaphor: Studies in the Yiddish and American Jewish Novel* (1971), Pinsker traces the possible origins of the character to a figure in Numbers, Shelumiel ben Zurishaddai (5). He accounts for the popularity and importance of the schlemiel within Jewish culture by suggesting that Jewish humor of this sort developed as "a weapon in the uphill battle for survival. . . . Powerless by any conventional standards, Jews became masters in the arts of self-mockery. . . . rather than merely turning the sharp edges of their humor against the oppressor, they tended to turn it inward, to establish their own humanity by comic extensions of universal follies" (14–15). That is to say, laughter inspired by the foibles of the schlemiel allowed Jews some relief (if not transcendence) from their own hapless predicaments as unwelcome inhabitants in their various host countries in the Diaspora. The ancient pedigree of the schlemiel reflects, among other things, the long legacy of Jewish persecution that culminated in the Holocaust.

The possible biblical origins of the schlemiel notwithstanding, the character gained a special prominence in Yiddish literature written during the nineteenth and early twentieth century, and it gained momentum in the highly popular Jewish American fiction of Saul Bellow, Bernard Malamud, and Philip Roth. Ruth Wisse considers Rabbi Nachman of Bratzlav's "A Story about a Clever Man and a Simple Man" (written about 1805) to be the first Yiddish tale that revolves around a schlemiel (*Schlemiel* 16). The more prominent schlemiels in Yiddish literature include I. L. Peretz's Bontshe (of "Bontshe Shvayg"), Sholom Aleichem's Sholom Shachnah (of "On Account of a Hat"), and I. B. Singer's Gimpel (of "Gimpel the Fool"). Saul Bellow, Bernard Malamud, and Philip Roth may have had these very characters in mind when they fashioned their own most prominent schlemiels, Moses Herzog, Morris Bober, and Lou Epstein, respectively (Bellow, incidentally, translated Singer's story into English and included it, along with Roth's "Epstein" and several other schlemiel stories, in a volume he edited, *Great Jewish Short Stories* [1963]). The schlemiel turned out to be a wildly successful character for these Jewish American writers. Bellow, Malamud, and Roth achieved mainstream success in the 1950s and 1960s—arguably the golden age of Jewish American fiction—in no small part because the reading public curiously identified with the plight of someone like, say, Morris Bober.

In recent years, as I hope I have demonstrated in previous chapters, Jewish American writers have set their sights on new fictional terrain. Indeed, with the exception of Steve Stern's fiction, the previous works explored in this study would seem to suggest that the new generation of Jewish American writers has little use these days for the schlemiel. Broadly speaking, the conditions that inspired the construction of schlemiel characters in the 1950s and 1960s—feelings of cultural marginality and spiritual alienation—no longer seem to dog contemporary Jews or Jewish American writers. Thus, as popular as the schlemiel remains in forums of mass culture (e.g., Woody Allen movies, television shows such as *Seinfeld*), the character now more than ever seems the earmark of a specific time and place in Jewish American literature.

Small wonder that Jay Halio smells a trace of dust on Gerald Shapiro's first collection of stories, *From Hunger* (1993), which is rife with schlemiels:

> Shapiro is one of a younger generation of Jewish American writers who are trying in some fashion to maintain the traditions of their forebears, storytellers like I. B. Singer or Bernard Malamud. . . . Although most of the charac-

> ters in Shapiro's stories are Jewish (or have Jewish names) and share attributes and experiences with the traditional schlemiel, they are otherwise far removed from the worlds of Sholem Aleichem, Singer, and even Malamud. These are third-generation Jewish Americans, fully assimilated in most respects. (703, 704)

Halio implies here that Shapiro and the "younger generation" of Jewish American writers generally are latecomers to a tradition that reached fruition at least one generation ago. He laments that Shapiro's characters are so "far removed" from the (presumably) rich cultural heritage of Aleichem, Singer, and Malamud. When it comes to contemporary Jewish American fiction, criticism of this ilk is as common as it is disconcerting—disconcerting, at least, to anyone with a keen interest and scholarly stake in these contemporary writers. Irving Howe, one should note, set the stage for this dour take on third-generation Jewish American fiction when he predicted in his introduction to *Jewish American Stories* (1977) that the younger generation of Jewish American writers would face an insuperable "thinning-out of materials and memories" (16). Halio, disappointed with what he perceives to be the thinning gruel of Shapiro's fiction, enacts the very criticism of contemporary Jewish American fiction that Howe glimpsed several years ago.

I wish to stand against this rather pervasive assumption that contemporary Jewish American writers offer up merely diluted concoctions of a once rich broth. More to the point of this chapter, Shapiro's treatment of the schlemiel character in *From Hunger* (which won the 1993 Edward Lewis Wallant Award given annually to the most distinguished work of Jewish American fiction) exemplifies the heady fictional possibilities for the contemporary Jewish American writer. Shapiro, like Stern, manages both to draw on a rich literary legacy and to make it his own. That is, in revisiting the schlemiel, he does not merely struggle to "maintain the traditions" of his predecessors, as Halio suggests. Rather, he revises and reconstructs the schlemiel to address his special contemporary concerns as a Jewish American writer.

Importantly, Shapiro's reconstruction of the schlemiel does not represent a new phenomenon. As both Wisse and Pinsker make abundantly clear in their separate studies of the schlemiel in literature, the character has proven remarkably dynamic. That this character can tolerate seemingly limitless permutations no doubt accounts partly for its resilience; there indeed seems no generation of writers who cannot put aspects of the character to some use or another. Peretz fashioned an utterly foolish and passive schlemiel in Bontshe Shvayg to expose the "grotesquerie of suffering silence" (Wisse, *Schlemiel* 22) to his fellow downtrodden Jews. Absorbed in socialist politics, he constructed an especially meek and oblivious schlemiel to convince his readers "that they had better learn to demand their due in life" (Wisse, "Introduction" xx). Alternatively, Singer—preoccupied by metaphysical rather than overtly political concerns—constructed a "wise fool" in Gimpel, one who meditates thoughtfully on higher and lower versions of the T/truth (Pinsker, "Jewish Novelists" 66). Malamud, who famously proclaimed that "all men are Jews," molded the schlemiel into a readily identifiable everyman, one who waffled when it came to following an abstract, humanistic moral code. Finally, Bellow, as Pinsker observes, fashioned numerous angst-ridden, psychological schlemiels to evoke the alienation that characterized his postimmigrant generation of Jewish Americans. A foot in both the Jewish world and the mainstream society beyond the Jewish hearth, the typical Bellow protagonist must agonizingly negotiate between these conflictive realms. To be sure, the schlemiel has hardly been as static a character in the hands of Yiddish and Jewish American fictionists as Halio's reference to a "traditional" schlemiel might suggest.

All of which brings us, finally, to Gerald Shapiro's own version of the schlemiel in *From Hunger* and what this version has to tell us about the current state of Jewish American literature and culture. (Shapiro's *Bad Jews* [1999], a collection also rife with schlemiels, was published too late for consideration in this chapter.) Although Shapiro does not cut each of his protagonists from precisely the same cloth, he tends to emphasize their isolation, both physical and spiritual. Through their bad luck and foolishness, Shapiro both highlights their isolation and leavens the story with humor. If his schlemiels triumph by the end of the story, they triumph by situating their lives within a larger framework of the human community. Although this human community is not always defined as specifically Jewish, I would argue that Shapiro's communal (rather than strictly individualistic) vision originates from a decidedly Jewish tradition. As Rabbi Morris N. Kertzer once put it, "It is hard to discuss Jews, Judaism, Jewish beliefs, Jewish spirituality, or Jewish anything, without first describing Jewish community" (3). Shapiro's protagonists inch toward a redemptive Jewish life as they manage (not unlike Robert Cohen's protagonists) to eschew their near solipsism and to realize their connectedness with others; herein, they follow the trajectory of rediscovery and repair (or *t'shuvah*) typical of the contemporary protagonist in Jewish American fiction.

The first and title story, "From Hunger," introduces the reader into the essential concerns that reverberate throughout the collection. The story revolves around a surprise visit that Altshuler receives from his aging, down-and-out Uncle Phil. It initially appears that the corpulent Phil, who cannot suppress his ravenous appetite, is the schlemiel of the story. Frustrated by his suicidal eating habits, his wife and daughters want to have nothing more to do with him. He seeks out his nephew, Altshuler, because he has no other place to go and no one else to go to. Additionally, Altshuler remembers that conversations around the dinner table when he was a child occasionally drifted to Uncle Phil's "grubby, incompetent life—a misspent youth followed by a series of bad jobs, a few disastrous forays into the jungle of self-employment, a long, tattered marriage" (*FH* 2). Phil's insatiable appetite and grotesque physical form—"a shade over five-six, he'd zoomed past two hundred fifty pounds years ago and never looked back"—adds dark comedy to his predicament (2).

Still, the schlemiel at the heart of this story is not Uncle Phil, but Altshuler. Shapiro takes pains to emphasize that his protagonist, like many of the protagonists in the collection, has lately endured a string of bad luck. In the past year, he and his wife had been divorced, his oldest friend had died suddenly of a parasitic disease, and an assortment of "little disasters had kept on nibbling away at him" (7). He visits the doctor for a skin rash only to discover that, on top of the rash, he is an inch shorter than he had always thought. True to the essential definition of a schlemiel, Altshuler is at least partially responsible for his decline, for, as Shapiro suggests, he has withdrawn himself emotionally from others, especially from his ex-wife, with whom he has no children owing to their "desultory" efforts (6). In fact, by the time Uncle Phil strolls into town, Altshuler has pretty much dropped out of life. He even carries out his intermittent sexual performances in a detached manner. They "faded into a series of halfhearted, disorganized overtures that never got off the ground" (7). One senses that all of Altshuler's misfortunes, even the rapid decline of his stock portfolio, somehow originate (rather than merely result) in his utter isolation.

Taking in Uncle Phil offers Altshuler a sorely needed opportunity to rejoin the human community, to participate in and take responsibility for the life of someone other than himself. Altshuler's father—who alternately calls Phil a schnorrer (beggar) and a "'dumb yutz'" (10, 2)—attempts to convince his son to turn Phil out of his home, but Altshuler steadfastly refuses, explaining to his father, "'I think it's important that I'm doing this. I think it's a big step for me'" (9). Altshuler realizes that the sudden emergence of his Uncle Phil offers him the opportunity to counter the forces of inertia that have led him further and further into a mean, isolated existence. He cannot save his uncle from literally eating himself to death, but Uncle Phil in a very real sense saves Altshuler. A schlemiel no longer (his status at work, for example, begins to improve), Altshuler embraces his responsibility for his uncle even after his uncle's death. The hospital needs to have releases and affidavits signed, whereupon Altshuler signs himself "as next of kin, as responsible party" (19).

In "Community Seder," Shapiro revisits the essential concerns of "From Hunger." He creates a disaffected schlemiel-like protagonist who ultimately embraces his relationship with the larger human community. That said, there are important distinctions to be made between the two stories. In "Community Seder," Shapiro intensifies the religious nature of his protagonist's crisis. It is a more distinctively Jewish community that the protagonist, Lenny Schrank, finally embraces by the end of the story. Moreover, perhaps because of the more distinctively Jewish community of Schrank's childhood, leading a fiercely individualistic existence seems far less possible for Schrank than it does for Altshuler. The entire Jewish community from Schrank's childhood, rather than merely one sick uncle, conspire to draw him back into the communal fold.

In the opening paragraph, Shapiro evokes the theme of physical and spiritual return that characterizes the entire collection. Schrank, in fact, has returned to "the city of his father's . . . youth": "Although he'd been raised far away from the place, in his thirties Schrank moved to the city of his father's poverty-stricken youth, and settled down in luxury along its exquisite and privileged lakeshore. These wards were very different from the vile, desperate city his father had spoken of so bitterly when Schrank was a boy" (63). The passage says a great deal about Schrank and about the dilemma of some third-generation Jewish Americans generally. Schrank is the son of parents who largely left *yiddishkeit* behind in their (successful) effort to escape the material poverty of their own childhoods in immigrant, urban neighborhoods. However, although these parents gained material comfort in various leafy suburbs, they tended to impose a measure of cultural and spiritual poverty on themselves and their children.

This dilemma began, of course, with the very first generation of Jewish Americans, as Jewish American fiction of this generation reflects. For example, by the end of Abraham Cahan's *The Rise of David Levinsky* (1917), the protagonist, David Levinsky, has achieved material riches in the garment industry but mourns the concomitant loss of his religious identity: "David, the poor lad swinging over a Talmud volume at the Preacher's Synagogue, seems to have more in common with my inner identity than David Levinsky, the well-known cloak-manufacturer" (529). Similarly, Anzia Yezierska's protagonist in *Bread Givers* (1925) adopts the New World ethos of rugged individualism and escapes from under the thumb of her pious father, but by the novel's conclusion, she, like David Levinsky, cannot quite turn her back on the values of the Old World. She reconciles with her father, who embodies these values, and salvages a crucial element of her own identity: "How could I have hated him and tried to blot him out of my life? Can I hate my arm, my hand that is part of me?" (286). The second-generation Jewish American writers (e.g., Saul Bellow, Philip Roth, Bernard Malamud, Grace Paley) felt this burden even more acutely as *yiddishkeit* faded further back into their collective memory. In fact, certain Jewish critics were not above taking potshots at the waning Jewish identity of the second-generation writer. Most memorably, perhaps, in his landmark essay in *Commentary,* "Philip Roth Reconsidered," Irving Howe saw fit to excoriate Roth for his "thin personal culture" (73).

In the opening passage of "Community Seder," Shapiro suggests how desperate matters have become for the third generation. Schrank, it would appear, does not have even a culturally rich childhood of his own to return to; instead, he returns to the site of his *father's* youth to recapture all that has been lost over three generations of assimilation. That the squalid tenements of his father's childhood have been replaced by upscale housing (which Schrank, apparently, can afford) illustrates the futility of his efforts to rediscover the cultural richness of his father's youth. Indeed, the delicatessen Schrank frequents to eat chopped liver with *schmaltz* (chicken fat) and hear a cacophony of thick, Eastern European accents seems as close as he can get to reconnecting with his father's Jewish past.

Shapiro, however, does not mean to suggest that Judaism has irretrievably waned as third- and fourth-generation Jewish Americans come of age. Rather, in "Community Seder," the site of Schrank's own childhood, it turns out, contains a cultural and religious richness that he has overlooked. What makes Schrank a schlemiel is that he returns to the wrong place to realize a meaningful Jewish existence. He wishes to lead a more meaningful life, but, like Bellow's celebrated schlemiel, Moses Herzog, *"kept tripping, never reached the scene of the struggle"* (*Herzog* 128).

Fortunately for Schrank, Shapiro imbues the story with just enough magic to bring the scene of the struggle to him. One might see the story as a twist on the adage "you can't go home again," for, hard as Schrank might try, he cannot escape his home. Indeed, Schrank's childhood home (for which he apparently feels little affinity) literally follows him to the childhood home of his father. First, at a deli counter, Schrank runs into the mother of a childhood friend from Hebrew school. The next day, he actually stumbles across one of his Hebrew school friends on a bus, who exclaims excitedly to fellow passengers, "'We went to Hebrew school together. . . . A million miles from here! Can you believe it? I haven't seen him in about twenty years!'" (*FH* 69). These coincidental brushes with figures from Schrank's past eventually give way to the more magical intrusion of his past into his present as he receives an invitation from his childhood synagogue for a community Passover Seder. Illustrating his marginal Jewish identity and his general disaffection, Schrank puzzles over the bizarre invitation, which contains no address, date, or time. He wonders how they could have found him, as "[h]e didn't belong to any Jewish organizations, not even the Jewish Community Center. Nor had he given money to any Jewish causes in recent memory" (71).

Although Schrank does not have the inclination to seek out the community Seder, the community Seder seeks out him when the sexton from Schrank's old synagogue catches him urinating in an alley and ushers him into the Seder. Schrank attempts to beg out by describing the dime-thin Jewish element of his American identity: "'The thing is, I'm—you know what I mean? It's like on those census forms, where they say 'religion,' I always just leave it blank'" (74). The sexton, however, forces him to recognize that he cannot simply opt out of his Judaism: "You're a Jew?" he asks Schrank rhetorically (74). Inside the synagogue, Schrank sees hundreds of the congregants from his childhood synagogue, several of whom he knows have already died:

> There was Tarr, the banker, with his three strawberry blonde daughters, and Dekovnick, the tympanist with the symphony, with his brilliant, neurasthenic son, Walter. . . . Wasn't that Irving Mandelbaum the ACLU lawyer, who'd died years before of heart failure? And wait a second, that was—it had to be—Shifra Axelrod, the smartest girl he'd known in high school, who'd killed herself and her *shaygetz* boyfriend with carbon monoxide the night of their senior prom. (78)

Nonplussed by what he sees, Schrank wishes to flee. The Jewish legacy of suffering, specifically, proves almost too much for him to bear. In the most poignant scene of the story, Rothblatt, a Holocaust survivor, recounts his tragic losses during the atrocity and his theological doubts, but also his refusal to abandon the Jewish rituals that imbue his life with meaning nonetheless. Schrank cries, "'I'm not cut out for all of this! I did my part, I went to Hebrew school, I learned my *haftorah,* I fasted, I prayed—it just didn't *take,* that's all. . . . I'm sorry I came to this crummy city, this stinking place'" (82–83).

What Schrank must overcome, Shapiro suggests, is primarily his conviction that his fate as a materially prosperous, contemporary Jewish American is no longer bound up in the fate of Jews worldwide in *galut* (exile). He has not laid eyes on his fellow Jews from his childhood for twenty years, so he feels that he has removed himself too far from his Jewish roots to return. The sexton, however, assures him that twenty years is only a blink in God's eyes (78). Shapiro thus evokes the crucial Jewish precept that Jews of every epoch form links in a single chain of Jewish continuity—that all Jews, in fact, were spiritually present as God handed down the gift of the Law to Moses atop Mount Sinai. As Cynthia Ozick tersely puts it, "there are no latecomers in Judaism" ("Literature" 194).

By the end of the story, Schrank triumphs by renouncing (implicitly at least) his wrongheaded assumption of a latecomer Jewish status. Specifically, he situates his own exile from Judaism within the larger context of Jewish exile that Jews acknowledge each year during the Passover Seder, especially in the phrase that concludes most Passover Seders, *Lashannah habbah birushalayim* (next year in Jerusalem). His own lament, "I'm so far from home" merges with the exilic lament of the entire Jewish community at the Seder, "We are so far from home. . . . So far, so far from home. So far, so far, we are so far from home" (*FH* 83). Schrank, ultimately, can "no longer distinguish their voices from his own" (83). He, thus, takes his place along the continuum of Jews in *galut* and overcomes his psychic alienation.

On the surface, "Golders Greer" seems not to have much in common with "The Community Seder." After all, it revolves around a foundering scholar working abroad, who agrees to check in on the sister of his parents' friend while he is in London (an entirely different scenario). That said, the schlemiel-hero of "Golders Greer," Ted Lustig, suffers from a dilemma strikingly similar to Lenny Schrank's. A thoroughly assimilated Jewish American, Lustig feels only a remote affinity for Judaism or for his Jewish identity; this rootlessness exacerbates his general disaffection. In the first sentences of the story, Shapiro belabors Lustig's isolation. The woman whom his parents wish him to call is "the elderly sister of a man they knew from their synagogue" (*FH* 149). It is, tellingly, not Lustig's synagogue, and one infers that Lustig himself probably does not even belong to one. Moreover, Shapiro characterizes Lustig as a schlemiel to illustrate his alienation from the world outside the Jewish community as well: "when he was in Europe he still felt, after five summers, like a yokel. His French was barely passable, his German halting and crude. He had difficulty with even the smallest tasks of everyday life on the Continent; he was overcharged continually by sharp-eyed hotel clerks and waiters, and had had his pocket picked in Rome, Amsterdam, Paris, even Lucerne" (150). One suspects that his alienation from himself and his own identity precludes meaningful relationships with others, specifically the women he only reluctantly (and briefly) dates. His sheer loneli-ness is what, no doubt, provokes him to go beyond the call of duty, as it were, to ask Anna Peltzman, the sister of his parents' friend, to meet him for lunch.

Lustig's encounter with Peltzman forces him to confront his waning Jewish identity. Specifically, the Holocaust has scarred Peltzman profoundly, which forces Lustig to consider his own lackluster response to the atrocity and what that response means. Peltzman tells him,

> "[W]e had family left in Germany, you know. They all died. . . . In some cases they were just names I'd seen in the front of our family album. . . . But then there were a few of them I'd met on trips during the twenties when I was quite young—we went to Belgium once on holiday, and to Paris and Brittany, and our relatives joined us. Everyone spoke Yiddish. Mine was pretty rough, and I don't think I understood them, or liked them very much, really. . . . They

> seemed so wretched, most of them. But I'd seen them and broken bread with them," she went on, "and they were quite real to me, these relatives. And when they'd been gassed it shocked me in a way I shall never forget." (159–60)

The Jewish victims of the Holocaust are not quite "real" to Lustig. He feels little connection to them. Whereas Peltzman can see Germany only as a "nation of pigs and murderers," Lustig acknowledges that "'I'm too young to feel that kind of hatred of the Germans. I mean, I hate them, I guess, but it's not the same thing. I don't hate them for what they did to me, because really they didn't do anything to me. I hate them for what they did to a bunch of people I'm probably related to distantly, but I never met any of them and don't even know their names'" (160). Peltzman chastises Lustig for his lack of empathy, chalking it up to his Americanization: "'You're so awfully sweet to one another in superficial ways . . . but you don't sense a connection with the world'" (160, ellipses in original). What is more, Lustig's scholarly interest in the German writer Heinrich von Kleist also betrays his dislocation from recent Jewish history. (Again, Bellow's *Herzog* resonates: Moses Herzog's own scholarship, specifically his monograph, *Romanticism and Christianity,* also illustrates his waning Jewish identity.) Peltzman chides the Jewish protagonist for his decidedly un-Jewish scholarly pursuits: "'you'll forgive me if I tell you I've no stomach for German literature'" (158).

Lustig's afternoon with Peltzman emerges as a watershed event in his life. Consciously or unconsciously, Peltzman pressures him, through her acute sensitivity toward her Jewish identity, to recognize his own connectedness to the Jewish past, present, and future. As they walk through Golders Greer, Lustig feels the persistent "tug of her on his arm" (165). Lamentably, however, he does not respond to this "tug"; he does not experience a Schrank-like epiphany. "So much for making contact" (166), he muses after lunch, wishing to be on his way. Clearly, he does not come to realize his place along the continuum of Jewish existence. Rather, he clings to the false hope that his scholarship on the German writer will reveal the connectedness of things: "Surely the wisdom, the insight, the perception of the connectedness of things that he hoped his work would bring him—all these lay waiting on . . . some forgotten scrap of paper he'd failed to find. He'd made no progress; he understood nothing, Lustig realized, and this thought came over him now with the finality of a shroud" (168). That the connectedness Lustig seeks might be found in the tug of an arm rather than on a scrap of scholarly paper is something that he fails to consider.

The affinities between these stories forces one to reckon with their starkly contrasting conclusions. The point Shapiro wishes to make, it seems, is that a meaningful contemporary Jewish identity must be comprised of more substantial stuff than a mere identification with Jewish suffering. After all, Schrank, like Lustig, cannot quite identify with the suffering experienced by European Jews in the Holocaust. To the Holocaust survivor's description of his spiritual plight in "The Community Seder," Schrank merely responds, "'I don't know if I understand you exactly'" (81). Importantly, the meaningful Jewish ritual of the Passover Seder—not his affinity for Jewish suffering in the Holocaust—inspires Schrank's *t'shuvah.* To put it another way, *yiddishkeit* offers Schrank something from within Jewish culture that he can say yes to, something that he can affirm. In "Golders Greer," Peltzman describes plenty of influences from without Judaism against which Lustig could rebel (e.g., the persecution of Jews in the Holocaust, the insidious anti-Semitism in modern-day England), but offers him precious little from within the Jewish religion or culture for him to celebrate. A contemporary Jewish American ethos, Shapiro suggests, must be forged substantially from Judaism.

In "Levidow," Shapiro draws more overtly on Judaic sources (biblical stories, specifically) to emphasize the continuity of the Jewish experience, while again drawing on the schlemiel tradition. In Morris Levidow, Shapiro creates a hapless protagonist continually beset by misfortunes great and small. Consider, for example, the opening lines of the story:

> To say that this past year had been a bad one would be to insult all the other bad years of Levidow's long life. As he was apt to tell anyone who would listen, every day fresh misery poured on his head. Fruit spoiled as he carried it home from the market. Cars splashed mud and slush on him, even on the sunniest of afternoons. . . . Pigeons flew for miles to soil his shoulders. A piece of bad fish at a lunch counter landed him in the emergency room at Mount Sinai, where someone stole his glasses.(38)

And on and on and on. Despite Levidow's superficial resemblance to any number of schlemiels in Yiddish and Jewish American fiction, one cannot dismiss him as merely a stock figure, for theological concerns play a far more central role in the story than in the schlemiel narratives of other writers such as Singer, Malamud, Roth, and Bellow. Indeed, biblical stories, as I have suggested, resonate throughout "Levidow." Levidow, for example, leaves New York to see "America" after God tells him to "[g]et out of town" in one of Levidow's fevered dreams (38–39). Shapiro, I contend, quite consciously evokes God's command to Abraham here, "'Get thee out of thy country, and from thy kindred, and from thy father's house, unto the land that I will show thee" (Genesis 12:1). Levidow's flight, however, unlike Abraham's, represents a rejection of his covenant with God. Indeed, the biblical story of Jonah reverberates even more significantly in the story as Levidow, like Jonah, attempts to flee God. Instructed by God to go to Nineveh and warn the non-Jewish town of its imminent destruction, Jonah "rose up to flee unto Tarshish from the presence of the Lord" (Jonah 1:3). Levidow, similarly, wishes to escape God's presence through his journey westward to the heart of America: "Let God, that scamp, that bully, try to follow him into the wilds! Levidow chuckled at the thought. America lay ahead of him, green and embraceable, short on concrete, full of soft spots. He felt free" (41). He thus succumbs to idolatry; he confuses the created with the Creator, worshiping a natural world that he (mistakenly) dissociates from God's realm. By consciously evoking biblical stories but tweaking them in essential ways, Shapiro affirms the essential continuity of the Jewish experience throughout the epochs without neglecting the special burdens of his contemporary Jewish American protagonist.

Broadly speaking, Levidow suffers from a crisis of faith to which Jews have always been susceptible, and he foolishly seeks to write himself out of Jewish history. His crisis, however, originates in thoroughly American temptations, in secular dreams and distractions unique to the Jewish American experience. Levidow views America as a land "still fresh and full of promise" (43). Material riches, specifically, seem attainable to him. Thus, when God tempts him with a gaudy Italian sharkskin suit, he dons the suit and embraces the opportunity to become a "new," rather than Jew, man (41).

Levidow's Jewish identity as a schlemiel plays a crucial role in the story. It intensifies his desire to embrace a new, American identity and originates in the first place from his Jewish desire to repair a broken world. After Levidow's car breaks down somewhere in the Alleghenies, God sends Levidow's childhood self to visit the old Levidow and to guide him. The child cajoles Levidow into reexamining his lifelong efforts to repair the world. It seems that practically all of Levidow's efforts, true to schlemiel form, resulted in disaster. But, as he reflects, "I have always my whole life had a problem leaving things alone" (48). For example, he recalls his ill-fated effort to restore the hearing of a deaf woman. Although technically he fixes the woman's problem, his efforts only heap a more burdensome agony upon her: "It's a terrible thing, she never again had a good night's sleep. Heard *everything.* She couldn't stop; it was terrible. She begged me to do something about it. 'Turn down the volume!' she begged me. What could I do? I threw up my hands" (50). As the child Levidow observes, "You were a handyman, a fixer, weren't you? Only something always went a little haywire" (50). Interestingly, try as Levidow might to eschew his old ways and embrace a new identity in America's heartland, he cannot resist the temptation to fix things. A grotesque demon lady visits him on the side of the road, whereupon he succumbs to the urge to beautify her: "He pressed her flesh this way and that; he pinched her nose down, spread the flesh of her cheeks flat against the bones beneath them, wiped beneath her chin at the sack of flesh that hung there, then took hold of a piece of bone at her chin and pulled it out gracefully, as though it were made of moist clay" (57). Predictably, Levidow's efforts in the present lead to disaster when the now beautiful woman abandons him and the child Levidow at the side of the road for a strapping young man in a convertible. As the convertible disappears off into the horizon, Levidow laments, "no matter how I try, something always goes wrong!" (61).

The sheer volume of the surreal material in "Levidow" leaves one breathless by the end of the story, grasping for answers to the weighty questions that the story poses: What precisely does Shapiro think and want us to think about his schlemiel? Does he condemn or celebrate Levidow's ill-fated efforts to fix the world about him? And, finally, what do the answers to these questions tell us about the evolving concerns of the Jewish American writer? Clearly, the story reaffirms the biblical lesson of Jonah; like Jonah, Levidow realizes the futility of his effort to flee the presence of God. Upon encountering his childhood self by the side of the road, who tells Levidow that God has sent him, he realizes that he cannot escape God; the fact that he heeds the child's instructions betrays his implicit cry of *Hineni* (Here I am). Regarding the more vexing question concerning Levidow's identity as an inept "fixer," Shapiro undoubtedly pokes fun at his hero's foibles but lauds his irrepressible inclination to repair a broken world. That is, he affirms the efforts of his schlemiel even though, as Levidow admits, something always goes wrong. As Levidow bemoans his lifelong blunders, his childhood self instructs him, "'All the more reason never to be disappointed,'" whereupon cans upon cans of ice-cold soda drop from Levidow's sleeves to slake their thirst (62). Through the schlemiel, then, Shapiro challenges but then affirms a central principle of Judaism, *tikkun olam*: to repair or heal the world in preparation for the Messiah.

The stories that I have explored illustrate how one Jewish American writer, Gerald Shapiro, revisits the age-old but dynamic tradition of the schlemiel to engage concerns that bear down on the contemporary Jewish American ethos and that preoccupy his imagination as a contemporary Jewish American writer. Lenny Schrank, Ted Lustig, and even Altshuler are schlemiels not because they are too good (like I. B. Singer's Gimpel or Malamud's Morris Bober) or too long on book smarts (like Bellow's Herzog), but primarily because they have withdrawn from the human community. If they manage to shake off their string of bad luck and blunders by the end of the story, they do so through various expressions of *t'shuvah*: Schrank's return to the Jewish community in "The Community Seder"; Levidow's rejection of his impulse to flee God and his renewed efforts toward *tikkun* in "Levidow"; and even, I would argue, Altshuler's recognition of his responsibility for the welfare of someone other than himself. As previous chapters suggest, *t'shuvah* has emerged as one of the predominant themes of the contemporary Jewish American writer as increasing numbers of contemporary Jews in America (and of contemporary Jewish American protagonists) seek to rediscover the Judaism that their "alienated" parents and often their grandparents eschewed.

Above all, the stories in *From Hunger* demonstrate how durable a character the schlemiel continues to be in Jewish American literature. Jews needed these characters during times of persecution so that they might laugh through their tears. The good-natured schlemiel also tended to affirm their moral, if not physical, superiority over their anti-Semitic persecutors. Shapiro's fiction suggests that the contemporary battle over the Jewish American ethos is also fertile ground for the schlemiel. As long as Jews in this country continue to grapple with their hyphenated identities, there will be those who cannot quite get it right; as long as Jews seek to repair a broken world, there will be those who blunder in often humorous ways. In short, there will always be room for the schlemiel in Jewish American fiction. One both suspects and hopes that Gerald Shapiro will continue to revisit the character in the many works that will surely follow *From Hunger.*

10

Conclusion

Toward a New Century of Jewish American Fiction—Emergent Voices, Emergent Visions

First, an anecdote. Just after I received my first tenure-track job offer (only a few years ago), I delivered a paper on a Jewish American writer at a regional conference of the Modern Language Association. Upon excitedly sharing my good news with a colleague on my panel, she replied, "Are they going to let you just publish on Jewish American writers?" What intrigued me about my colleague's response was not so much what it revealed about the marginalized role of Jewish American literature in English departments across the country (after all, two fruitless years of job hunting had already told me all I needed to know on that front), but rather what was revealed by the *tone* of my colleague's remark, which suggested to me that, at least to a certain extent, she had internalized the wrongheaded assumptions of the "they" in her remark. That is, even to this eminent scholar of Jewish literature, devoting one's research time solely to Jewish American writers had come to seem a less than noble enterprise. Similar exchanges with other colleagues have since convinced me that her views are the norm rather than the exception among scholars with a particular interest in Jewish writers.

I have taken to pointing out to such colleagues that the scholars I know who publish fairly exclusively on African American, American Indian, Asian American, or U.S. Latino/a writers do not feel the least bit insecure about it—nor should they, in my view. Scholars of other multicultural literatures currently bask in the sunshine of their scholarly confidence; they entertain no doubts about the value of their work. By contrast, most scholars interested in Jewish American fiction these days guiltily drum up their article on, say, Thane Rosenbaum between more "worthy" scholarly projects and behind closed office doors (as if they were partaking in some mildly shameful act, like listening to a Michael Bolton CD). To sum up the current state of Jewish American letters in a single sentence: at the very moment that Jewish American fiction is enjoying a revival, scholars of that fiction are still in recovery mode from its fairly lackluster showing in the 1970s.

The 1970s were admittedly bear-market years for Jewish American fiction. The dazzling postimmigrant fiction of marginality and alienation, as Irving Howe observed, had pretty much run its course, and the modest output of quality Jewish American fiction by younger writers in the 1970s heralded at best an uncertain future for the genre. For whatever reason (the overwhelming power of their work, the definitive claim they seemed to stake on the subject of Jewish American identity), Bellow, Roth, Malamud, and Ozick had largely devoured the generation of their literary children. What we thankfully began to see in the 1980s, I believe, was the emergence of a generation of literary grandchildren to Bellow and the others, who set the stage for the current revival of Jewish American literature. These grandchildren and their works of the 1980s include Nessa Rapoport's *Preparing for Sabbath* (1981), Rebecca Goldstein's *The Mind-Body Problem* (1983), Steve Stern's *Lazar Malkin Enters Heaven* (1986), Tova Reich's *Master of the Return* (1988), Robert Cohen's *The Organ Builder* (1988), and the most precocious of grandchildren, Allegra Goodman, and her first collection of stories that rounds out the decade, *Total Immersion* (1989). For those who were paying attention, these writers and a handful of others announced that the regeneration of Jewish American fiction had begun.

In the 1990s, as the previous chapters should make clear, we have enjoyed the full flowering of this literary renaissance. Practically all of the "grandchildren" listed above went on to produce stronger, more mature work (for example, Allegra Goodman's first novel, *Kaaterskill Falls* [1998], was a finalist for the National Book Award), and new grandchildren emerged, most notably Melvin Jules Bukiet, Thane Rosenbaum, Gerald Shapiro, Pearl Abraham, Jonathan Rosen, Joseph Skibell, Lev Raphael, Benjamin Taylor, Jyl Lynn Felman, Dani Shapiro, and Michael Chabon. Several fine works by these and other Jewish American writers emerged too late to receive adequate attention in this study (works such as Saul Bellow's *Ravelstein* [2000], Philip Roth's *I Married a Communist* [1998] and *The Human Stain* [2000], Gerald Shapiro's *Bad Jews* [1999], Steve Stern's *The Wedding Jester* [1999], Melvin

Bukiet's *Signs and Wonders* [1999], Pearl Abraham's *Giving Up America* [1999], Nathan Englander's *For the Relief of Unbearable Urges* [1999], Tova Mirvis's *The Ladies Auxiliary* [1999], Ehud Havazelet's *Like Never Before* [1998], Eileen Pollack's *Paradise, New York* [1998], and Ross Feld's *Zwilling's Dream* [1999]). Indeed, these are heady times for those interested in the distinct cadences of the Jewish American literary voice, as even a cursory glance at some recent special issues of both academic and popular journals suggests. The prestigious academic journal *Contemporary Literature* published a special issue entitled "Contemporary American Jewish Literature" in 1993. The issue was highly important for scholars interested in Jewish American literature. Given the prominence of *Contemporary Literature* within the academic community, it went a long way toward reestablishing the significance (dare I say legitimacy?) of Jewish American literature as a discrete subject of literary study. The issue includes an important interview with Cynthia Ozick and fine essays by such eminent scholars as Elaine M. Kauvar, Murray Baumgarten, Mark Krupnick, and S. Lillian Kremer. Still, the thrust of "Contemporary American Jewish Literature" is not quite as "contemporary" as its title suggests. That the usual suspects in Jewish American fiction—Bellow, Malamud, Ozick, Roth, and Paley—figure so prominently in the issue (Rebecca Goldstein is the only literary "grandchild" of the postimmigrant Jewish American writers to receive substantial attention) was one of the factors that motivated me to work on the book you now hold in your hand.

Thankfully, special issues of periodicals that followed *Contemporary Literature* have been substantially more forward looking. In 1996, *Response* published an issue entitled "Perspectives on Jewish Literature," which included articles that emphasized the currency of Jewish American literature. The editors emphasized contemporary Jewish American writers not least of all by publishing contemporary fiction and poetry written by emergent writers (the resurgence of Jewish American poetry is a topic for an entirely separate study). In 1997, *Prairie Schooner*—one of the oldest and most prestigious literary quarterlies in the country—published a special issue, "Jewish American Writers." Also contemporary in its focus, the editors published prose and poetry, including stories by Steve Stern and Rebecca Goldstein, as well as an essay by Sanford Pinsker, "Dares, Double-Dares, and the Jewish-American Writer," in which Pinsker explores how contemporary Jewish American fiction writers (most notably, Thane Rosenbaum and Melvin Bukiet) have emerged to stake out new fictional terrain. *"Double-dare,"* Pinsker observes, "may be as good a term as any to describe what the new crop of Jewish American writers is doing, and gives every promise of continuing to do" ("Dares" 285).

Thane Rosenbaum, the literary editor of *Tikkun,* recently put together an impressive literary symposium of his own, "The Jewish Literary Revival," in the November–December 1997 issue of the magazine. The symposium includes seven essays written by an impressive mix of scholars and fiction writers (Morris Dickstein, Nessa Rapoport, Mark Shechner, Rebecca Goldstein, Melvin Bukiet, Steve Stern, and Sanford Pinsker). Refreshingly, there is nary a mention of Bellow, Roth, and Malamud in the symposium as each of the contributors focus on the resurgence of Jewish American writing in the 1990s. A useful reading list of more than thirty emergent Jewish novelists is nestled between two essays in the symposium, reflecting *Tikkun*'s apparent (and laudable) effort to effect a stretching of the Jewish American fiction course syllabus. Additional special issues of journals devoted to Jewish American literature have appeared, including *Shofar*'s special issue (vol. 16, no. 2 [winter 1998]) on Jewish American literature about Israel and Israeli literature about the United States. Perhaps most importantly, the first Norton anthology of Jewish American literature is scheduled to appear in 2000.

Finally, it is worth noting that the Jewish American literary renaissance was the subject of a special 1997 symposium of the American Literature Association, "Revisioning Jewish American and Holocaust Literature" (this symposium on Jewish American literature has developed into an annual conference in Delray Beach, Florida) and of a 1997 panel discussion, "The Jewish Literary Revival," cosponsored by *Tikkun* and New York's New School (most of the fiction writers explored in the previous chapters—with the exception of Goodman, Shapiro, and Roth—were featured participants of this panel discussion). Despite the factors limned in my introduction that discourage the study of Jewish American fiction, the most recent scholarly and critical attention lavished on these writers heralds a more promising future for the field.

Those readers who enjoy turning the pages of quality Jewish American fiction have much to be optimistic about as we look forward to a new century of Jewish American writing. I devoted the previous chapters to a diverse grouping of the strongest contemporary writers to present a fairly accurate portrait of what this new century of Jewish writing, at least the first decade or so of it, will look like. Still, a plethora of emergent artists will contribute their own distinct brush strokes to this family portrait. To bring this study to a satisfactory conclusion, I would like to consider briefly the contributions of a few additional writers most likely to leave their own indelible mark on Jewish American fiction, in my estimation.

In his beautifully wrought debut novel, *Eve's Apple* (1997), Jonathan Rosen, the cultural editor of the *Forward*, examines the contemporary, largely assimilated Jewish American middle class with an aesthetic rigor that evokes Saul Bellow's work. Rosen deftly immerses us in the lives of his two principle characters: Ruth Simon, a lovely and artistic young woman struggling to stave off a relapse of anorexia, and her compassionate lover, Joseph Zimmerman, who desperately plumbs the depths of her illness in his effort to save her. Joseph comes to understand through the course of the novel that in saving Ruth, he also seeks to redeem his own life, sullied (so he believes) by his inability to thwart his sister's suicide many years earlier.

Although the novel's twenty-something protagonists give little thought to their Judaism or to the issue of their hyphenated identities, several elements of the novel distinguish it, in my view, as a work of the Jewish American imagination: Rosen revels in the ironic play of language, a characteristic that earmarks so many Jewish American writers; allusions to the Holocaust pervade the novel (Ruth, we learn, was obsessed with the story of Anne Frank as a child); Joseph teaches English to Russian immigrants for a living; he reflects occasionally on the high holidays and his upbringing in a kosher home; he recites the mourner's kaddish (for whom, I shall not reveal); he seeks redemption. None of these factors alone, or even combined for that matter, truly make it a Jewish American novel, however.

To my mind, what makes *Eve's Apple* a stunning contemporary Jewish American novel is that Joseph self-consciously identifies himself and Ruth (and his sister, Evelyn, for that matter) as Jewish Americans grappling with their own historically and culturally specific problems. Joseph at least partly attributes his sister's melancholia and Ruth's anorexia to the rootlessness that defines their fairly affluent contemporary Jewish milieu, so far removed from the immigrant experience of their great-grandparents. Consider, for example, his reflections on New York's Jewish Lower East Side: "The Jewish Lower East Side was hidden, an overgrown garden. It was a place my sister had wished us all to return to—boisterous, intimate, familial. The childhood of American Jews. I knew from my students how brutal immigrant life could be, but in Evelyn's mind it was the great antidote to the inert suburban world. . . . What had happened—to my sister and then to Ruth?" (*EA* 294). To be sure, these characters' identities as third-generation Jewish Americans are of central significance. The problems of poverty and cultural marginality, Rosen implicitly suggests, were the problems that dogged an earlier generation of Jewish Americans (unsurprisingly, these problems permeate the fiction of Rosen's literary "grandparents"). But, as Joseph gleans above, his own suburban generation must reckon with poverty of a different ilk, a more nebulous emotional poverty that all the same reduces its victims to skin and bones. Through Joseph's decidedly unneurotic cultural identification as a Jew, Rosen illustrates what has been gained along with the postwar social mobility that characterizes the Jewish experience in this country; through the diseases that starve Ruth and Evelyn, he offers us a glimpse at what has been lost. I suspect that Rosen will continue in the years ahead to bring his considerable artistic gifts to bear on the distinct burdens and preoccupations of his young Jewish American generation.

As several of the previous chapters suggest, the Holocaust continues (more strongly than ever) to stake its claim on the Jewish American imagination. Recent works by Dani Shapiro, Joseph Skibell, Harvey Grossinger, and Aryeh Lev Stollman further illustrate this point. Dani Shapiro's *Picturing the Wreck* (1996) revolves around a New York psychoanalyst, Solomon Grossman, whose parents had the foresight and the luck to escape Germany just before the onset of the Holocaust. In America, Solomon's parents lead a meager existence and die while he is in college, leaving him rootless because all of their relatives perished in the concentration camps. Solomon seems to shut his painful past out of his life by marrying the Jewish debutante Ruth Lenski. However, his past intrudes on his present once he engages in an illicit affair with a patient, Katrina Volk, the daughter of a Nazi.

In his debut novel, *A Blessing on the Moon* (1997), Joseph Skibell, like Melvin Bukiet, journeys through his imagination to the European milieu of his forebears. However, whereas Bukiet tends to focus on the time just before the Holocaust (*Stories of an Imaginary Childhood*) or just after the atrocity (*After*), Skibell sets his sights squarely on the "during." Several Jewish American fiction writers, of course, have previously explored this terrain: Bellow's *Mr. Sammler's Planet* (1970), Edward Lewis Wallant's *The Pawnbroker* (1961), Ozick's *The Shawl* (1989). What sets *A Blessing on the Moon* apart from these works is Skibell's haunting depiction of his Jewish protagonist's tortured afterlife. By the time we reach the novel's second page, Chaim Skibelski (Skibell uses the name of his great-grandfather for his protagonist) has already been rounded up along with his fellow Jews and murdered by a Nazi firing squad. The rest of the novel details Skibelski's poignant search for an elusive World to Come. In one particularly powerful scene, Skibelski vents his pent up rage and claims his home from its usurpers by befouling it with the blood of his mangled corpse:

> The bleeding has begun again. There is apparently nothing I can do. . . . Instead of suffering politely and considerately this time, waiting for the wounds to drain, in the tub, for instance, or in the garage with my old car on top of the straw, I walk through the house, leaving trails in the hallways, through the rooms, on the staircases. . . . I open the kitchen drawers and shake my moistened sleeves over their utensils and their pots. My blood rains down in a vibrant cascade. May they eat with it in their mouths! (Skibell 18–19)

Lev Raphael, the son of Holocaust survivors, also grapples with the legacy of the Holocaust in his fiction, most notably in his award-winning collection of stories *Dancing on Tisha B'Av* (1990) and in his first novel, *Winter Eyes* (1992). Raphael's protagonists, however, must reckon with their identities as both gay and Jewish American children of Holocaust survivors. Ludger Brinker observes that "[w]hile other gay and lesbian Jews have attempted to reconcile their different roles and identities as Jews and gays and lesbians, Raphael's writing so far offers the single most articulate, sustained vision of how to enrich and balance the often opposing demands of the different aspects of one's personality" (297). Raphael's evocative depiction of the psychic wounds that dog Holocaust survivors and their children, and his adroit exploration of the rifts between these generations, represents the greatest strength of his fiction. The protagonist of "Fresh Air," for example, reflects poignantly on his particular tensions with his survivor parents: "So I was a child of necessity, of duty to the past, named not just for one lost relative but a whole family of cousins in Lublin: the Franks. Frank. My incongruously American first name was their memorial. Perhaps that explained my mother's distance, my father's rage—how could you be intimate or loving with a block of stone?" (Raphael 109). In "Inheritance," Raphael also powerfully evokes the tensions between survivor parents and their children as the protagonist (a child of Holocaust survivors) remembers intruding on his mother during a moment of grief and fear: "I crept down the hall to find her on her back on the gold-threaded overstuffed red couch. Her face was foreign, squeezed, and she moaned in what sounded like Russian. Beginning to cry, I poked at her leg and she rolled onto her side away from me. I ran to the bathroom to wash and wash my hands, as if they were stained by her fear" (187). The most powerful of Raphael's stories are the ones in which the Holocaust figures prominently, and both Ludger Brinker and Alan Berger have examined these stories in some detail (see Brinker's "Lev Raphael" Berger's *Children*).

The stories in *Dancing on Tisha B'Av* that engage gay issues more exclusively (e.g., "Remind Me to Smile," "Sanctuary," "The Prince and the Pauper") are also carefully crafted and often moving. However, although Brinker argues that Raphael's "best tales link Jewish and gay experiences, drawing connections between both" (298), I must admit that I recoil at some (though not all) of the connections that Raphael seeks to make between homophobia and anti-Semitism. For example, in "The Life You Have," the mother of a gay character succumbs to her husband's desire to have a child "because of all the lives lost in the war" (212). Raphael situates their parenthood in direct opposition to Hitler's effort to murder all of the world's Jews. Having done this, he proceeds to draw a parallel between the mother's homophobia and Nazism when, upon learning of her son's sexual orientation, she expresses her wish to obliterate his existence. Raphael thus enacts a narrative leveling, of sorts, between homophobia and Nazism. As Alan Berger argues, "Raphael is willing to indict the mother's homophobia no less than Nazism's murder of the Jews" (*Children* 112). Such leveling does justice neither to the Jewish victims of the Holocaust in Europe nor to the victims of antigay violence in present-day America. That said, Raphael dramatizes with considerable subtlety the homophobia of the mainstream Jewish American community, while managing to resist the temptation to conflate homophobia and Nazism in such stories as "Dancing on Tisha B'Av," "Caravans," and "Shouts of Joy," all collected in *Dancing on Tisha B'Av.*

For Lev Stollman and Harvey Grossinger (like Bukiet and Rosenbaum), the difficulty of imagining the Holocaust has become an inescapable subject rather than a creative impediment. Grossinger's debut collection, *The Quarry* (1997), winner of both the Edward Lewis Wallant Award and the Flannery O'Connor Award, represents one of the most aesthetically satisfying articulations of this emergent theme in Jewish American fiction. Through two collaborating and competing narrators (a father, Jacob, and his son, Mickey),

Grossinger tells essentially two stories in the title novella, "The Quarry": the story of the mysterious illness and tragic death of Eve, Jacob's wife and Mickey's mother, and the story of Esther Mermelstein and her son, Uriel—Holocaust survivors whose lives and fates intersect with the narrators' once they find themselves adrift in Jacob and Mickey's small Indiana town. As compelling as these stories are, Grossinger never allows the reader to forget that the novella is primarily about his narrators' *memories* concerning these events. "Nursed by intimate misfortunes," Jacob reflects, "our memories, it seems, have powerful lives of their own. . . . All I have left is my impoverished *memory* of what happened to my wife, and *that* is an illusive thing indeed" (Grossinger 179). Jacob's reflections concerning the simultaneous illusiveness and centrality of memory prepare us for the sections in which Jacob and Mickey (who slowly wrests control of the narrative) remember and, more precisely, reconstruct the Mermelsteins' story.

Grossinger takes pains to depict the Holocaust—including Esther Mermelstein's experiences in the camps—at full-arm's length through Mickey's rather than Jacob's perspective. It is a choice worth reflecting on because Jacob (who witnessed the suffering of Hitler's victims while serving in the U.S. military during the war) would seem the natural choice to narrate these sections. "The war in Europe," Mickey reflects, "first came to members of my generation from Fox Movietone Newsreels, then as lyricized history, the rarefied domain of professional historians, as sanitized as Gettysburg or Gallipoli, or the Punic Wars. But he [Jacob] was *there*" (185, emphasis in original). So why, one wonders, doesn't Grossinger allow Jacob to relate his experiences in Europe or to be the one to translate Esther's experiences? He doesn't, it becomes clear, because "The Quarry" is finally about Mickey's burdens as one who must grapple with the haunting strangeness of the Holocaust. It exists for him and for those of his generation, Grossinger implicitly argues, only through the treacherous imagination:

> My father said that when the Americans entered the camp they found masses of sick and dying people lying helpless or else roaming among the putrefying dead, bewildered skeletons in their gruesome, maggot-stained pajamas. He said the bodies were stacked like blackened cordwood. The mild spring breeze had the fragrance of burnt sandalwood and rotten meat, and the grass was waxed with blood. . . . His eyes as he told me all this were filled with urgency. (182)

Grossinger here renders a son's perceptions of his father's perceptions of the misery inflicted on the victims of the Holocaust. Mickey's insistence that he is giving his *father's* description of the concentration camp ("my father said," "he said," "his eyes") evokes the distance between the terrible event and Mickey's unreliable, thirdhand perception of that event. It is indeed difficult to determine where the father's account leaves off and the son's imaginative reconstruction of the father's account begins.

As the novella progresses, Mickey becomes more and more self-conscious as a narrator; he realizes that the imagination necessary to reconstruct the Mermelsteins' story threatens to usurp the events themselves. His tale, he realizes, is an "imperfect memoir," the product of "deficient recollections" (215). Rather than stifle his recollections, his discovery of the "blurry and ill-defined" line between "truth and distortion" liberates Mickey creatively, for he also realizes that "what we remembered about the past may, of course, be more *significant* than what had actually happened" (215). Armed with this knowledge, Mickey is free for the remainder of his narrative to retrieve what memories he can. Beholden not to what "actually happened," but to his own recollection of events, Mickey imagines Esther Mermelstein's experiences and even adopts her persona. It is a testament to Grossinger's technical proficiency that these italicized sections of the story emerge clearly as a projection of Mickey's imagination. When Esther challenges Father Rook's redemptive vision of the atrocity, for example—*"Father Rook—there was no protected place in the camps. . . . Informers were everywhere. Prisoners would bribe their torturers for a piece of dirty bread, for a frozen potato. I saw decent people betray their friends for some extra soup. Men smeared their lips with urine to ease their thirst"*—we know that it is really Mickey (and Grossinger) who is doing the challenging (229).

The sensitive young protagonist of Lev Stollman's debut novel, *The Far Euphrates* (1997), like Grossinger's Mickey, also struggles with the legacy of the increasingly nebulous Holocaust of his ancestors. Stollman deftly controls the narrative to evoke Alexander's complex interior life and its associated pain. In praise of Stollman's artistry, Alvin Rosenfeld notes "an alternating rhythm of contraction and expansion, the hidden and the disclosed, that runs delicately over the course of the narrative. . . . the substance of individual experience is incrementally shaped by a hidden, grievously burdened past" (16). Indeed, the secrets of the past that the sensitive Alexander uncovers (secrets I shall not reveal here) prove almost too much for him to bear. If he is to affirm a meaningful Jewish existence in the post-Holocaust world, he must first withdraw from the material world by tapping into the mythic past of Judaism: "I knew that at Creation, God performed *tzimtzum.* He withdrew into Himself, contracting His very being, and made within Himself an isolated place in which to set His universe—an infinite creation within an even greater infinity. There He organized all the attributes of His being in harmony. . . . This was something I then felt I needed to do for myself" (Stollman 140). Given the horror of the past, it is to Stollman's credit that the novel culminates with only an equivocal intimation of redemption.

In her debut novel, *The Romance Reader* (1995), Pearl Abraham, like Tova Reich, writes about ultra-Orthodox Jewish life as an insider particularly sensitive to its patriarchal mores. In the novel, Rachel Benjamin, faced with the prospect of a traditionally arranged marriage, struggles to reconcile her religious ardor and the love for her family and community with her creative and fiercely independent nature. In Rachel's Hasidic realm, speaking English (rather than Yiddish) and wearing sheer beige stockings count as small acts of rebellion, and she intensifies the rebellion by reading romance novels, to her parents' consternation. Power to Rachel means, among other things, being able to choose what to read and owning her own books. "One day," she reflects, "I will have my own bookcase. On my shelves I'll have at least one book for every letter of the alphabet, with room for more. They'll be my books. I'll build a bookcase like Father built" (Abraham 39). The novel unfolds as Rachel tests out several modes of existence both within and without the traditions of her Hasidic community.

Michael Chabon and Paul Hond engage a vastly different, secular Jewish American milieu in their work. If the implacable demands of the Jewish community burden Rachel Benjamin in *The Romance Reader,* it is the absence of a tangible Jewish community that leaves Chabon's secular Jews in *A Model World* (1991) emotionally adrift (not unlike Jonathan Rosen's characters). In "S Angel," Chabon's protagonist cringes at the dour, Conservative synagogue while attending his cousin's wedding, but nonetheless finds himself "awash in a nostalgic tedium, and he fell to wishing for irretrievable things" (Chabon 17). In his debut novel, *The Baker* (1998), Paul Hond explores the contemporary tensions between blacks and Jews in the inner-city, and offers readers an unflinching look at Jewish racism and black anti-Semitism. The novel recalls the gritty social realism of Bernard Malamud's fiction, especially *The Tenants* (1971) and "Black Is My Favorite Color," wherein Malamud engages black-Jewish relations as well. In Nelson Childs, Hond arguably manages to create the most fully realized black character in Jewish American fiction.

Finally, in *Tales out of School* (1995), Benjamin Taylor traces the immigration and assimilation of several generations of Mehmels in Galveston Island, Texas, artfully evoking a site of Jewish American existence largely unexplored by Jewish American fiction writers. Taylor's novel (like Allegra Goodman's early stories set in Hawaii) suggests how Jewish American writers are beginning, with unprecedented intensity, to look beyond the familiar urban environment of Jewish American fiction to engage largely untapped realms of the Jewish experience in America. "From up where clouds were packing," Taylor writes, "from up where heaven was, Galveston must only have looked like a ridge of marl. Or like a floating spar, flotsam of some wrack. But what is essential to say is that his place existed, that these people existed, and were in one another's keeping, and stood still in the lee of an instant" (282). Hear, hear!

The literary grandchildren of the postimmigrant Jewish American writers interestingly share the same aspirations as Rebecca Goldstein's Sasha and her fellow members of the Bilbul Art Theater in Warsaw: "How could there be time enough to touch it all, absorb it all, and then—yes—contribute something of one's own? A piece of the melody, an equation, a theory, a canvas—something of one's own that will make a difference . . . *something* to show that one is there, *there,* inhabiting the text itself, no longer stranded in the despair of those despicably narrow margins" (*Mazel* 202). I fear that the grandchildren will remain stranded in the narrow margins of our literary culture for as long as our current oppositional rather than inclusive multiculturalism holds sway. Contemporary Jewish American fiction writers simply lack the attentive audience that their literary grandparents enjoyed, even as they continue to create a body of work that is larger, more diverse, and ultimately richer than the canon of Jewish American fiction has ever been. Which brings to mind a more economical reply to those who question the full-time study of Jewish American fiction writers: it is, quite simply, a full-time job, one worthy of the effort and one that currently has plenty of openings and opportunities for advancement. Reader, please apply.

A Selected Reading List of Contemporary Jewish American Fiction

Works Cited

Index

A Selected Reading List of Contemporary Jewish American Fiction

Novels and Short Story Collections

Abraham, Pearl. *Giving Up America.* New York: Riverhead, 1998.

———. *The Romance Reader.* 1995. Reprint. New York: Riverhead Books, 1996.

Apple, Max. *Free Agents.* New York: HarperCollins, 1984.

Bellow, Saul. *The Actual.* New York: Viking, 1997.

———. *Ravelstein.* New York: Viking, 2000.

Black, David. *An Impossible Life: A Novel, a Bobeh Myseh.* New York: Moyer Bell, 1998.

Bloom, Steven. *No New Jokes.* New York: W. W. Norton, 1997.

Bukiet, Melvin Jules. *After.* New York: St. Martin's, 1996.

———. *Signs and Wonders.* New York: Picador, 1999.

———. *Stories of an Imaginary Childhood.* 1991. Reprint. Evanston, Ill.: Northwestern Univ. Press, 1992.

———. *While the Messiah Tarries.* 1995. Reprint. Syracuse, N.Y.: Syracuse Univ. Press, 1997.

Chabon, Michael. *A Model World.* New York: William Morrow, 1991.

———. *The Wonder Boys.* New York: Villard Books, 1995.

Clayton, John J. *Radiance.* Columbus: Ohio State Univ. Press, 1998.

Cohen, Robert. *The Here and Now.* New York: Scribner, 1996.

———. *The Organ Builder.* 1988. Reprint. New York: Perennial Library, 1989.

Elkin, Stanley. *Mrs. Ted Bliss.* New York: Hyperion, 1995.

Englander, Nathan. *For the Relief of Unbearable Urges.* New York: Alfred A. Knopf, 1999.

Epstein, Leslie. *King of the Jews: A Novel of the Holocaust.* New York: Coward, McCann, and Geoghegan, 1979.

Feld, Ross. *Zwilling's Dream.* Washington, D.C.: Counterpoint, 1999.

Goldstein, Rebecca. *Mazel.* New York: Viking Penguin, 1995.

———. *The Mind-Body Problem.* New York: Dell, 1983.

———. *Strange Attractors.* New York: Viking Penguin, 1993.

Goodman, Allegra. *The Family Markowitz.* New York: Farrar, Straus and Giroux, 1996.
——. *Kaaterskill Falls.* New York: Dial, 1998.
——. *Total Immersion.* New York: Harper, 1989.
Grossinger, Harvey. *The Quarry.* Athens: Univ. of Georgia Press, 1997.
Havazelet, Ehud. *Like Never Before.* New York: Farrar, Straus and Giroux, 1998.
Henkin, Joshua. *Swimming Across the Hudson.* New York: G. P. Putnam's Sons, 1997.
Hershman, Marcie. *Safe in America: A Novel.* New York: HarperCollins, 1995.
Hoffman, Allen. *Small Worlds.* New York: Abbeville, 1996.
Hond, Paul. *The Baker.* New York: Random House, 1997.
Kaplan, Johanna. *O My America!* 1980. Reprint. Syracuse, N.Y.: Syracuse Univ. Press, 1995.
Lerman, Rhoda. *God's Ear.* 1989. Reprint. Syracuse, N.Y.: Syracuse Univ. Press, 1997.
Leviant, Curt. *The Man Who Thought He Was Messiah.* Philadelphia: Jewish Publication Society, 1990.
Merkin, Daphne. *Enchantment.* New York: Harcourt Brace, 1986.
Mirvis, Tova. *The Ladies Auxiliary.* New York: W. W. Norton, 1999.
Nattel, Lilian. *The River Midnight.* New York: Scribner, 1999.
Neugeboren, Jay. *The Stolen Jew.* 1981. Reprint. Syracuse, N.Y.: Syracuse Univ. Press, 1998.
Nissenson, Hugh. *The Elephant and My Jewish Problem: Selected Stories and Journals.* New York: HarperCollins, 1988.
Ozick, Cynthia. *The Messiah of Stockholm.* 1986. Reprint. New York: Vintage, 1988.
——. *The Puttermesser Papers.* New York: Knopf, 1997.
——. *The Shawl.* 1989. New York: Vintage, 1990.
Pollack, Eileen. *Paradise, New York.* Philadelphia: Temple Univ. Press, 1998.
Raphael, Lev. *Dancing on Tisha B'Av.* New York: St. Martin's, 1991.
Rapoport, Nessa. *Preparing for Sabbath.* 1981. Reprint. New York: Biblio, 1988.
Reich, Tova. *The Jewish War.* 1995. Reprint. Syracuse, N.Y.: Syracuse Univ. Press, 1997.
——. *Mara.* New York: Farrar, Straus and Giroux, 1978.
——. *Master of the Return.* 1988. Reprint. Syracuse, N.Y.: Syracuse Univ. Press, 1999.
Roiphe, Anne. *Lovingkindness.* 1987. Reprint. New York: Warner, 1989.
——. *The Pursuit of Happiness.* New York: Summit, 1991.
Rosen, Jonathan. *Eve's Apple.* New York: Random House, 1997.
Rosenbaum, Thane. *Elijah Visible.* New York: St. Martin's, 1996.
——. *Second Hand Smoke.* New York: St. Martin's, 1999.
Roth, Philip. *American Pastoral.* New York: Houghton Mifflin, 1997.
——. *The Counterlife.* 1986. New York: Vintage, 1996.
——. *The Human Stain.* New York: Houghton Mifflin, 2000.
——. *I Married a Communist.* New York: Houghton Mifflin, 1998.

——. *Operation Shylock: A Confession.* 1993. Reprint. New York: Vintage, 1994.
——. *Sabbath's Theater.* 1995. Reprint. New York: Vintage, 1996.
Schulman, Helen. *The Revisionist.* New York: Crown, 1998.
Schwartz, Lynne Sharon. *Disturbances in the Field.* 1983. New York: Bantam Doubleday, 1985.
Segal, Lore. *Her First American.* 1985. Reprint. New York: New Press, 1994.
Shapiro, Dani. *Picturing the Wreck.* 1996. Reprint. New York: Plume, 1997.
Shapiro, Gerald. *Bad Jews.* Cambridge, Mass.: Zoland Books, 1999.
——. *From Hunger.* Columbia.: Univ. of Missouri Press, 1993.
Shomer, Enid. *Imaginary Men.* Iowa City: Univ. of Iowa Press, 1993.
Skibell, Joseph. *A Blessing on the Moon.* New York: Algonquin, 1997.
Stern, Steve. *Lazar Malkin Enters Heaven.* 1986. Reprint. Syracuse, N.Y.: Syracuse Univ. Press, 1995.
——. *A Plague of Dreamers: Three Novellas.* 1994. Reprint. Syracuse, N.Y.: Syracuse Univ. Press, 1997.
——. *The Wedding Jester.* Saint Paul: Graywolf, 1999.
Stollman, Aryeh Lev. *The Far Euphrates.* New York: Riverhead, 1997.
Taylor, Benjamin. *Tales out of School.* 1995. Reprint. New York: Warner, 1997.

Anthologies

Bukiet, Melvin, ed. *Neurotica: Jewish Writers on Sex.* New York: W. W. Norton, 1999.
Raz, Hilda, ed. *The Prairie Schooner Anthology of Contemporary Jewish American Writing.* Lincoln and London: Univ. of Nebraska Press, 1998.
Shapiro, Gerald, ed. *American Jewish Fiction: A Century of Stories.* Lincoln and London: Univ. of Nebraska Press, 1998.
Solotaroff, Ted, and Nessa Rapoport, eds. *Writing Our Way Home: Contemporary Stories by American Jewish Writers.* New York: Schocken, 1992. Reprinted as *The Schocken Book of Contemporary Jewish Fiction.* New York: Schocken, 1996.
Stavans, Ilan, ed. *The Oxford Book of Jewish Stories.* New York: Oxford Univ. Press, 1998.

Works Cited

Abraham, Pearl. *The Romance Reader.* New York: Riverhead, 1995.

Allen, Walter. Afterword to *Call It Sleep,* by Henry Roth. 1934. Reprint. New York: Avon Books, 1962, 442–47.

Allen, Woody. "Am I Reading the Papers Correctly?" *New York Times* 28 Jan. 1988: A27.

Alter, Robert. "Confronting the Holocaust: Three Israeli Novels." *Commentary,* Mar. (1966): 67–73.

——. "Defenders of the Faith." *Commentary,* July (1987): 52–55.

——. "The Jewish Voice." *Commentary,* Oct. (1995): 39–45.

Baumgarten, Murray. *City Scriptures: Modern Jewish Writing.* Cambridge, Mass.: Harvard Univ. Press, 1982.

Beck, Evelyn Torton. "Jews and the Multicultural University Curriculum." In *The Narrow Bridge: Jewish Views on Multiculturalism,* edited by Marla Brettschneider, 163–77. New Brunswick, N.J.: Rutgers Univ. Press, 1996.

Bellow, Saul. *Herzog.* 1964. Reprint. New York: Viking Penguin, 1996.

——. *The Victim.* 1947. Reprint. New York: Penguin, 1988.

Berger, Alan L. "American Jewish Fiction." *Modern Judaism* 10 (1990): 221–41.

——. "Ashes and Hope." In *Reflections of the Holocaust in Art and Literature,* edited by Randolph L. Braham, 97–116. New York: Columbia Univ. Press, 1990.

——. "Bearing Witness." *Modern Judaism* 10 (1990): 43–63.

——. *Children of Job: American Second-Generation Witnesses to the Holocaust.* Albany: State Univ. of New York Press, 1997.

——. *Crisis and Covenant: The Holocaust in American Jewish Fiction.* Albany, N.Y.: State Univ. of New York Press, 1985.

——. "Memory and Meaning." In *Methodology in the Academic Teaching of the Holocaust,* edited by Zev Garber, Alan L. Berger, and Richard Libowitz. Lanham, Md.: Univ. Press of America, 1988.

Bershtel, Sara, and Allen Graubard. *Saving Remnants: Feeling Jewish in America.* New York: Free Press, 1992.

Biale, David. "The Melting Pot and Beyond: Jews and the Politics of American Identity." In *Insider/Outsider: American Jews and Multiculturalism,* edited by David Biale, Michael Galchinsky, and Susannah Heschel, 17–33. Berkeley and Los Angeles: Univ. of California Press, 1998.

Biale, David, Michael Galchinsky, and Susannah Heschel. "Introduction: The Dialectic of Jewish Enlightenment." In *Insider/Outsider: American Jews and Multiculturalism,* edited by David Biale, Michael Galchinsky, and Susannah Heschel, 1–13. Berkeley and Los Angeles: Univ. of California Press, 1998.

Birkets, Sven. "Mapping the New Reality." *Wilson Quarterly* 16, no. 2 (spring 1992): 102–10.

Boyers, Robert. Review of *American Pastoral,* by Philip Roth. *New Republic,* 7 July 1997: 36–41.

Brawarsky, Sandee. "Rebecca Goldstein: Mining Intellectual Dilemmas." *Publisher's Weekly,* 23 Oct. 1995: 48–49.

Brinker, Ludger. "Lev Raphael." In *Contemporary Jewish-American Novelists: A Bio-Critical Sourcebook,* edited by Joel Shatzky and Michael Taub, 295–304. Westport, Conn.: Greenwood, 1997.

Brown, Rosellen. "What's New in American Jewish Writing." In *The Writer in the Jewish Community: An Israeli–North American Dialogue,* edited by Richard Siegel and Tamar Sofer, 77–84. Cranbury, N.J.: Associated Univ. Presses, 1993.

Bukiet, Melvin Jules. *After.* New York: St. Martin's, 1996.

——. "Looking at Roth; or 'I Always Wanted You to Admire My Hookshot.'" *Studies in American Jewish Literature* 12 (1993): 122–25.

——. "Master of the Bad Name." Review of *Sabbath's Theater,* by Philip Roth. *Tikkun* Sept.–Oct. (1995): 84–86.

——. *Stories of an Imaginary Childhood.* 1991. Reprint. Evanston, Ill.: Northwestern Univ. Press, 1992.

——. *While the Messiah Tarries.* New York: Harcourt Brace, 1995.

Burch, C. Beth. "Allegra Goodman (1967–)." In *Jewish-American Women Writers,* edited by Ann R. Shapiro, Sara R. Horowitz, Ellen Schiff, and Miryam Glazer, 88–94. Westport: Greenwood, 1994.

Cahan, Abraham. *The Rise of David Levinsky.* New York: Harper and Row, 1917.

Chabon, Michael. *A Model World, and Other Stories.* New York: William Morrow, 1991.

Chertok, Haim. "My American Problem . . . and Ours." *Israeli Preoccupations,* 185–89. New York: Fordham Univ. Press, 1994.

Cheyette, Bryan. "Within the Borders." Review of *Stories of an Imaginary Childhood,* by Melvin Jules Bukiet. *Times Literary Supplement,* 26 June 1992, 21.

Chicago Cultural Studies Group. "Critical Multiculturalism." In *Multiculturalism: A*

Critical Reader, edited by David Theo Goldberg, 107–39. Oxford: Basil Blackwell, 1994.

Cohen, Arthur A. "Nathaniel West's Holy Fool." In *An Arthur A. Cohen Reader: Selected Fiction and Writings on Judaism, Theology, Literature, and Culture,* edited by David Stern and Paul Mendes-Flohr, 447–52. Detriot: Wayne State Univ. Press, 1998.

Cohen, Robert. *The Here and Now.* New York: Scribner, 1996.

——. *The Organ Builder.* 1988. Reprint. New York: Perennial Library, 1989.

Cooper, Alan. *Philip Roth and the Jews.* Albany: State Univ. of New York Press, 1996.

Dickstein, Morris. "Dybbuks in Dixie." Review of *Lazar Malkin Enters Heaven,* by Steve Stern. *New York Times Book Review,* 1 Mar. 1987, 11.

Emerson, Ralph Waldo. "The American Scholar." In *Selected Writings of Emerson,* edited by Donald McQuade, 45–63. New York: Modern Library, 1981.

Epstein, Joseph. "America Is Where the Action Is . . ." *Forward,* 21 Aug. 1998: 11–12.

Felman, Jyl Lynn. "If Only I'd Been Born a Kosher Chicken." In *Nice Jewish Girls: Growing Up in America,* edited by Marlene Adler Marks, 83–87. New York: Penguin, 1996.

Feingold, Henry L. "American Zionism *In Extremis?*" *Midstream,* June/July (1994): 22–25.

Fiedler, Leslie. *Fiedler on the Roof: Essays on Literature and Jewish Identity.* 1991. Reprint. Boston: Godine, 1992.

Field, Leslie. "Israel Revisited in American Jewish Literature." *Midstream,* Nov. (1982): 50–54.

Finkelstein, Norman. "Nostalgia and Futurity: Jewish Literature in Transition." In *The Ritual of New Creation: Jewish Tradition and Contemporary Literature,* 127–40. Albany, N.Y.: State Univ. of New York Press, 1992.

Fishman, Sylvia Barack. "Rebecca Goldstein (1950–)." In *Jewish American Women Writers: A Bio-Bibliographical and Critical Sourcebook,* edited by Ann R. Shapiro, 80–87. Westport, Conn.: Greenwood, 1994.

Franzen, Jonathan. "Perchance to Dream." *Harper's,* Apr. (1996): 35–54.

Friedman, Thomas L. *From Beirut to Jerusalem.* 1989. Reprint. New York: Doubleday, 1990.

Frosch, Mary. Preface to *Coming of Age in America: A Multicultural Anthology,* edited by Mary Frosch. New York: New Press, 1994.

Gates, Henry Louis, Jr. "Goodbye, Columbus? Notes on the Culture of Criticism." *American Literary History* 3 (1991): 711–27.

Gilman, Sander L. "Introduction: Ethnicity-Ethnicities-Literature-Literatures." *PMLA* 113, no. 1 (Jan. 1998): 19–27.

Golan, Matti. *With Friends Like You: What Israelis Really Think about American Jews.* Translated by Hillel Halkin. New York: Free Press, 1992.

Goldstein, Rebecca. "Looking Back at Lot's Wife." *Commentary,* Sept. (1992): 37–41.

——. *Mazel.* New York: Viking Penguin, 1995.

——. *The Mind-Body Problem.* New York: Dell, 1983.

——. *Strange Attractors.* New York: Viking Penguin, 1993.

——. "Writing the Second Novel: A Symposium." *New York Times Book Review,* 17 Mar. 1985, 1, 40, 41, 43.

Goodman, Allegra. *The Family Markowitz.* New York: Farrar, Straus and Giroux, 1996.

——. "Writing Jewish Fiction in and out of the Multicultural Context." In *Daughters of Valor: Contemporary Jewish American Women Writers,* edited by Jay L. Halio and Ben Siegel, 268–74. Newark, N.J.: Univ. of Delaware Press, 1997.

Green, Daniel. Review of *A Plague of Dreamers,* by Steve Stern. *Georgia Review* 49 (winter 1995): 960–67.

Grossinger, Harvey. *The Quarry.* Athens: Univ. of Georgia Press, 1997.

Hadda, Janet. "Ashkenaz on the Mississippi." *YIVO Annual* 19 (1990): 93–103.

Halio, Jay. Review of *From Hunger,* by Gerald Shapiro. *Studies in Short Fiction* 31, no. 4 (1994): 703–4.

Halkin, Hillel. "How to Read Philip Roth." *Commentary,* Feb. (1994): 43–48.

Hertzberg, Arthur. *The Jews in America: Four Centuries of an Uneasy Encounter, A History.* New York: Simon and Schuster, 1989.

Hicks, Granville. "One Man to Stand for Six Million." *Saturday Review,* 10 Sept. 1966: 37–39.

Hollinger, David. *Postethnic America: Beyond Multiculturalism.* New York: Basic, 1995.

Hond, Paul. *The Baker.* New York: Random House, 1997.

Horowitz, Sara R. "The Paradox of Jewish Studies in the New Academy." In *Insider/Outsider: American Jews and Multiculturalism,* edited by David Biale, Michael Galchinsky, and Susannah Heschel, 116–30. Berkeley and Los Angeles: Univ. of California Press, 1998.

Howe, Irving. "American Jews and Israel." *Tikkun,* May/June (1989): 71–74.

——. Introduction to *Jewish American Stories,* edited by Irving Howe, 1–17. New York: NAL Penguin, 1977.

——. "Philip Roth Reconsidered." *Commentary,* Dec. (1972): 69–77.

Howe, Irving, and Eliezer Greenberg. Introduction to *A Treasury of Yiddish Stories,* edited by Irving Howe and Eliezer Greenberg, 1–71. 1954. Reprint. New York: Penguin, 1990.

Hughes, Robert. *The Culture of Complaint: The Fraying of America.* New York: Oxford Univ. Press, 1993.

Jay, Gregory S. "Jewish Writers in a Multicultural Literature Class." *Heath Anthology of American Literature Newsletter* 16 (fall 1997): 8–9, 11.

——. "Taking Multiculturalism Personally." In *American Literature and the Culture Wars,* 103–35. Ithaca and London: Cornell Univ. Press, 1997.

Kakutani, Michiko. Review of *American Pastoral,* by Philip Roth. *New York Times* 15 Apr. 1997, B1.

——. "Through Life and Strife, the Tales of a Family." Review of *The Family Markowitz,* by Allegra Goodman. *New York Times* 22 Oct. 1996, B2.

Kauvar, Elaine M. "Introduction: Some Reflections on Contemporary American Jewish Culture." *Contemporary Literature* 34, no. 3 (fall 1993): 337–57.

Kazin, Alfred. *Writing Was Everything.* Cambridge, Mass.: Harvard Univ. Press, 1995.

Kertzer, Rabbi Morris N. *What Is a Jew?* Revised by Rabbi Lawrence A. Hoffman. 1953. Reprint. New York: Collier, 1993.

Klingenstein, Susanne. "Destructive Intimacy: The Shoah Between Mother and Daughter in Fictions by Cynthia Ozick, Norma Rosen, and Rebecca Goldstein." *Studies in American Jewish Literature* 11, no. 2 (fall 1992): 162–73.

——. "Visits to Germany in Recent Jewish-American Writing." *Contemporary Literature* 34, no. 3 (fall 1993): 538–70.

Klinghoffer, David. "What Do American Jews Believe?" *Commentary,* Aug. (1996): 55–57.

Knippling, Alpana Sharma, ed. *New Immigrant Literatures in the United States: A Sourcebook to Our Multicultural Literary Heritage.* Westport, Conn.: Greenwood, 1996.

Kremer, S. Lillian. "Post-Alienation: Recent Directions in Jewish-American Literature." *Contemporary Literature* 34, no. 3 (fall 1993): 571–91.

——. *Witness Through the Imagination: Jewish American Holocaust Literature.* Detroit, Mich.: Wayne State Univ. Press, 1989.

Krupnick, Mark. "Jewish-American Literature." In *New Immigrant Literatures in the United States: A Sourcebook to Our Multicultural Literary Heritage,* edited by Alpana Sharma Knippling, 295–308. Westport, Conn: Greenwood, 1996.

——. "New Writers, Old Stories." Review of *Writing Our Way Home: Contemporary Stories by American Jewish Writers,* edited by Ted Solotaroff and Nessa Rapoport. *Forward Books,* 6 Nov. 1992: 14.

Langer, Lawrence L. "Home, Before Dark." Review of *Stories of an Imaginary Childhood,* by Melvin Jules Bukiet. *Tikkun,* Nov.–Dec. (1994): 75, 79.

Lauter, Paul, ed. *The Heath Anthology of American Literature.* Vol. 2. 2d ed. Lexington, Mass: D. C. Heath, 1994.

——. "The Literatures of America: A Comparative Discipline." In *Redefining American Literary History,* edited by A. LaVonne Brown Ruoff and Jerry W. Ward Jr., 9–34. New York: MLA, 1990.

Lester, Julius. "The Lives People Live." In *Blacks and Jews: Alliances and Arguments,* edited by Paul Berman, 164–77. New York: Delacorte, 1994.

Marcus, Amy Dockser. "American Jews Grapple with an Identity Crisis as Peril to Israel Ebbs." *Wall Street Journal* 14 Sept. 1994: A1, A4.

Menand, Louis. Review of *American Pastoral,* by Philip Roth. *New Yorker,* 19 May 1997: 88–94.

Merkin, Daphne. "Philip Roth's Diasporism: A Symposium." *Tikkun,* May–June (1993): 41–45, 73.

Naylor, Gloria. *Bailey's Café.* 1992. Reprint. New York: Vintage Books, 1993.

Ozick, Cynthia. "The Art of Fiction XCV." *Paris Review* 29 (1987): 155–90.

——. "Innovation and Redemption: What Literature Means." In *Art & Ardor,* 238–48. New York: Knopf, 1983.

——. "An Interview with Cynthia Ozick." Interview by Elaine M. Kauvar. *Contemporary Literature* 34, no. 3 (fall 1993): 359–94.

——. "Literature as Idol: Harold Bloom." In *Art & Ardor,* 178–99. New York: Knopf, 1983.

——. "'Making Our Way Back to the Mother Ship.'" *Forward* 14 (Nov. 1995): 11–13.

——. "The Pagan Rabbi." 1971. Reprinted in *The Pagan Rabbi and Other Stories,* 1–38. Syracuse, N.Y.: Syracuse Univ. Press, 1995.

——. "Toward a New Yiddish." In *Art & Ardor,* 154–77. New York: Knopf, 1983.

Pack, Robert, and Jay Parini, eds. *American Identities: Contemporary Multicultural Voices.* Hanover, N.H.: Middlebury College Press, 1994.

Peretz, I. L. "Bontshe Shvayg." 1894. Reprinted in *The I. L. Peretz Reader,* edited by Ruth R. Wisse, 146–52. New York: Schocken, 1990.

Pinsker, Sanford. "Dares, Double-Dares, and the Jewish-American Writer." *Prairie Schooner* 71, no. 1 (spring 1997): 278–85.

——. "Earthly Brushes with the Eternal." Review of *While the Messiah Tarries,* by Melvin Jules Bukiet. *Midstream,* Aug.–Sept. (1995): 44.

——. "Jewish Novelists: The Next Generation." *Reform Judaism* (spring 1997): 64–66.

——. "Jews, Jewish Traditions, and the Disarming Individual Artist." Review of *Total Immersion,* by Allegra Goodman. *Forward* 8 (Dec. 1989): 8.

——. "The Lives and Deaths of Nathan Zuckerman." Review of *The Counterlife,* by Philip Roth. *Midstream,* June–July (1987): 52–54.

——. "Satire, Social Realism, and Moral Seriousness: The Case of Allegra Goodman." *Studies in American Jewish Literature* 11, no. 2 (1992): 182–84.

——. *The Schlemiel as Metaphor: Studies in the Yiddish and American Jewish Novel.* Carbondale and Edwardsville: Southern Illinois Univ. Press, 1971.

Plaskow, Judith. *Standing Again at Sinai: Judaism from a Feminist Perspective.* 1990. Reprint. New York: HarperCollins, 1991.

Podhoretz, Norman. "A Statement on the Peace Process." *Commentary,* April (1993): 19–23.

Potok, Chaim. "A Conversation with Chaim Potok." Interview by S. Lillian Kremer. In *Dictionary of Literary Biography Yearbook: 1984,* edited by Jean W. Ross, 83–87. Detroit: Gale, 1985.

——. "The Invisible Map of Meaning: A Writer's Confrontations." *Tri-Quarterly* 84 (spring–summer 1992): 17–45.

Prager, Dennis, and Joseph Telushkin. *The Nine Questions People Ask about Judaism.* New York: Simon and Schuster, 1981.

Pritchard, William H. "Roth Unbound." Review of *Sabbath's Theater,* by Philip Roth. *New York Times Book Review,* 10 Sept. 1995, 6, 9.

Quint, Alyssa P. "Bearing the Weight: A Plea for Jewish Literacy." *Response* 65 (winter–spring 1996): 23–29.

Raphael, Lev. *Dancing on Tisha B'Av.* New York: St. Martin's, 1991.

Rapoport, Nessa. "Afterword: The Jewish Writer Unmasked." In *The Writer in the Jewish Community: An Israeli–North American Dialogue,* edited by Richard Siegel and Tamar Sofer, 142–47. Cranbury, N.J.: Associated University Presses, 1993.

——. "Summoned to the Feast." In *Writing Our Way Home: Contemporary Stories by American Jewish Writers,* edited by Ted Solotaroff and Nessa Rapoport, xxvii–xxx. New York: Schocken, 1992.

——. "Text, Language, and the Hope of Redemption." In *The Writer in the Jewish Community: An Israeli–North American Dialogue,* edited by Richard Siegel and Tamar Sofer, 41–44. Cranbury, N.J.: Associated University Presses, 1993.

Review of *The Organ Builder,* by Robert Cohen. *Antioch Review* 47 (winter 1989): 115.

Revel, Hirschel. "Schlemiel." In *The Universal Jewish Encyclopedia,* 115. New York: Ktav, 1943.

Rogoff, Jay. "Hymn to Dreams and Fallibility." Review of *Harry Kaplan's Adventures Underground,* by Steve Stern. *Sewanee Review* 101 (winter 1993): xxx–xxxii.

Roiphe, Anne. *Generation Without Memory: A Jewish Journey in Christian America.* New York: Simon and Schuster, 1981.

Rosen, Jonathan. *Eve's Apple.* New York: Random House, 1997.

Rosen, Norma. "'Making Our Way Back to the Mother Ship.'" *Forward,* 14 Nov. 1995: 11–13.

Rosenbaum, Thane. *Elijah Visible.* New York: St. Martin's, 1996.

——. *Second Hand Smoke.* New York: St. Martin's, 1999.

Rosenfeld, Alvin. "Two Mystical First Novels Haunted by Visions of Evil." Review of *A Blessing on the Moon,* by Joseph Skibell, and *The Far Euphrates,* by Aryeh Lev Stollman. *Forward,* 31 Oct. 1997: 15–16.

Roth, Henry. *Call It Sleep.* 1934. Reprint. New York: Farrar, Straus and Giroux, 1991.

Roth, Philip. *American Pastoral.* New York: Houghton, Mifflin, 1997.

——. "A Bit of Jewish Mischief." *New York Times Book Review,* 7 Mar. 1993, 1, 20.

——. *The Breast.* New York: Holt, Rinehart, and Winston, 1972.

——. *The Counterlife.* 1986. Reprint. New York: Viking, 1988.

——. "Eli, the Fanatic." In *Goodbye, Columbus,* 180–216. 1959. Reprint. New York: Bantam, 1970.

——. *The Ghost Writer.* New York: Farrar, Straus and Giroux, 1979.

——. "'I Always Wanted You to Admire My Fasting'; or, Looking at Kafka." 1973. Reprinted in *Reading Myself and Others,* 303–26. New York: Farrar, Straus and Giroux, 1975. Reprint. New York: Penguin, 1985.

——. "An Interview with Philip Roth." Interview by Asher Z. Milbauer and Donald G. Watson. In *Conversations with Philip Roth,* edited by George J. Searles, 242–53. Jackson: Univ. Press of Mississippi, 1992.

——. "The NBA Winner Talks Back." Interview by Martha McGregor. In *Conversations with Philip Roth,* edited by George J. Searles, 1–2. Jackson: Univ. Press of Mississippi, 1992.

——. *Operation Shylock: A Confession.* New York: Simon and Schuster, 1993.

——. *Sabbath's Theater.* New York: Houghton Mifflin, 1995.

——. "Writing about Jews." In *Reading Myself and Others,* 205–25. 1975. Reprint. New York: Penguin, 1985.

Rothchild, Sylvia. Review of *Total Immersion,* by Allegra Goodman. *Jewish Advocate,* July (1989): 16.

Rothstein, Mervyn. "To Newark, with Love. Philip Roth." In *Conversations with Philip Roth,* edited by George J. Searles, 274–79. Jackson: Univ. Press of Mississippi, 1992.

Ruoff, A. LaVonne Brown, and Jerry W. Ward Jr., eds. *Redefining American Literary History.* New York: MLA, 1990.

Seebohm, Caroline. "Husbands, Lovers, and Parents." Review of *The Mind-Body Problem,* by Rebecca Goldstein, and of *Nights in Aruba,* by Andrew Holleran. *New York Times Book Review,* 25 Sept. 1983, 14, 30.

Shapiro, Dani. *Picturing the Wreck.* 1996. Reprint. New York: Plume, 1997.

Shapiro, Gerald. *From Hunger.* Columbia: Univ. of Missouri Press, 1993.

Shechner, Mark. "Is This Picasso, or Is It the Jews?" *Tikkun,* Nov.–Dec. (1997): 39–41.

——. "Steve Stern." In *Contemporary Jewish-American Novelists: A Bio-Critical Sourcebook,* edited by Joel Shatzky and Michael Taub, 414–21. Westport, Conn.: Greenwood, 1997.

——. "Zuckerman's Travels." *American Literary History* 1 (1989): 219–30.

Silverman, Hilda. "Palestinian Holocaust Memorial?" *Palestinian Perspectives,* Sept./Oct. (1988): 4.

Simonson, Rick, and Scott Walker, eds. *The Graywolf Annual Five: Multi-Cultural Literacy.* St. Paul: Graywolf, 1988.

Singer, I. B. "Gimpel the Fool." 1954. Reprinted in *The Collected Stories of Isaac Bashevis Singer,* 3–14. New York: Farrar, Straus and Giroux, 1981.

Skibell, Joseph. *A Blessing on the Moon.* New York: Algonquin, 1997.

Sokoloff, Naomi. "Imagining Israel in American Jewish Fiction: Anne Roiphe's *Lov-*

ingkindness and Philip Roth's *The Counterlife*." *Studies in American Jewish Literature* 10 (1991): 65–80.

Sollors, Werner. *Beyond Ethnicity: Consent and Descent in American Culture*. New York: Oxford Univ. Press, 1986.

Solotaroff, Ted. "American Jewish Writers: On Edge Once More." *New York Times Book Review*, 18 Dec. 1988, 1, 31, 33.

——. "The Open Community." In *Writing Our Way Home: Contemporary Stories by American Jewish Writers*, edited by Ted Solotaroff and Nessa Rapoport, xiii–xxvi. New York: Schocken Books, 1992.

——. "Philip Roth and the Jewish Moralists." *Chicago Review* 8 (1959): 87–99.

Sonenberg, Nina. "In Short." Review of *The Organ Builder*, by Robert Cohen. *New York Times Book Review*, 25 Sept. 1988, 30.

Staub, Michael E. "The Shoah Goes On and On: Remembrance and Representation in Art Spiegelman's *Maus*." *MELUS* 20, no. 3 (fall 1995): 33–46.

Stern, Gerald. "Behaving Like a Jew." In *Lucky Life*, 55–56. Boston: Houghton Mifflin, 1977.

Stern, Steve. "After the Law." *Tikkun*, Nov.–Dec. (1997): 47–48, 76.

——. "A Brief Account of a Long Way Home." *YIVO Annual* 19 (1990): 81–91.

——. *Lazar Malkin Enters Heaven*. New York: Viking, 1986.

——. *A Plague of Dreamers: Three Novellas*. New York: Scribner's, 1994.

——. "Stern un Ikh, or Ambushed by Jewishness." *Tikkun*, Sept.–Oct. (1994): 51–52, 94.

——. "The Tale of a Kite." *Reform Judaism* (spring 1997): 68–75.

Stollman, Aryeh Lev. *The Far Euphrates*. New York: Riverhead, 1997.

Strandberg, Victor. *Greek Mind/Jewish Soul: The Conflicted Art of Cynthia Ozick*. Madison: Univ. of Wisconsin Press, 1994.

Sumida, Stephen H. "Centers Without Margins: Responses to Centrism in Asian American Literature." *American Literature* 66, no. 4 (1994): 803–15.

Talese, Gay. "The Italian-American Voice: Where Is It?" In *American Identities: Contemporary Multicultural Writers*, edited by Robert Pack and Jay Parini, 311–21. Hanover: Middlebury College Press, 1994.

Taliaferro, Frances. Review of *The Mind-Body Problem*, by Rebecca Goldstein. *Harper's*, Dec. (1983): 74–75.

Taylor, Benjamin. *Tales out of School*. New York: Turtle Point, 1995.

Teicher, Morton I. "Act Three." Review of *Sabbath's Theater*, by Philip Roth. *Midstream*, Jan. (1996): 45–46.

Trilling, Lionel. *The Liberal Imagination*. Garden City, N.Y.: Doubleday, 1953.

Ross, Jean W. "Steve Stern." In *Contemporary Authors*, vol. 132, edited by Susan M. Trosky, 402–6. Detroit: Gale Research, 1991.

Walzer, Michael. "Multiculturalism and the Politics of Interest." In *Insider/Outsider: American Jews and Multiculturalism,* edited by David Biale, Michael Galchinsky, and Susannah Heschel, 88–98. Berkeley and Los Angeles: Univ. of California Press, 1998.

Waters, Mary C. *Ethnic Options: Choosing Identities in America.* Berkeley and Los Angeles: Univ. of California Press, 1990.

Wirth-Nesher, Hana. "Defining the Indefinable: What Is Jewish Literature?" Introduction to *What Is Jewish Literature?* edited by Hana Wirth-Nesher, 3–12. Philadelphia: Jewish Publication Society, 1994.

———. "From Newark to Prague: Roth's Place in the American Jewish Literary Tradition." In *What Is Jewish Literature?* edited by Hana Wirth-Nesher, 216–229. Philadelphia: Jewish Publication Society, 1994.

———. "Language as Homeland in Jewish-American Literature." In *Insider/Outsider: American Jews and Multiculturalism,* edited by David Biale, Michael Galchinsky, and Susannah Heschel, 212–30. Berkeley and Los Angeles: Univ. of California Press, 1998.

Wisse, Ruth R. "American Jewish Writing, Act II." *Commentary,* June (1976): 40–45.

———. Introduction to *The I. L. Peretz Reader,* edited by Ruth R. Wisse, xxiii–xxx. New York: Schocken, 1990.

———. *The Schlemiel as Modern Hero.* Chicago: Univ. of Chicago Press, 1971.

Yezierska, Anzia. *Bread Givers.* New York: Persea, 1925.

Index